BRITAIN IN A BOTTLE

A VISITOR'S GUIDE

DISTILLERIES | BREWERIES | VINEYARDS | CIDER MILLS

TED BRUNING | RUPERT WHEELER

www.bradtguides.com
Bradt Travel Guides Ltd, UK
The Globe Pequot Press Inc, USA

First edition published April 2020
Bradt Travel Guides Ltd
31a High Street, Chesham, Buckinghamshire, HP5 1BW, England
www.bradtguides.com
Print edition published in the USA by The Globe Pequot Press Inc,
PO Box 480, Guilford, Connecticut 06437-0480

Text copyright © 2020 Ted Bruning and Rupert Wheeler
Maps copyright © 2020 Bradt Travel Guides
Photographs copyright © 2020 Individual photographers (see opposite)
Project Manager: Rupert Wheeler
Cover research and design: Josse Pickard

ISBN: 978 1 78477 591 9

British Library Cataloguing in Publication Data
A catalogue record for this book is available from the British Library

Front cover image from Sonsam/Getty Images

Maps Posthouse Publishing

Typeset and designed by Posthouse Publishing
Production managed by Jellyfish Print Solutions; printed in Turkey
Digital conversion by www.dataworks.co.in

ABOUT THE AUTHORS

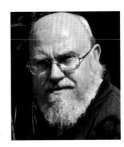

Ted Bruning has been a journalist and author in the licensed trade and hospitality industry since 1986, when he joined the publicans' paper *The Morning Advertiser*. He worked for 13 years on the Campaign for Real Ale's monthly paper, *What's Brewing*, and has freelanced for trade titles including *The Publican*, *The Brewers' Guardian*, *Caterer & Hotelkeeper*, and *On Trade Preview*. Book credits include *Historic Pubs of London*, *London by Pub*, *Brewery Breaks*, *The Microbrewers' Handbook* and *The Craft Distillers' Handbook*.

Rupert Wheeler has been involved in publishing for over 30 years and was previously the managing editor of *Whisky Magazine*. He is a judge in the World Whiskies Awards and has recently moved to Orkney. He now works part time at Highland Park Distillery, taking tours and running tasting events.

ACKNOWLEDGEMENTS

The authors would like to thank all the locations who have supplied photographs and helped in providing the most up-to-date information.

PHOTOGRAPHS

Dan Fawcett, Rachel Phipps, Keith Murray, DAC, Rachel Davies, Getty Images, Diageo, Stephen R Sizer, Dave_S, Chris Fleetwod, Quisnovus, YoYotes, Femma Anderson, Julia, Visit Kent, Ian Docwra, Derek Finch, Mario Frias Ducoudray, Adrian Pink, Werner-Q, Rob Young, Tammy, Kamal, Samanta Jackson, Andy, Wooly Maverick, Tom Blackwell, Torfaen Corvine, Philip McGraa, Alan Austin, Michael Stalker, James Brown, Jamie Wilson, Ellen Cross, Chris, Mike Mather, Ian Lamb, Alexandre Vingtier, Haltse, Bernt Rostad, Jade Ching, Jen Riehle McFarland, Derek Gray, Joe Collver, Alexandre Vingtier, ScottSim Photography, Stuart Anthony, Peter Goodhall, SamRoss1, Tom68*, Ewan Graham, Alison Giguere, David Woods, Nige Aus, John, cizetta111, Alan George, Chris Smith and Brian Hamilton. Shutterstock: JASPERIMAGE, Francesco Dazzi, Alistair McDonald, Lukassek, Jeffrey B. Banke, duchy. iStock: HildaWeges.

CONTENTS

CLOSEUPS 🔍

INTRODUCTION

It's not that many years since the idea of regarding breweries and distilleries as tourist attractions would have seemed distinctly odd. Cider farms – more aptly spelled *zoider* in this context – always proved a lure for townee tourists braving the folkloric flavours of Devon and Somerset, all the more so since until the 2003 Licensing Act zoider makers were allowed to sell wholesale (ie: stupefying) quantities of their product at the farm gate without a licence. English vineyards too, from their inception in the 1970s, attracted the curious, most of whom would rather have been in Burgundy or Tuscany, but who would put up with slumming it in Sussex. But the notion of undertaking a guided tour of a gloomy Victorian pile in the least appetising quarter of some industrial city with any expectation of being treated as an honoured guest rather than a bloomin' nuisance was absurd.

All that changed on 1 September 1987, with the airing of the first instalment of *Floyd on France*, in which the louche Bristolian, wine glass in one hand and cigarette in the other, cooked his languid but unsteady way round Provence. This wasn't the first TV cookery show by any means; nor even was it Keith Floyd's – he had made *Floyd on Fish* in 1984. But the idiosyncrasies of the host, the beauty of the Provençal landscape, and the beckoning finger of the food itself combined to turn that first airing into 'a moment', when that part of the demographic with well-stocked wallets suddenly realised that food and drink sprang from the soil; that they were part of the countryside and shared its beauty; and that a vineyard was the ideal venue for a spot of (fully clad) *déjeuner sur l'herbe*.

Food and drink tourism was still slow to take off in Britain: brewers distillers and the makers of heritage pork pies alike all regarded their premises as places of work where potential breaches of health and safety regulations lurked on every steep, narrow staircase and wet, slippery floor. The more visually appealing Scotch malt whisky distilleries led the way in opening up to tourists: sales in the bottle-shop and fees for guided tours were all good for cashflow, and word-of-mouth was great marketing. The more handsome breweries – Elgood's of Wisbech, Eldridge Pope of Dorchester, Young's of Wandsworth – one by one followed suit, at the same time developing informative and comfortable visitor centres and inviting brewery taps until, by the opening of the new millennium, you didn't have to be an enthusiast to regard a guided tour and maybe even lunch at a distillery, brewery or vineyard as anything out of the ordinary in the slightest.

More recently still the proliferating craft brewers, artisan distillers and boutique winemakers of this parish have come to realise that their production bases are also excellent shop windows. Fees for tours and tastings, tea and/or tapas in the café and, especially, *après-tour* bottle sales at full retail price represent good business for them.

Of course, we haven't been able to include here every facility that awaits your visit – there are too many of them, and the rate of new openings is too fast to keep track of. But here are the ones we know and love, so let us introduce you.

Cheers!

▲ *Whisky Show, London*

FESTIVALS & SHOWS

There are a considerable number of festivals and shows throughout Great Britain. We have listed just some of the major ones and websites where you can find out further information below.

BEER
CAMRA ⌖ camra.org.uk
Great British Beer Festival London ⌖ gbbf.org.uk
Beer Festival Calendar ⌖ beer-festival-calendar. co.uk

CIDER
Craft Nectar ⌖ craftynectar.com

GIN
Gin Festival, London & Edinburgh
⌖ ginfestivalsuk.com

WHISKY
For a complete list of festivals and shows in Scotland, visit ⌖ visitscotland.com/blog/whisky/whisky-festivals/

Feis Ile, Islay ⌖ islayfestival.com
Glasgow Whisky Festival
⌖ glasgowswhiskyfestival.com
Whisky Live, London ⌖ whiskylive.com
Whisky Show, London ⌖ whiskyshow.com
Whisky Show Old and Rare, Glasgow
⌖ whiskyshow.com/old-and-rare/
Spirit of Speyside ⌖ spiritofspeyside.com
World Whisky Day ⌖ worldwhiskyday.com

WINE
London Festival of Wine ⌖ festival-of-wine. com/london-wine-festival/. And also in Glasgow & Edinburgh.

HOW TO USE THIS GUIDE

Our guiding principles in compiling and arranging this book have been twofold: to place you, wherever you live or are on holiday, as physically close to a tour destination as we can; and to select, as far as possible (although not always with complete success), destinations where you can just turn up to kill an hour or escape the rain without having to book or pay an admission charge. Even so, it is still always wise to ring ahead to check that the place is actually open and awaiting your arrival. We have detailed where it is absolutely necessary to pre-book.

With the first of our guiding principles in mind we have divided each country into counties and move through each country – England, Wales and Scotland – in a southerly to northerly direction. The counties within each chapter run alphabetically.

The entries in each county are listed by the type of beverage they produce – brewery, cider mill, gin distillery, whisky distillery and vineyard/winery, in strict alphabetical order. Each listing comes with its full postal address for the traditional road atlas user, its postcode for the satnav jockey, and a telephone number for the hopelessly lost. Some destinations are extremely remote and hard to find, so always check the website for directions before setting off. And in some cases the official postcode will confuse the satnav and guide you to a back gate or a car park on the wrong side of a churning river – again, check the website!

Our criterion for all locations detailed in this book is that you are able to do a tour of the site, and in most cases guided tours need to be booked, often quite far in advance. And in some cases, especially when it's an old and rambling brewery or distillery you want to tour, there may be difficult staircases and gantries which the elderly and less able might find too challenging. For all these, and to find out whether children and/or dogs are welcome, it's the same old story… check the website!

FEEDBACK REQUEST

Have you visited one of the businesses recommended in this guide? Or want to suggest one that you feel should have been included? Or fancy sending us an update on the businesses we have recommended? Why not write and tell us about your experiences? You can send your feedback to us on ✆ 01753 893444 or ✉ info@bradtguides.com. We will forward emails to the authors, who may post updates on the Bradt website at ⬧ bradtupdates.com/bottle. Alternatively you can add a review of the book to ⬧ bradtguides.com or Amazon. Please also communicate your adventures on Twitter, Instagram, Facebook and YouTube using the hashtag #BritainInABottle and we'll share it for you.

f BradtGuides 🐦 @BradtGuides
📷 @bradtguides 📌 bradtguides
▶ bradtguides

▶ *Coopers at work in Theakstons (page 184)*

PART ONE
ENGLAND

CHAPTER ONE
WEST
COUNTRY

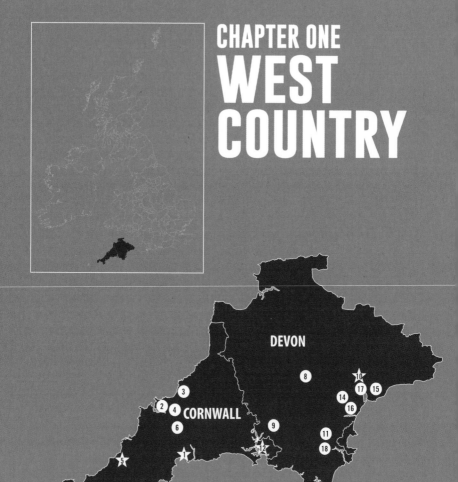

CORNWALL

1 ST AUSTELL BREWERY

MORE DR WHO THAN POLDARK: CORNWALL'S BIGGEST BREWERY IS A PRODUCT OF INDUSTRY, NOT SMUGGLING.

✉ 63 Trevarthian Rd, St Austell PL25 4BY ✐ 01726 66022 ✐ staustellbrewery.co.uk ☉ year-round 09.00–17.30 daily.

▲ *The entrance to the interactive brewing experience, which reveals the secrets behind 160 years of brewing*

St Austell may be one of Cornwall's bigger towns, but it's certainly not one of its prettiest or one of its more historic. The rather fine parish church is 15th century, but as far as medieval landmarks go that's it. St Austell didn't even have a market until 1638.

Standing some miles inland, it has none of the fishing and smuggling heritage of more favoured Cornish towns. Don't be put off, though: there's plenty of chocolate-box or perhaps fudge-tin-pretty Cornwall close at hand. Charlestown, St Austell's little port a few miles off, ranks with

Robin Hood's Bay and Clovelly for quaintness and was a favourite location for filming the BBC *Poldark* series, and the Eden Project is nearby.

But St Austell itself gets its rather dour character from its industrial past. Tregooth nearby was one of the region's biggest tin mines from the mid-18th century to modern times, and vast china clay deposits here gave the town a new and generous source of prosperity in the 19th century. The industry's characteristic conical spoil-heaps, the so-called Cornish Alps, are still a feature of the district and have also had their moments of TV fame: in the 1960s, worked-out Cornish claypits regularly stood in for alien planets in *Dr Who*.

The brewery owes its fortune to St Austell's Victorian boom years. It goes back to 1851 when local farmer Walter Hicks founded a maltings, which is a familiar enough story: in mid-century the rail network was still evolving, and for expanding towns it made more sense to supply local brewers with local malt than to haul it from distant regions. And perhaps it's the founder's background as a maltster that has influenced the character of the house beers. The best-known – Tribute, Proper Job, and HSD – describe themselves perfectly fairly as pale ales, but there's a warming maltiness to them that evokes hard-working labourers and their need for calories. Even among the more recent and craft-influenced additions to the range there are malty delights such as Ruby Jack red ale and Mena Dhu Cornish stout.

In 1863 Hicks – again, like many others in his situation – took the next step and bought a pub and brewhouse: the Seven Stars in East Hill. As there wasn't much competition he did well and

in 1867 bought the London Inn on Market Street, which he replaced with an impressive four-storey steam brewery whose shell, Tregonissey House, you can still see today.

Hicks soon grew out of his new home. The town's continuing growth and the lack of competition necessitated the construction of today's much bigger brewery in 1893. It's a classic tower brewery of the sort that was springing up all over the country: water and malt were pumped and hauled by steam power up to the top, and each step in the brewing process took place on a

"THE BREWERY OWES ITS FORTUNE TO ST AUSTELL'S VICTORIAN BOOM YEARS"

successively lower floor. As you approach its rather stern grey stone bulk, you might think that it looks a little forbidding, but you couldn't be more wrong. St Austell was an early adopter of the idea of welcoming its customers in to see and hear the story behind what they were drinking and today there is an absorbing visitor centre including the welcoming Hicks bar and restaurant, a shop and an interactive brewing exhibition. There are three grades of brewery tour you can book – each one including a complimentary Cornish pasty.

> **THE BEER** Tribute 4.2% ABV, a Cornish pale ale – it's light, hoppy and easy to drink. The zesty orange and grapefruit flavours are balanced with biscuit malt. For those wanting a more traditional bitter, try Hicks 5% ABV or Trelawny, a best bitter at 3.8% ABV.

BREWERIES

2 SHARP'S
⌂ St Minver Lowlands, Rock, Wadebridge PL27 6NU ✆ 01580 862121 ⌨ sharpsbrewery co.uk ◷ year-round 09.00–17.00 Mon–Sat; shop, visitor centre, guided tours. Founded by former silversmith Bill Sharp in 1994 on the Camel Estuary on North Cornwall's dramatic coast, Sharp's quickly became one of the superstars of the small independent brewing scene thanks largely to its best bitter, Doom Bar, named after a sandbar at the mouth of the estuary of the River Camel. In 2004 it was sold to a group of sharp-eyed local businessmen who continued to build the beer's popularity until 2011 when it attracted the attention of the mighty Molson Coors, who bought the brewery and made Doom Bar Britain's top real ale. The brewery is brand new and very modern.

3 TINTAGEL
⌂ Condolden Farm, Tintagel PL34 0HJ ✆ 01840 212475 ⌨ tintagelbrewery.co.uk ◷ year-round 09.30–17.30 Tue–Sat, 11.30–17.30 Sun; shop, bar/bistro, tours & tastings. High in the hills just inland from Tintagel Castle itself, Tintagel Brewery's rather stark new brewhouse and visitor centre with its timber cladding suits the rugged surroundings to a T. There's nothing bleak about the stylish bistro, though – Wagyu beef from the farm itself (the highest in Cornwall) is a speciality. The beers range from a mild at 3% ABV to the strong dark Caliburn at 5.8% ABV. Dogs on a lead are welcome, there's a play area for the kids and unusually for Cornwall there's plenty of space for parking.

CIDER MILLS

4 HAYWOOD FARM CIDER
⌂ St Mabyn, Wadebridge PL30 3BU ✆ 01208 8840140 ⌨ haywoodfarmciderco.uk. ◷ year-round 9.00–18.00 Mon–Sat, 10.00–16.00 Sun; walking & tractor tours must be booked. A stone mill that could be centuries old shows that cider had been made here for generations. It was restarted in 2003 by Tom Bray, who also planted 14 acres of orchards and whose apples are pressed the old-fashioned way in alternate layers of apple pulp and straw. The remote farm is plain and down-to-earth but comes to life on selected Sunday afternoons (see website) when the barn's complement of old sofas, barrels and bales are turfed out into the yard to be the auditorium for live bands, a barbecue and copious supplies of Tom's sweet, medium and dry farm ciders.

5 HEALEYS CORNISH CYDER FARM
See page 20.

◀ *Building the cheese on the cider press at Haywood Farm Cider*
▶ *The magnificent views over the Camel Valley*

VINEYARDS

6 CAMEL VALLEY

✉ Nanstallon, Bodmin PL30 5LG ✆ 01208 77959 ⌂ camelvalley.com ◷ year-round 09.00–17.00 Mon–Fri, Apr–Sep 10.00–17.00 Sat. Camel Valley was established in 1989 when retired squadron leader Bob Lindo and his wife Annie planted the first vines on the slatey south-facing slopes of their 82-acre farm. Ideal terroir and assiduous winemaking propelled them to success in international competitions, and they ventured into making traditionally bottle-fermented sparkling wines that have gained international recognition. Sip them on the sun terrace of the vineyard shop while taking in the magnificent views of the valley.

7 POLGOON

✉ Rosehill Meadow, Penzance TR20 8TE ✆ 01736 333946 ⌂ polgoon.com ◷ year-round 09.00–17.30 Mon–Sat, 10.30–16.00 Sun; tours alter according to season – must book. Fish merchants Kim and John Coulson from the seaside town of Newlyn founded the vineyard to make both still and sparkling wines on what had been a flower-farm, when they decided they wanted a change of occupation. They added bottle-fermented sparkling cider, Aval, to the range when disastrous harvests in 2007 and 2008 left them with no wine to sell. Since then they've won many awards and have added Raspberry Aval to their portfolio. The vineyard is on a sheltered slope overlooking Mount's Bay; the Vine House Kitchen has an outdoor terrace with sweeping sea views.

ALCOHOLIC STRENGTH?

HOW STRONG IS YOUR DRINK? IT TOOK A FRENCH CHEMIST TO FIND OUT FOR CERTAIN.

Most people these days have probably forgotten about proof, degrees proof, percent proof and the confusion that descended on the nation's drinking folk when proof was superseded in 1980 by percent alcohol by volume. That was the year that Britain went metric and, although the new system of measuring strength wasn't exactly metric, it had been defined by a Frenchman (the great chemist Joseph Gay-Lussac, 1778–1850), so it might as well have been.

To be fair, the change to a more rational system was long overdue. British proof was the strength at which gunpowder soaked in spirit would still catch fire. If the spirit were any more dilute than that it would still ignite, but the powder wouldn't because it was waterlogged. It might seem an odd test of alcoholic strength, but spirits and gunpowder were constant companions among navy gunners: a paste of the two was used to waterproof linstocks and fuses, and spirit was often used to swab out the guns between broadsides because water in the barrel could prevent it going off.

The Dutch had a more practical method of determining proof, which was universally used by British distillers (who tended not to keep gunpowder lying around) for day-to-day use: they half-filled a bottle with the spirit to be tested, sealed it and gave it a vigorous shake. The denser the liquid – ie: the more water it contained – the more slowly the bubbles or 'blebs' would disperse. At proof, a distinct foamy head would form. To muddy the waters, 100 proof in the UK was 57.15% ABV; in the US, and by the Dutch method of testing, it was a more convenient 50% ABV. But, just to make matters more complicated, British proof was commonly expressed as a percentage of 57.15: '26% proof' may sound like a nonsense but was adopted in 1861 as the dividing line between table and fortified wines and equated roughly to 15% ABV. To add to the confusion, 'degrees below proof' was another common means of expressing alcoholic strength.

Before ABV came in, the strength of beer was tested by an even more obtuse method. The gravity or density of the wort was measured

by hydrometer before fermentation and again afterwards. By subtracting the second reading from the first, the brewer could calculate roughly how much sugar there was at the start and how much of it had been converted to alcohol by the end, alcohol being lighter than sugar. It wasn't a very accurate system: a beer of 1040 OG ought to be around 4% ABV but might very well have been less if all the sugar was not converted. Unlike pounds, miles and pints, no-one rushed to the defence of the old system when it was threatened with metrication!

"BRITISH PROOF WAS THE STRENGTH AT WHICH GUNPOWDER SOAKED IN SPIRIT WOULD STILL CATCH FIRE"

It might come as a surprise to know that for the most part alcoholic strength isn't actually regulated. It's manipulated by a very complicated duty regime that has grown up higgledy-piggledy over generations and makes no obvious sense at all: for instance a woman in Dorset who made traditional nettle 'beer' using sugar found herself charged the duty rate for wine, and went bust as a result; had she used malt extract she would have been charged the rate for beer and would presumably be living happily ever after right now.

The exception is that some spirits have a minimum permitted strength of 37.5% ABV, while Scotch whisky may not be less than 40% ABV. This came about during World War I when the government sought to restrict the consumption of spirits simply by diluting them. Before the war they had usually been bottled at 15–22% under proof or 44.6–48.6% ABV. In 1915 the government wanted a cut to 35% under proof or 37.2% ABV, and then sought a further reduction to 50% under proof or 28.5% ABV. However, after negotiation with the distillers it settled on 30% under proof or 40% ABV for Scotch, which has been the minimum strength ever since.

5 HEALEYS CORNISH CYDER FARM

IT SAYS 'CYDER FARM' – SO WHAT'S WITH THE DISTILLERY?

⌂ Penhallow, Truro TR4 9LW ✆ 01872 573356 ⊘ healeyscyder.co.uk ⊙ year-round 09.00–20.00 daily.

If you could imagine all the things you could get up to on a Cornish cider farm that had thrown its gates open to the public, what would be on your list? Watching apples being squished, maybe; guzzling scones and cream and jam (or is that scones and jam and cream?) in the tea room; snoozing under an apple tree having sampled a few ciders; being introduced to a shire horse and maybe some baa-lambs; tasting new make spirit in a cobbled cellar lined with tiers of slumbering barrels of whisky... hang on! Do what? This is supposed to be a cider farm!

But just as Tesco's philosophy is to 'sell everything to everybody everywhere', so Healeys' is to offer tourists the complete package. Since arriving at Porthallow from a smallholding and off-licence in the village of Mevagissey in 1986, the Healey family – David, wife Kay and young sons Joe and Sam (now joined by wives Georgie and Lara) – have transformed the place, mainly by the sweat of their own brows, from a semi-derelict farm without electricity or mains water into Cornwall's biggest cidermaker, which was always David's original plan. He sold a lot of cider in the shop, but it was all from small farms or from... Devon! He succeeded within the first ten years of planting, grafting, pruning and picking in getting output up to 60,000 gallons, and growth has been

steady ever since; but he also expanded sideways. Apart from the cider apple trees the Healeys were planting, there were a lot of other fruits to get stuck into. You sell scones? You've got to have jam. Healeys makes jam. You can make jam? You can make chutney. Healeys makes chutney. You've got a mill and a press to make your cider? You can make country wines. Healeys also makes country wines.

"FROM A SEMI-DERELICT FARM WITHOUT ELECTRICITY OR MAINS WATER INTO CORNWALL'S BIGGEST CIDERMAKER"

The opening of a small distillery was not quite such a natural progression. Plenty of cidermakers have discovered since 1990 that good cider makes amazing cider brandy, but Healeys didn't set out to make cider brandy. They wanted to make whisky and in 2000, having installed a small copper pot-still and suborned St Austell Brewery into producing the wash to fill it, that's exactly what Healeys did. But everything at Porthallow has to earn its living, and today the still makes cider brandy and apple eau de vie as well. No gin yet, but it can't be long.

Healeys' ciders (ranging from old-school scrumpy to on-trend fruit-flavoured fizzies) and

▲ The well-established orchards contain over 3,000 trees producing 1,000 tonnes of apples every year

its other products (except the jam) are widely distributed throughout Cornwall. The new visitor centre includes a museum with artefacts including a 16th-century trough mill and cooper's tools, a tea room, a shop selling all manner of local produce, a restaurant best described as hearty and a small collection of Austin-Healey two-seaters (the clue is in the name). Tours range from a self-guided ramble round the orchard to a veritable odyssey (that should be booked) embracing a look at the press, a peek into the jam factory, a tour of the museum, a look at the still and its cellarage, a tractor ride through the orchards and a full sampling session. Keep your ears open and by the end of it you'll know enough to set up your own cider business.

Healeys has recently invested in a 190-acre farm nearby called Tregoninny, where a vineyard will soon be added to 80 acres of orchard and where the farmhouse and a number of other cottages have been turned into luxury self-catering accommodation. So there's absolutely no reason to leave.

THE CIDER The Rattler Original comes in at 6% ABV, giving you a cloudy, crisp apple finish. Rattler 4% ABV, Rattler Pear 4% ABV, Rattler Berry 4% ABV, Rattler Mulled 4% ABV and the new Rattler Strawberry and Lime 4% ABV. They also produce Cornish Gold, which has a champagne-style finish.

21

DEVON

CIDER MILLS

8 THE CIDER VAT AT SAMPFORD COURTENAY CIDER

✉ Solland Farm, Solland Ln, Sampford Courtenay EX20 3OT ☎ 01837 851638 ☌ devoncider.com ⏱ year-round 10.00–18.00 Tue–Sat, 11.00–16.00 Sun; special events some evenings; ring for information on tours. They had been making a highly regarded cider at Solland Farm, including a rare natural sweet, for over 20 years when in 2016 they decided to open a purpose-built showcase for their products. But the Cider Vat is much, much more than just an outlet for Sampford Courtenay's own range: it stocks some 300 lines from more than 60 Devonian food and drink producers. Its tea room and restaurant also focuses on home-cooked local produce and often hosts live events, as well as being the starting point for orchard trails.

9 COUNTRYMAN

✉ Felldownhead, Tavistock PL19 0QR ☎ 01822 870226 ☌ crying-fox.com/cider1.htm ⏱ year-round 09.00–18.30 Mon–Sat, closed Oct–Apr Sat. For many aficionados, this simple family-run farm is the epitome of Devon cider. Originally the stable-block of an inn called the Kelly Arms (now the farmhouse), it's been making cider since the mid-19th century. Other than the acquisition of today's mechanised mill and press in the 1960s, little has changed. The simple shop stocks and gives tastings of Countryman's sweet, medium and dry ciders and also sells apple brandy, cider vinegar, mead and country wines. Feel free to wander around the orchard and peek into the cider barn itself.

10 KILLERTON ESTATE

See page 24.

GIN DISTILLERIES

11 DEVON DISTILLERY

✉ The Shops at Dartington, Shinner's Bridge, Dartington TQ9 6TQ ☎ 01803 812509 ☌ devondistillery.com ⏱ 09.30–17.30 Mon–Sat, 10.00–17.00 Sun; gin school 2 sessions daily. The 1,200-acre Dartington Hall Estate with the mainly 14th-century hall and its exquisite gardens at its centre has been home to a host of educational, artistic and artisanal enterprises since it was rescued from dereliction by Leonard and Dorothy Elmhirst in 1925. One of the denizens of the Shops at Dartington, formerly the Cider Press Centre, is the Devon Distillery, where the Elmhirsts' great grandson Cosmo Caddy makes Elmhirst Gin and runs gin schools every day. But as he's also the grandson of the founder of Sharpham Vineyard (page 31), he also makes grappa (or Dappa), which is a form of pomace brandy, made from the skins, pulp and seeds of grapes used in winemaking, and Devoncello – Devon's answer to Limoncello. Unmissable for so many reasons!

12 PLYMOUTH GIN

See page 26.

▲ *Dartmoor Whisky Distillery*

13 SALCOMBE GIN

⌂ The Boathouse, 28 Island St, Salcombe TQ8 8DP
✆ 01548 288180 ⌖ salcombegin.com ☻ year-round 10.00–22.00 Tue–Thu, 10.00–23.00 Fri–Sat, 10.00–17.00 Sun; gin school sessions must be booked. Salcombe, at Devon's southernmost point, has been a *port de plaisance* since its role as a trading harbour died a death before the war. The distillery is located in an area known for its boatbuilding but also now fast becoming an area known for its art scene. As is the custom, all gin stills are named and this one is called Provident – named after a Brixham sailing trawler that was the founding vessel of the Island Cruising Club in Salcombe, which once stood on the same site as the distillery does today. If you really want to know more about making gin then make sure you attend their gin school, where you can take home your own personalised 70cl bottle.

WHISKY DISTILLERY

14 DARTMOOR WHISKY DISTILLERY

⌂ Old Town Hall, Bovey Tracey TQ13 9EG
✆ 07967 836275 ⌖ dartmoorwhiskydistillery.co.uk ☻ year-round 10.00–16.00 Mon–Sat; tours 11.00, 14.00 on distilling days, booking is essential. Dartmoor Whisky had its genesis in 2014 when enthusiasts Greg Millar and Simon Crow clubbed together and bought an old French alembic to restore. In 2016 they bought the rather grand but redundant Victorian town hall in Bovey Tracey, restored that as well and then put the two together. The first spirit ran in 2017 and the partners distil a new batch every week; you can't have a dram yet because it has to mature for three years. You can still visit, try your hand at distilling or have a good time at one of the foodie events for which the hall is the perfect venue.

10 KILLERTON ESTATE

CIDER FOR THE RICH MAN'S TABLE AND THE LABOURER'S PAY.

✉ Broadclyst EX5 3LE ✆ 01392 881345 ⊘ nationaltrust.org.uk/killerton ⊙ House year-round 11.00–17.00, gardens 10.00–dusk, facilities 10.00–17.30, park 08.00–19.00.

It's cheating, you might think, to direct you to a National Trust-owned 6,500-acre estate of farms, barns, mills and outbuildings, with a splendid pink-brick late Georgian mansion at the heart of it all, just to look at a shed where they make a bit of cider. But Killerton Estate is definitely worth a visit whatever the excuse, and the 50-plus acres of traditional cider orchards scattered among its 20 farms have a story to tell.

The estate was the property and home of the Acland family from 1680 until 1944, when they handed it over to the National Trust. The existing house dates to 1778 – a larger one was planned but never completed and its demolished remains have recently been discovered hidden under a plantation of laurels. It's packed with fine paintings and furniture and is home to a significant collection of 19th- and 20th-century costumes. The exquisite gardens (watch out for the ha-ha!) were laid out and planted by the noted 18th-century designer John Veitch. Other buildings include not one chapel but two – the original and its flamboyant 1841 Gothic successor – an icehouse and a stableyard where you'll find the shop and tea room (there's also a highly regarded restaurant). Then beyond the parkland and out into the working part of the estate there's a working watermill, the aforementioned 20 farms and 250 cottages, including a well-preserved 1950s village post office and a medieval forge built of cob.

"EVERY AUTUMN THIS IS WHERE VOLUNTEER PICKERS BRING THE SPOILS FROM ALL THOSE ORCHARDS TO BE MILLED AND PRESSED BY YET MORE VOLUNTEERS"

All these treasures are well worth visiting in their own right, and every year more than a quarter of a million people do indeed come to explore. But our attention is focused on the old Forestry Yard where, in a little shed, we find a 19th-century twin-screw flatbed cider press. Every autumn this is where volunteer pickers bring the spoils from all those orchards to be milled and pressed by yet more volunteers. There are 700 of them all told: in a good year they've been known to bring in six tonnes of windfall. And that shows how important those little pockets and scraps of orchard – old-style standard orchards with trees 7.6–9.1m tall – were to the tenant farmers of yesteryear. The best cider fetched a high price: one good tree would pay a cottager's rent, and the very finest ciders in the 17th and 18th centuries were rated as highly as any French wine and fit for any

▲ *The very distinctive pink-brick Georgian mansion at Killerton Estate*

table. But they also yielded 'ciderkin', once-pressed pomace rehydrated and pressed again to yield a watery beverage of maybe 3% alcohol that part-paid the workers (much to their resentment: they'd rather have had the cash), mistletoe for the Christmas trade, firewood from old or diseased trees and good straight spurs or poles for the lathe. The grass beneath the trees nurtured poultry and fattened lambs, who also fertilised the soil and nibbled the bramble shoots.

Those 50 acres have been increased since 2016, when the National Trust took over the collection of Haney May of Tidnor in Herefordshire and planted out saplings of rare heritage varieties around eight of its properties. They should start bearing by 2024 but there are already 100 varieties represented here, two of them – Killerton Sharp and Killerton Sweet – unique to the estate. They're good regular croppers and, according to connoisseurs, they import a pleasant softness to the estate's award-winning blend.

THE CIDER The cider is on sale, from the estate, only in mid-October, when the legendary annual Apple Festival is held. Past years have seen the cider full-flavoured with a complex character and notes of toffee apple.

12 PLYMOUTH GIN

HOW OLD IS OLD? NOBODY KNOWS FOR CERTAIN, BUT IT'S CERTAINLY VERY OLD.

✉ 60 Southside, Plymouth PL1 2LQ ✐ 01752 665292 ✐ plymouthgin.com ⏰ year-round 10.00–17.00 Mon–Sat, 11.00–17.00 Sun; Barbican Kitchen 12.00–22.00 Mon–Sat; reservations: ✐ 01752 604448.

The Plymouth Gin distillery, in the quarter of the historic city centre that survived the Luftwaffe bombardment, always claims to be England's oldest, with a charter date of 1793. Supposedly, though, it's even older as that's the year in which a Mr Coates (who later gave the company the name it bore until 2004) joined the established firm of Fox & Williamson. It's all a bit murky as the Luftwaffe destroyed not only most of the old city but also all the records it housed. Suffice it to say that in the 1880s, Coates & Co. was trying to stop London distillers passing their products off as Plymouth-style, and produced in evidence a single bottle label bearing the legend 'established 1793'. Which has since disappeared.

Not to worry, though, because distilling on the site goes back several centuries before 1793. From the 1430s to the 1530s the site was a Dominican friary, whose refectory is today an absolutely wonderful cocktail bar. Healing the sick was a monastic duty, and by the 15th century every abbey had an infirmarer – a person who took care of unwell people – who distilled wine to make a spirit that would extract the active ingredients from medicinal plants. At about this time, northern European infirmarers were learning to distil their own spirit from cheap and plentiful malt liquor rather than wine; so the infirmarer here was undoubtedly making a crude proto-gin.

In the 19th century, Coates & Co's gin became very popular with the many naval officers based in the city, selling 1,000 barrels a year to seagoing customers. Ratings and petty officers had their rum, taken well-watered and medicated with lemon or lime juice to ward off scurvy, paid for by the Admiralty. Officers had to buy their own cabin stores, and gin as a drink of higher status than rum

▲ *The Refectory Bar*
▶ *Some of the botanicals used in a classic Plymouth Gin*

was favoured by those who couldn't afford to buy brandy. The Navy, being frequently deployed to the Caribbean, medicated its gin not with quinine but with Angostura bitters from South America; hence 'Harry Pinkers'.

"AN INFIRMARER – A PERSON WHO TOOK CARE OF UNWELL PEOPLE – WHO DISTILLED WINE TO MAKE A SPIRIT THAT WOULD EXTRACT THE ACTIVE INGREDIENTS FROM MEDICINAL PLANTS"

You may find all this history absorbing or it may leave you a little cold. What really matters is the gin, and Plymouth Gin is something special. It's not actually a separate style, although from the 1880s right up until 2015 the name was legally protected. Its botanicals are weighted towards orris root and liquorice, making it fuller bodied and less aromatic than other gins. It has also traditionally been a smidgeon stronger than its rivals at 41.2% ABV, with a 100 proof or 57.15% ABV 'Navy strength' version being much the same as those seafarers in the Victorian navy used to enjoy. In the 1930s its somewhat richer texture made it a huge favourite as a cocktail base: if, on your visit, you repair to the aforementioned Refectory Bar you will have ample opportunity to discover why. (The quality of the gin actually inspired Charles Rolls, MD from 1997 to 2001, to spark the mixer revolution by formulating a tonic brand called Fever Tree.)

Given its location on the edge of the Barbican district (the name given to the western and northern sides of Sutton Harbour in Plymouth), its history (there are possible links to the Pilgrim Fathers), its facilities (the Barbican Kitchen, a modern brasserie specialising in seafood, is as highly regarded as the Refectory Bar) and of course its gin, the distillery is a hugely popular attraction and has been for many years.

> **THE GIN** Plymouth is rich and smooth, the Navy strength is bold and aromatic, the Sloe gives you that classic English style and the Fruit Cup is the traditional base for fruity summer pitchers.

ENGLISH SPARKLING WINE

ENGLISH WINEMAKERS HAVE MASTERED THE *MÉTHODE CHAMPENOISE* AND NOW THEY MAKE THE WORLD'S BEST BUBBLES.

By the mid-1950s, the English wine revival may have been on but it was slow to reach full speed. Many people were prepared to give it a go, but few were prepared – or were able – to do it on much of a scale. By the early 1990s there were more than 400 vineyards in England and Wales but most were very small, some less than an acre and few that were bigger than five.

One of the factors holding the first growers back was that they didn't know what English wine was supposed to be. Comparing the climate of southeast England with those of other wine regions, they concluded that it was most like the Rhine's, which they thought no bad thing since Liebfraumilch and Hock were huge sellers. They were also very cheap and sweet, which wasn't such

good news. Others, perhaps more courageously, have seen their role as creating a distinctive English identity with idiosyncratic hybrids such as cream wine, a blend of white and sweet red.

The true answer had been under the fledgling industry's nose all along. The pioneer George Ordish had been inspired by the many similarities between the southeast and the Champagne region; and if anything, he concluded, England's climate was the milder. But it took a while for an industry that had grown up on the fairly limited ambition of producing a half-Riesling to fix its gaze upon the impossibly lofty peak of the greatest wine in the world.

The first to experiment with the *méthode champenoise* – ie: allowing a secondary fermentation in the bottle using Müller-Thurgau

and Seyval Blanc were – Nigel Godden of Pilton Manor, Somerset, who started up in 1966, and Graham Barrett at Felsted Vineyard, Essex, who started a year later. In 1970, Sir Guy Salisbury-Jones planted 1,000 Chardonnay vines – widely used in Champagne itself – as well as Pinot Auxerrois and Pinot Meunier at Hambledon in Hertfordshire, and tested bottle-fermentation; sadly the high production costs and long maturation meant his experiment was a financial flop. It all looked like a dead end. Then in 1987 Carr Taylor Vineyard of Hastings, Sussex, decided to give the idea another go and after a hesitant start this time it took off to an extent that inspired others to follow its lead.

> ## "ALTHOUGH NOT ALL OF THEM PERSEVERED, THE QUALITY OF THEIR SPARKLING WINES WAS GOOD ENOUGH TO ATTRACT HUGE ATTENTION BOTH AT HOME AND ABROAD"

Lamberhurst in Kent (then the UK's largest vineyard and winery), New Hall in Essex, Tenterden in Kent (now Chapel Down; page 96), Rock Lodge and Nyetimber, both in Sussex, Camel Valley (page 17) in Cornwall and others were early adopters. Although not all of them persevered, they were numerous enough and the quality of their sparkling wines was good enough to attract huge attention both at home and abroad. More

and more growers and makers saw the potential, and throughout the 1990s the number of English sparkling wine producers grew steadily and their income became a more and more significant proportion of their output.

So what had changed? The first experimenters produced small volumes and were tentative rather than confident. They were using the wrong varieties of grape. And more to the point, the most prominent wine merchants – on whom success or failure would depend – regarded them as amusing eccentrics rather than serious players. But by 1987 English winemakers had gained credibility in the right circles. They were producing more serious volumes and of superb quality. They were planting the classic Champagne varieties rather than making the best of whatever they thought they could grow. They were charging serious prices in the belief that their wines could retail at £30–40 a bottle. They were making friends in the right places and even the most patrician of buyers would answer their calls. In short, as so often happens, the settlers stepped over the bodies of the pioneers.

Today sparkling accounts for 68% of the industry's sales, and the three classic varieties cover 71% of its acreage. Bottle-fermented sparkling wine has emerged as an agricultural product at which the English are supremely good. So Ordish was right: when it comes to bubbles, Rathfinny is every bit as good as Rheims!

VINEYARDS

15 LILY FARM

⌂ Dalditch Ln, Knowle EX9 7AH 🖉 01395 443877/07977 057864 🖉 lilyfarmvineyard. com ⏱ year-round 10.30–19.00 Thu–Sat; tours with tasting start at 14.00, booking is essential. At a mere 1½ acres, Lily Farm is a microcosm of English winemaking and everything that makes it special, and it would be your ideal introductory tour. The first vines were planted by Alan and Faye Pratt in 2005 on a steep south-facing slope amid sheltering hills (and with spectacular views from the top). The vines get exactly the right amount of sun and rain and are planted in a sandy soil absolutely perfect for Pinot Noir, Précoce, Bacchus, Seyval Blanc and most recently Reichensteiner. The wines – two sparkling and four still – are not made on site but by an expert contractor.

16 OLD WALLS

⌂ Old Walls Rd, Bishopsteignton TQ14 9PQ 🖉 01626 770877 🖉 oldwallsvineyard.co.uk ⏱ year-round 09.00–17.00 Sun–Wed, 09.00–11.00 Thu–Sat. Named after the ruined 13th-century Bishop's Palace nearby – of which only a few old walls remain standing – the vineyard was first planted in 2002 on ideal sheltered south-facing slopes overlooking the River Teign. Over the years it has evolved into a holiday destination in its own right, with a restaurant of quite some renown and six smart and very comfortable lodges that were added in 2017, where you can take a blissful mini-break or even go on a three-day artists' retreat complete with resident artist. Oh yes, there's wine,

▲ *Sharpham Vineyard & Dairy*

too: sparkling white and rosé and still red, white and rosé. The three grades of vineyard tour must be booked.

17 PEBBLEBED

⌂ Marianne Pool Farm, Clyst St George, Exeter EX3 0NZ 🖉 01392 661810/875908 🖉 pebblebed. co.uk ⏱ year-round 09.00–17.00 Mon–Fri (vineyard), 17.30–22.00 Tue–Sat (Tasting Cellar), vineyard & winery tours 16.00 Thu, 11.00 & 15.00 Sat; booking of tours & tastings is essential. Pebblebed is the vineyard that famously financed its expansion via an appearance on *Dragons' Den* in 2011. The vineyard and winery are up in the hills a couple of miles inland from Topsham, and although there is a sample room at the winery

for the post-tour tastings it's more usual to head down into Topsham to round off the trip with locally made tapas and a glass or two of Pebblebed's sparkling white and rosé and/or its still red, white and rosé at the Tasting Cellar, a converted warehouse in Fore Street.

18 SHARPHAM VINEYARD & DAIRY

✉ Sharpham Estate, Totnes TQ9 7UT ✆ 01803 732203 🖰 sharpham.com ☺ year-round daily – check website for hours; for self-guided tours & mini-tastings no booking is required, but booking is essential for tutored tastings, guided & private tours running Apr–Oct. Sharpham's creamery, vineyards and winery, beautifully set on the banks of the Dart, were established in 1981 by distinguished philanthropists, environmentalists and promoters of artisan production Ruth and Maurice Ash (who were also the daughter and son-in-law of Leonard and Dorothy Elmhirst of Dartington fame). After Maurice's death in 2003 (Ruth died in 1986) the business continued under the direction of Mark Sharman and has flourished. Its 38 acres of vines produce three competitively priced but serial award-winning sparkling wines as well as a wide range of table wines. Its herd of Jerseys produce the creamy milk that goes into the vegetarian and unpasteurised cheeses, including Sharpham, and the Cellar Door restaurant specialises in fine dining made with local produce but is only open during the main season of April to October.

CHAPTER TWO
SOUTHWEST

GLOUCESTERSHIRE

10 8 7
6

9

SOMERSET

14 17
19 20
18 12 11
15 16
13

DORSET

1

4 5
2 3

DORSET

BREWERIES

1 HALL & WOODHOUSE

✉ The Brewery, Blandford St Mary DT11 9LS
✆ 01258 486004 ⌖ hall-woodhouse.co.uk
🕐 shop 08.30–17.00 Mon–Wed, 08.30–19.00 Thu–Fri, 09.00–16.00 Sat. Brewery Tap bar-restaurant 09.00–17.00 Mon–Tue, 09.00–11.00 Wed, 08.30–11.00 Thu–Fri, 09.00–11.00 Sat. Tours start 10.30 Mon–Sat. Few people will have heard of Hall & Woodhouse, even though with 200 pubs spread across the south of England and a nationally distributed range of bottled beers it's one of Britain's biggest surviving family brewers. That's because since 1875 it has traded mainly under its logo, which is a badger. By then the company was already more than a century old, having been founded by a farmer by the name of Charles Hall in 1771. Its Badger bottled beers predated craft brewers by years in the use of ingredients such as elderflower, orange and peach blossom; it's also long been a national name in soft drinks, producing the Panda range until 2005 and now the maker of Rio. The big square red-brick brewery was built in 1900 and its industrial character is echoed by the décor of the Brewery Tap, shop and visitor centre.

2 PALMERS

✉ Old Brewery, West Bay Rd, Bridport DT6 4JA
✆ 01308 422396 ⌖ palmersbrewery.com
🕐 08.30–17.00 Mon–Fri; tours 11.00 every w/day Easter–Oct, which must be booked in advance. Palmers is probably the perfect tour for any curious beer-drinker who wants to simply and clearly see the various ingredients and processes involved in producing an absolutely traditional pint. The range even includes a strong, dark, roasty bitter called Tally Ho, first brewed in 1943, which is effectively a Victorian porter. Founded in 1794, Palmers is traditional in other ways too: like any local brewer before the 1960s, it's a jack-of-all-trades. A wine shipper and merchant of repute, its legendary wine store is in effect its visitor centre. It blends its own high-malt whisky called Golden Cap, once common practice but now rare. It even has its own range of ciders made in Somerset but from Dorset apples. The impressive waterwheel was installed in 1879, and parts of the oldest building on the site are actually thatched!

▲ *Palmers Brewery*

CIDER MILL

3 MILL HOUSE CIDER MUSEUM & DORSET CLOCK MUSEUM

✉ 33 Moreton Rd, Owermoigne DT2 8HZ
✆ 01305 852220 ◌ millhousecider.com
◷ 10.00–17.00 Tue–Sun. This most eclectic, not to say eccentric, of small museums happened by accident in the 1980s and has been progressing by a series of accidents ever since. First, local man Derek Whatmoor bought an antique mill-and-press rig from a farmer to make cider for himself and his brothers. Then they started making enough to sell and therefore opened a shop. Soon they amassed enough old rigs (42 now!) to qualify as a museum so they would qualify for brown road signs which would help people find them. Next they built a bigger shop to sell local produce including cheese, sausages, chutneys, pickles and preserves and plants from the nursery next door. And then they assembled the 30 grandfather clocks and four turret clocks they owned between them as a separate museum. Visitors who expect a more formal operation might be dismayed, but turn up with the right attitude and you'll soon enjoy the spirit of things.

◀ *Some of the beers from Hall & Woodhouse*

▲ *The tasting room at Langham Wine Estate*

VINEYARDS

4 FURLEIGH ESTATE

⌂ Furleigh Farm, Salway Ash DT6 5JF ✆ 01308 488991 ⟋ furleighestate.co.uk ⏲ 11.00–17.00 Mon–Sat; tours 11.00, 14.30 Wed, Fri, Sat. In 2004 Rebecca Hansford and Ian Edwards were changing careers as actuaries in the pensions industry when the opportunity came up to buy the 85-acre dairy farm Rebecca's father had once owned. So of course they did. Some 17 acres of the gently rolling land were found to be perfect for Chardonnay, Pinot Noir and Pinot Meunier, so they planted 22,000 vines (including some Rondo and Bacchus for still wines) and built a modern winery. Their bottle-fermented bubbles are world-beaters, but another factor that sets Furleigh apart is its absolutely gorgeous location. With its lakes, woods and meadows (not to mention its vine rows), it's a Dorset idyll, which is also the name of one of its finest sparkling wines.

5 LANGHAM WINE ESTATE

⌂ Crawthorne Farm, Crawthorne DT2 7NG ✆ 01258 839095 ⟋ langhamwine.co.uk ⏲ 10.00–16.00 Tue–Sun; guided & self-guided tours must be booked in advance. The Langham Estate is a 2,500-acre oyster with not one but two pearls: the largely 16th-century Bingham's Melcombe House and Crawthorne Farm, where in 2009 Justin Langham planted 30 acres of Chardonnay, Pinot Noir and Pinot Meunier vines and installed a winery in a historic barn. An equally old and picturesque milking parlour was converted into a café, tasting room and shop with sweeping views over the rolling vine-clad hills. Langham produces only bottle-fermented sparkling wines (a blended cuvée, a Chardonnay Blanc de Blancs, a Pinot Noir/Pinot Meunier rosé and Blanc de Noirs) which epitomise English sparkling wine. They continue to try and reduce the amount of chemical intervention by employing canopy management.

GLOUCESTERSHIRE

CIDER MILLS

6 DUNKERTONS

🏠 Dowdeswell Park, London Rd, Charlton Kings GL52 6UT 📞 01242 650145 🌐 dunkertonscider.co.uk 🕐 10.00–18.00 Mon–Fri, 10.00–17.00 Sat–Sun. Tours, tastings and masterclasses must be booked in advance. In 1982, Ivor and Suzie Dunkerton abandoned their media careers and fled to Herefordshire to restore a neglected cider orchard and live the bucolic dream. In the process they became the first certified all-organic cidermakers and pioneered bottled single-varietals and perries. Their products appealed to refined urban wine drinkers rather than traditional cider fans, and their superb ciders and perries quickly acquired legendary status among buffs. In 2014 son Julian, of Superdry and Lucky Onion hotels fame, took over and moved the entire operation to refined urban Cheltenham, where instead of oak and cobwebs there are rows of giant stainless-steel tanks and a very chic boutique. However, the cider hasn't changed. The apples still come from the same orchards; they're still organic; they're still legendary. Only now they're hip too.

7 HAYLES FRUIT FARM

🏠 Winchcombe GL54 5PB 📞 01242 602123 🌐 haylesfruitfarm.co.uk 🕐 shop 09.00–17.00 (Jan–Mar closed Mon), café 09.00–17.00 (Nov–Mar closed Mon). Established in 1880 by the local landowner, Lord Sudeley, to produce apples and

▲ *The shop at Dunkertons Cider*

cobnuts, the farm started diversifying after World War II into stone fruit and soft fruit, then into leisure. With camping, nature trails, coarse fishing, clay pigeon shooting, PYO (in season), a well-stocked farm shop and the highly regarded Orchard Café all thriving, it's more a farm holiday camp than just a farm. Cider has been made in the district, and possibly on this very site, since the late 12th century, but today's Badger's Bottom range (three still, a sparkling and an authentic perry) is rather more sophisticated than traditional farm scrumpy, and it all makes camping on the farm a more memorable experience.

8 NATIONAL PERRY PEAR COLLECTION

⌂ Orchard Centre, Blackwell's End, Hartpury GL19 3DB ⌀ nationalperrypearcentre.org.uk ☉ Visitors are welcome at any time – parking (if gates closed) is on hardstanding outside the main gate & access is via kissing gates. It's a cheat including the Orchard Centre in a visitors' guide since the facilities amount to an information board. Nevertheless it's a place of pilgrimage for everybody who loves perry. Essentially it comprises 30 acres of wetland and orchards, the latter including more than 100 varieties of perry pears, many of them endangered and rescued from hedgerows and paddocks by enthusiasts as a DNA bank in case of future need. The collection was formed in 2003 by the merger of two smaller units and found a home on a very appropriate parcel of donated land: the '-pury' element in Hartpury means 'place of pears' and Blackwell's End is a prehistoric trackway lined with wild service, wild pears and crabs. The site teems with wildlife and you are welcome to roam at your leisure provided your dog stays on the lead – sheep and cattle graze the orchard. One thing you'll notice if you visit at the right time of year is that most perry pears aren't pear-shaped!

VINEYARDS

9 POULTON HILL ESTATE

⌂ Poulton, Cirencester GL7 5JA ⌀ 01285 850257 ⌀ poultonhillestate.co.uk ☉ 09.00–17.00 Mon–Fri; tours/tastings Jun–Oct 11.00 Mon–Fri. Founded in 2010 by local businessman Mark Thomas, Poulton Hill produces a wide range of white and rosé still and sparkling wines on seven acres of Bacchus, Seyval Blanc, Pinot Noir, Regent and Rondo vines, as well as a grape brandy and an award-winning sloe eau de vie. It is perhaps best known in the wine world for trademarking the word 'bulari' (from the Latin 'bulla', as in 'ebullient') as a generic term to describe English sparkling wine. Visitors may stay in a Cotswold stone barn recently converted into a three-bedroom luxury guesthouse.

10 THREE CHOIRS

⌂ Ledbury Rd, Newent GL18 1LS ⌀ 01531 890223 ⌀ three-choirs-vineyards.co.uk ☉ shop 09.00–12.00 Mon, 10.00–17.00 Tue, 09.00–17.00 Wed–Sun; brasserie 12.00–14.00 & 18.30–21.00, closed Mon; tours 11.30 Wed, Fri, Sat. One of England's oldest and largest vineyards, Three Choirs started off as half an acre planted on Fairfield Fruit Farm by owner Alan McKechnie in 1973. After his retirement in 1986 the new owner, John Oldacre, renamed it after the Three Choirs Festival that rotated annually between Gloucester, Worcester and Hereford cathedrals. He also extended the planting to 75 acres, turned the farmhouse into a luxury hotel and built a brand-new winery and visitor centre. After his death in 2001 three exclusive lodges were built right among the vine rows and, with its top-end brasserie, Three Choirs is not just a place to visit but a Tuscan hideaway in Gloucestershire. It and its sister vineyard in Hampshire (Wickham Estate) focus on a broad and varied range of still table wines but they also produce a non-vintage cuvée at a surprisingly reasonable price.

▲ *Three Choirs Vineyard*

SOMERSET

CIDER MILLS

11 EMILY ESTATE

✉ Hadspen Hall, Castle Cary BH7 7NG ✆ 01963 359172 ☷ thenewtinsomerset.com ⏲ May–Oct 10.00–18.00 daily, Nov–Apr 10.00–16.30 daily. The painstaking restoration of Hadspen Hall, a Palladian mansion built in 1680, and its spectacular gardens by South African telecoms magnate Koos Bekker and designer Karen Roos has been one of the wonders of the West Country in recent years. The gardens – colloquially called The Newt because they include a habitat for the rare great crested newt – run to 20 acres, laid out by some of the great names in 19th- and 20th-century garden design. The work here echoes a similar project by the pair in South Africa that included a vineyard; this being Somerset, though, there are plenty of apples. A collection of 3,500 trees of 500 varieties has been planted so far, including a 500-tree maze, a 1,900-tree orchard of standards and others such as espaliers and cordons. The apples are, of course, used to make cider, which you can enjoy in the bar or in the glass-fronted restaurant and also buy in the delicatessen.

12 HECKS
See page 40.

12 HECKS

SOMERSET CIDERMAKING ANCIENT & MODERN.

✉ 9–11 Middle Leigh, Street BA16 0LB ✆ 01458 442367 🖰 heckscider.com 🕘 09.00–17.00 Mon–Sat, 10.00–12.30 Sun/bank holidays.

Between 1887 when the last Truck Act finally outlawed payment of wages in kind and 2003 when the Licensing Act banned the unlicensed 'farm gate' sale of alcoholic liquor, the highways and byways of the South West, especially Somerset and Devon, were literally lined with farms that still made small quantities of cider for their own use but sold their surpluses to passers-by. This nod to the tourist trade was officially sanctioned as late as 1976 when Chancellor Denis Healey formally exempted producers of up to 1,500 gallons a year from liability for duty – an exemption that is still relevant today, albeit in metric. Nevertheless, the number of 'scrumpy farms' inexorably dwindled so much that when the 2003 Act took effect, there were fewer than a couple of dozen left, and not many of them bothered with all the faff of taking out a liquor licence.

One of those that did was Hecks – not a smallholding down a maze of lanes, but a common-or-garden working farm in the middle of Street, a large industrial village once the home of Clarks shoes. Perhaps because of the proximity of Glastonbury, or maybe because the old Clarks factory had been turned into a renowned shopping village that attracted visitors by the thousands, or possibly because of the quality of its cider, Hecks was already a revered institution when the Act came into force. The head of the family at the time, the late John Heck, decided to continue and to expand. It was a difficult decision, but it meant the continuation of a family tradition established as long ago as the 1840s.

In those days the Heck family farmed in Chard and like any Somerset farmer they made cider for themselves and their labourers. In or around 1870 they seem to have started making enough for farm-gate sales as well as for their own use, a sideline they continued when they migrated to

"HECKS WAS ALREADY A REVERED INSTITUTION WHEN THE ACT CAME INTO FORCE"

Street in 1914. However, after the 2003 Act the pace had to change. The family was already selling single-variety fresh-pressed apple juice; but it also broke with the old orthodoxy that with a few exceptions, such as Kingston Black, only blended ciders are reliably consistent. Today, the family

▶ Somerset scenes at Hecks: orchards in fruit and in blossom; maturing stocks; an Aladdin's cave

makes 15 single-varietal ciders and two of them, to pile heresy upon heresy, are made from dessert varieties. That's not the only change: you can still get your cider drawn from oak into ye olde plastic flagons, but you don't have to – they have a bottling line now as well. They also make mead. And since 2015 they've been exporting to the US – the height of heresy, surely!

Despite all this breathtaking innovation, the place still feels pretty traditional: a fairly nondescript yard studded with odds and ends of cidermaking gear ancient and modern; the shop no more than a barn, with some unidentifiable bits of ironmongery – mole traps, bull ticklers, trout spears and suchlike – hanging from the whitewashed walls; oak barrels in sturdy tiers; cheese – so much cheese!; and of course the inevitable jars of chutney pickle preserve. No tractor tours of the orchards at blossom time, no interactive displays, no DVDs spoken in drama-school Mummerset – just stuff you want to eat and drink. There may not be much to look at, but just smell the soul.

THE CIDER There are three basic ciders, dry, medium and sweet, all at 6.5% ABV. You could also try Portwine of Glastonbury at 6.5% ABV, giving you light effervesence and lemon tones.

APPLES

HUNDREDS OF VARIETIES OF APPLES GO INTO BRITAIN'S FINE CIDERS, BUT THEY DON'T ALL HAVE TO BE CIDER APPLES!

Contrary to West Country propaganda, perfectly good cider can be made from both the special apple varieties developed and grown in the South West and the West Midlands and the cookers and eaters more commonly found in East Anglia and the South East.

The difference lies mainly in their different balances of sugar, acid and tannin. Cider apples are classified as either bittersharp or bittersweet owing to their high tannin content, while eaters are generally sweets and cookers are sharps. Sweets and bittersweets can have the same sugar content,

but bittersharps taste less sweet because of their tannin while sweets taste sweeter because of their low acidity. The low tannin of eastern apples makes for a less astringent cider, but the higher tannin of the cider apple is a preservative that enables it to age and mature. A handful of cider apples can also be eaten straight from the tree – not many, mind, but among them is the king of cider apples, Kingston Black, which is also one of the few traditionally thought sufficiently rounded and balanced to make a good single-varietal.

Within those broad categories there are literally thousands of varieties cultivated over the centuries for all sorts of reasons: to suit local soils, to extend the picking season, for juice content, for sugar content, for hardiness, for weight of crop, for keeping qualities – you name it. Naturally each new variety had a slightly different chemical balance from all the others and, although the fresh, woody terpene farnesene is the dominant flavour component of pretty much all apples, there are so many other chemicals (as many as 300 aromatics alone) that the variety is, to quote Shakespeare, infinite. What people like most about them, though, is their funny names, which can themselves be pretty Shakespearean sometimes: Chelston Piemaker, Sheep's Nose, Fair Maid of Taunton, Fill Barrel, Slack Ma Girdle, Greasy Pippin, Golden Knob... with such a long list to choose from, it's hard to know when to stop.

Many of these old varieties are very rustic and are no longer suitable for large-scale cultivation. They are all descended from wildings found by chance to have the right qualities for cidermaking, and since they are propagated from grafts and are therefore clones, their immune systems never evolve. Inevitably they succumb to diseases which they can't fight off. There are heritage orchards and collections dotted across the country all dedicated to their preservation, but the cider industry is dominated by a handful of trusty all-rounders including Dabinett, Yarlington Mill, Foxwhelp and Harry Master's Jersey.

England's southwestern counties – Herefordshire, Worcestershire, Gloucestershire, Somerset, Devon and to a lesser extent Cornwall and Dorset – are the traditional heartlands of cidermaking, partly because their tracts of hilly terrain and thin soil and the region's changeable climate have always required multiple use to guarantee a decent return. Of course specialisation and a drive for efficiency as consequences of the cider industry's great strides from 1900 on have seen many traditional orchards of standard trees grubbed up and replaced by uniform and somewhat uninspiring rows of dwarf or bush trees, which were developed in the 1980s. But beside and sometimes behind all the regimented modernity you will find, if you look hard enough, that Zummerzet is still there.

"MANY OF THESE OLD VARIETIES ARE VERY RUSTIC AND ARE NO LONGER SUITABLE FOR LARGE-SCALE CULTIVATION"

The backstory of the eastern cider region – principally Norfolk, Suffolk, Essex, Cambridgeshire, Kent and Sussex – is the very opposite. These counties surround London in a vast crescent, and from them produce of all kinds flowed directly to the capital's processors and markets. Top fruit, soft fruit, salad veg, leafy veg, roots, hops, the finest malting barley, saffron and cut flowers, to name a few. But what to do with the surpluses of good years? In the case of soft fruit, make jam. Tiptree and Chivers are Essex names!

Crosse & Blackwell in London started pickling East Anglian veg in 1706. And as for the region's surplus apples? They don't have to be turned into jam or chutney... they could always be turned into cider!

13 PERRY BROS

⌂ Dowlish Wake, Ilminster TA19 0NY ☎ 01460 55195 ☞ perryscider.co.uk ⏲ 09.00–17.30 Mon–Fri, 09.30–16.30 Sat, 10.00–13.00 Sun; café 10.30–16.30, closed Sun. In a thatched stone barn dating from the 16th century you will find (if you keep a close eye on the sat nav) a cider mill so emblematic of all things Somerset you could exhibit it at travel shows around the world. Perry Brothers was founded in 1920 by one William Churchill, who bought Lot 9 in the auction at the dissolution of Dowlish Wake Manor due to unpaid death duties. Four generations on, his descendants still do things the right way. The ciders are 100% fresh-pressed juice, naturally fermented, unpasteurised and with no trace of rhubarb, mango or pineapple. (The Redstreak single-varietal is legendary.) The café does mammoth ploughman's lunches and cream teas and the shop is crammed with local produce. In addition, the collection of antique farming and cidermaking kit qualifies as a museum. All in all, a perfect Somerset day out.

14 RICH'S CIDER

⌂ Mill Farm, Watchfield, Highbridge TA9 4RD ☎ 01278 794537 ☞ richscider.co.uk ⏲ 09.00–18.00 Mon–Sat, 10.00–18.00 Sun. Gordon Rich started selling cider from Mill Farm in 1954, although his forebears had been making the stuff for maybe three centuries before that. Rationing had ended, the economy was recovering, people were beginning to enjoy life again and no touring or caravanning holiday in the West Country was complete without a cream tea

and a few flagons of genuine farm cider or perry to take home. Given its proximity to Burnham-on-Sea and Weston-super-Mare, Rich's soon became one of the region's best-known cider farms and one of the few whose all-natural products achieved a wider distribution. Now with the third generation involved, the business is as successful as ever, with the 70-cover Cider Press carvery and restaurant adding to the attraction of orchard walks, a play area, the traditional press and all those huge, imposing oak maturing vats.

15 SHEPPY'S

See page 46.

16 SOMERSET ROYAL CIDER BRANDY/ BURROW HILL CIDER

⌂ Pass Vale Farm, Kingsbury Episcopi, Martock TA12 6BU ☎ 01460 240782 ☞ somersetciderbrandy.com ⏲ shop 09.00–17.00 Mon–Sat; guided tours by arrangement. Self-guided orchard trails. Even before the first drop of Somerset Royal Cider Brandy fell from the sweet lips of Josephine the antique French copper pot still in 1989, Julian Temperley's Burrow Hill Cider was a powerful operation. At 150 acres it was the region's biggest orchard, producing 80,000 gallons of absolutely top-quality cider. That hasn't changed, but it's the distillery he founded after a long tussle with UK Customs to be granted England's first all-new distilling licence for the best part of a century that made headlines and history. Praise be that he stuck it out and won! Today the extended Somerset royal family of various expressions of brandy, liqueurs and

▲ *The Railway Inn*

aperitifs sits beside a cider range that includes perry, bottle-fermented sparkling cider and ice cider. Feel free to roam the orchards and climb Burrow Hill itself for a view over the levels to Glastonbury Tor.

17 THATCHERS

⌂ Myrtle Farm, Sandford BS25 5RA ✆ 01934 822862 ⊘ thatcherscider.co.uk ⊙ 09.00–18.00 Mon–Sat, 10.00–13.00 Sun. Thatchers has always been one of the Big Two independent cidermakers along with Westons (page 118) of Herefordshire. Now the Big Two national makers – Bulmers and Taunton – have been swallowed up, Thatchers and Westons are out there in front. Of the two, Westons has always been the more outgoing, Thatchers the more self-contained. Its buildings aren't especially mouthwatering and Sandford is no beauty spot, but since its centenary year in 2004 the company seems to have decided to stop hiding its light under a bushel. The new Jubilee Building is an architectural gem that houses the packaging and warehousing but the shop has been vastly extended and enhanced, the old Railway Inn next door has been reopened with a brand-new glass-sided barn-style bar and restaurant; tours (which must be booked) are often sold out weeks in advance. The cider range has been thoroughly revamped as well: Traditional and Rascal are still there but alongside them are craft bottled ciders as imaginative as anything an artisan maker could dream of.

15 SHEPPY'S

WHY, JUNIOR – LOOK HOW BIG YOU'VE GROWN!

✉ Three Bridges, Bradford-on-Tone TA4 1ER ✆ 01823 461233 ✆ sheppyscider.com ⏱ 09.00–17.30 Mon–Sat, 10.00–16.00 Sun. Orchard walks by appointment.

▲ *The brewery*

A few miles as the carrion crow flies from the giant Taunton Cider factory there once stood a medium-sized family-owned maker of ciders of high repute called Sheppy's. It had been there since 1917 when the Shepston family moved in. As dairy farmers from a neighbouring village, the family had made a bit of cider like Somerset farmers used to do; because if you ran livestock under standard trees you got two crops off one patch of ground – three if you counted mistletoe.

After the war farming got more and more mechanised and most farmers decided that cidermaking was no more than an interference

with more productive operations. For those that stuck with it, though, it became a bigger part of their sales and a serious business well worth a bit of time, effort and investment. Add to that the sudden availability of parcels of land – as high death duties forced country estates to sell a field or two whenever somebody died – and it's easy to see how the 1920s and 30s were a mini-golden age for small commercial cidermakers. Names like Coates, Perry Brothers, Wilkins, Coombe's, Inch's and the mighty Taunton itself are of that vintage; some of them are with us still.

▲ *The Apple Bay bar and restaurant*

One of them was Stanley Sheppy (after years of abbreviation the nickname had become official), who turned out to be a dab hand at cidermaking and the winner of a fair few prizes. Three Bridges continued as a dairy farm – and at nearly 400 acres a sizeable one – but more and more of the pastures and meadows were sprouting apple trees as Sheppy's reputation steadily grew. Like many of the mid-ranking independents it stuck to traditional methods – using only fresh-pressed juice, fermenting with natural yeast, maturing in giant oak vats – and kept well away from the corporate maelstrom of merger and takeover. One by one Showerings, Coates and in 1998 even Taunton laid off their workers and invited the bulldozers in. Not Sheppy's. Its gates opened right on to the A38 and as motoring holidays became the norm, more and more people chose to pull in en route for Devon for a cup of tea, a wander round the mountain of old kit the site was accumulating and a few bottles of Bullfinch or Goldfinch to make the B&B more bearable. (They'd pull in for a few more on the way home, too!) It was a cheerful place: a bit scruffy, a bit amateurish as visitor attractions go, but very laid-back, a welcome relief from the interminable road to Torquay, and a purveyor of some of the very best commercial ciders the West Country had to offer.

If the wraiths of the old Ford Popular and Morris Traveller drivers of the 1950s and 60s pulled in now, their spectral eyes would pop out of their ghostly sockets. They wouldn't recognise the place.

Success was long in the growing but great in the growth: single-varietal ciders, a novelty but made the traditional way as above, gave Sheppy's (as it did Thatchers, page 45) a distinctive place in the booming bottled cider market. A successful export drive added more sales and by 2015 it was time to build a completely new factory and open up the old red-brick buildings to a grateful public.

The Apple Bay bar and restaurant and the well-stocked farm shop specialise in local produce not just from Sheppy's itself (including premium beef from the Longhorns, which have supplanted the old dairy herd) but from other local producers too. The collection of antiques and curios is now a pukka Museum of Country Life, there are free try-before-you-buy tastings in the shop or you can buy up to four samples in the bar. The only thing that hasn't changed is that it's still a welcome relief along the interminable road to Torquay.

THE CIDER For those who like dry, try Kingston Black 6.5% ABV, finely balanced with some sparkle. For medium, taste the slightly stronger Vintage Reserve 7.4% ABV. And, for those who like sweet, Cider with Raspberry 4.0% ABV is summery with an elderflower finish, or go for the Original Cloudy 4.5% ABV.

18 TORRE CIDER

⌂ Washford, Watchet TA23 0LA ✆ 01984 640004 ⟲ torrecider.co.uk ◷ shop & tea room 09.00–17.00 daily; guided tours by arrangement. Although Torre Cider has only been going since the mid-1980s, everything about it conjures up images of 1940s and 50s-era innocence. The star of the play area is an old tractor the kids can climb all over in their baggy shorts and T-bar sandals; they can also charge about in the orchards to their hearts' content; there are ickle pigs and lambikins to see; the shop is an unfailing source of locally made fudge and other goodies; the tea room has cream teas with lashings of strawberry jam. Watch out for the cider, though: it's all naturally fermented from the fresh-pressed juice of the farm's own cider, dessert and culinary apple varieties, totally the real thing, undiluted and consequently strong – the strongest, the aptly named Sheep Stagger, is 7.4% alcohol. The kids should probably stick to the ginger beer...

....

19 WILKINS CIDER

⌂ Land's End Farm, Mudgley, Wedmore BS28 4TU ✆ 01934 712385 ⟲ wilkinscider.com ◷ 10.00–20.00 (10.00–13.00 Sun). Roger Wilkins's cider barn is a solid and uncompromising stone structure furnished with upturned crates and other improvised seats, and with great big barrels of incalculable age filled with Roger's ciders dry, medium and sweet. The cider's as real as it can be: blended by taste alone; fermented in oak by wild yeasts; left to work itself out however long it takes; unfiltered, unpasteurised, virgin from the vat to your flagon just as it was when Roger's

grandfather moved here in 1917 and when Roger as a 13-year-old started working alongside him. Turn up, sit on something, try a bit of this and a bit of that, buy some of Roger's unpasteurised cheddar – what more could anyone want?

VINEYARD

20 PENNARD ORGANIC WINES & CIDERS

⌂ Avalon Vineyard, The Drove, Shepton Mallet BA4 6UA ✆ 01749 86039 ⟲ pennardorganicwines.co.uk ◷ 10.00–18.00 Tue–Sat, 12.00–18.00 Sun; tours by arrangement only. There is a shop on site, but no other facilities: you are welcome to wander there, walk your dog, spread the picnic rug and afterwards call at the shop for a free tasting and perhaps buy some of their delicious wine. Avalon Vineyard sits at the very end of a long lane and beyond lies an uncertain sea of billowing green that Hugh and Hilary Tripp tend and nurture with careful understanding. Since 1981 when they planted their first half-acre of Orion and Seyval Blanc, not a drop of pesticide or fertiliser or even fungicide has been spilt upon it. They have introduced hybrid vines that have been crossed with native American vines, which helps a resistance to mildew and so eliminates the need to spray. They also built their own winery and planted their own orchards in 1987; they interplanted with soft and stone fruit for biodiversity and equally for fruit wines and liqueurs.

▶ *The Somerset Levels with Glastonbury Tor in the far distance*

GRAPES

GRAPES ARE PERFECT – THAT'S ALL.

Few fruits are more versatile than grapes. They flourish in a huge range of climates and are equally at home eaten straight off the vine, dried for storage or pressed for their sugar-rich juice. The leaves can be stuffed and eaten and even the debris is useful as animal feed or marc. Other sources of fermentable sugar, such as the honey, rice and fruit traces found in 9,000-year-old pottery vessels in China discovered in 2004, may well have helped humankind to make merry four millennia before the first evidence of winemaking; but grapes are definitely the best.

That's not to infuriate beer-lovers and others by suggesting that wine is superior to their beverage of choice, but as a single source the grape beats malt hands down. It has got absolutely everything you need to make liquor, and strong liquor at that – as strong as you can get without distilling it. And it's accessible. You don't have to steep it or cook it or grind it to a paste: the only process required is to squeeze and leave. You don't even have to drain it, and you definitely don't want to wash it before use. Yes, grapes are perfect. And here's why.

The skins contain red and yellow pigments, tannin, aromatics and minerals and are dusted with wild yeast, which if you don't kill off and replace it with a cultured strain will give you an uncertain fermentation. The pulp beneath the skin consists of large hollow cells whose vacuoles contain the juice, which makes up 70–85% of the berry's weight. Of course this is mostly water, but it has an array of dissolved compounds that makes it a little chemical factory in its own right. These include enough fermentable sugar (mostly fructose and glucose) to generate an alcohol content of 11–14%; acids that affect the wine's stability and create tart flavours; nitrogenous compounds including proteins to feed the yeast during fermentation; and aromatics including pyrazine, guaiacol and terpenes that will emerge during fermentation and develop during maturation. The pips also have their role: they contain yet more pigments and tannins that are critical to stable maturation.

So that's the grape: a status symbol, a ritual, an allegory, an accompaniment, a toast to love and friendship or just a really good party, all contained within a single skin as round and plump as a puppy's tummy. But there's more.

Not only is the berry packed full of juicy goodness, the vine that bears it is a tough customer that, in ancient times, made subsistence farming a lot more profitable as well as a lot more bearable. Vines actively reject both the most fertile arable land, which is often too rich for them, and the lushest pasture, which is generally too wet. They like a light, well-drained soil, sandy or even gravelly, on a slope or terrace otherwise uncultivable and only suitable for rough pasture. They are susceptible to frost, especially in March when their buds begin to break and a single ill-timed cold snap can ruin an entire vintage – hence the expression 'nipped in the bud'. They'd rather be halfway up a slope than in a valley that might be damp year-round and turn into a frost hollow in winter and early spring. They like to face southwest for maximum sunlight and

hence maximum sweetness; but you can tell by their range, from Algeria to Alsace, that they're not all that fussy about climate: over the centuries, varieties have been developed that can flourish in a huge range of climatic conditions, and climate change is extending their range still further.

"SO THAT'S THE GRAPE: A STATUS SYMBOL, A RITUAL, AN ALLEGORY, AN ACCOMPANIMENT, A TOAST TO LOVE AND FRIENDSHIP"

In fact they're perfect for the farmer's second-best soil, from which they, more than any other crop, can extract a harvest that princes and prelates will pay a king's ransom for. And even when a vine comes to the end of its life, it has one more gift to give: top-quality charcoal, equally prized by the artist and the pitmaster.

CHAPTER THREE
SOUTH

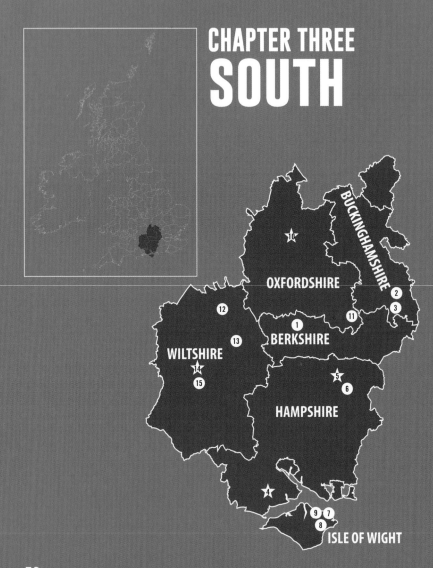

BUCKINGHAMSHIRE

OXFORDSHIRE

WILTSHIRE

BERKSHIRE

HAMPSHIRE

ISLE OF WIGHT

BERKSHIRE

BUCKINGHAMSHIRE

▲ *Stanlake Park, the coach house*

▲ *Ringwood Brewery tap room*

VINEYARD

BREWERY

1 STANLAKE PARK

✉ Waltham Rd, Twyford RG10 0BN ✆ 0118
934 0176 ⊘ stanlakepark.com ⏲ 12.00–17.00
Wed–Sun. The first planting of just 500 vines in
1979 puts Stanlake Park firmly in the first wave
of the English winemaking revival. In its early
years as Thames Valley Vineyard it flourished as
a producer of mainly German-style still whites
and contract winemaker for other growers. It now
has more than 25 acres under vines that include
the classic Champagne varieties, and produces
a highly regarded range of both single-varietal
and blended still whites and two very reasonably
priced sparkling wines. The 17th-century manor
house itself is not open to the public but Stanlake
Park makes good use of its outbuildings: the shop
and tasting room are in a Victorian greenhouse
with outdoor seating in a walled garden; the
winery is in a 17th-century barn; and another
historic barn is a popular wedding venue.

2 CHILTERN BREWERY

✉ Nash Lee Rd, Terrick HP17 ✆ 01296 613647
⊘ chilternbrewery.co.uk ⏲ year-round 10.00–
17.00 Mon, 10.00–18.00 Tue–Thu, 09.00–19.00
Fri, 09.00–17.00 Sat. Tours 14.00–15.30 Fri–Sat,
ring ahead to confirm availability. Group tours by
arrangement. Set in a little-visited but beautiful
stretch of the rolling and well-wooded Chiltern
Hills, the brewery was founded in 1980 on a
working farm by Richard and Lesley Jenkinson
who have now passed the baton to sons Tom
and George. Chiltern first found fame among
beer-lovers for its classic 8.5% ABV Bodger's
Barley Wine, named in honour of the region's
rustic wood-turners. Today it brews the gamut of
strengths, styles and shades but is still best-known
for strong, dark beers such as its three Vintage
Imperial Stouts and its Cream Porter. The brewery
shop is a cornucopia of English wines and spirits,
cheeses, sausages, beer, bread and things in jars.

GIN DISTILLERY

3 WAYFINDER SPIRITS
🏠 35 Aylebury End, Beaconsfield HP9 1LU
📞 01494 674104 🌐 wayfindersretreat.com
🕐 16.00–midnight Tue–Thu, 16.00–01.00 Fri–Sat. Tours need to be booked but they're not really tours: they're masterclasses in cocktail-mixing and botanical-blending. This is hardcore. Be prepared. Standing around glumly waiting for the tasting is not on the agenda for visitors touring the Wayfinder distillery at the Wayfinder's Retreat cocktail bar, formerly the Treehouse and before that the Charles Dickens and before that – since about 1600, in fact – The Star. The distillery was installed by a cadre of fanatical experimenters whose first product was a peach, clove and orange-infused American whiskey called Northern Discomfort and whose standard pouring gin has chilli, pimento and coriander seed among its botanicals. Limited editions, the weirder the better, are the house speciality.

HAMPSHIRE

BREWERY

4 RINGWOOD BREWERY
See page 56.

GIN DISTILLERY

5 BOMBAY SAPPHIRE DISTILLERY
See page 58.

VINEYARD

6 HATTINGLEY VALLEY
🏠 Wield Yard, Lower Wield, Alresford SO24 9AJ
📞 01256 389188 🌐 hattingleyvalley.com
🕐 09.00–17.00 Mon–Fri; winery tours must be booked; not available during harvest (mid-Sep–mid-Nov); vineyard tours occasionally available. Alresford was best known for its watercress before viticulturalists discovered that its rolling slopes, chalky soil and mild climate were ideal terroire for sparkling varieties including Chardonnay and the three Pinots. Simon Robinson was engaged when he heard a radio programme in 2000, on the rapidly developing English wine scene. After much thought and analysis, in May 2008, his Hattingley adventure began when planting started and in the same year Emma Rice joined as winemaker. The custom-built solar-powered winery was completed in 2010 and the first release was in 2013.

◀ *The Bombay Sapphire Distillery*

4 RINGWOOD BREWERY

IS THIS THE PLACE WHERE THE NEW AGE OF BREWING WAS BORN? WELL, ALMOST.

✉ 138 Christchurch Rd, Ringwood BH24 3AP ✆ 01425 470303 🖰 ringwoodbrewery.co.uk
🕘 09.30–17.00 Mon–Sat; tours must be booked in advance.

▲ *Vintage dray at Ringwood Distillery*

There's no visitor centre here, there's not even a brewery tap – just a shop with tasting bar and a few guided tours every week; but this is such an important shrine to beer-lovers that anyone who rates themselves a fan will make the hoppy pilgrimage at least once in their lifetime. For this was the headquarters of the Father of Microbrewing, Peter Austin.

Some would say the accolade is not entirely deserved. Many if not most of the founders of the early microbreweries had had distinguished careers in the mainstream brewing industry before redundancy drove them to set up on their own and provided the wherewithal to do it. Peter Austin was one of them. When Hull Brewery, where he was head brewer and worked for 30 years, was taken over by Northern Foods in 1975 Peter withdrew to Hampshire, aged only 54. Three years of the quiet life was plenty, and in 1978 he founded Ringwood in an old bakery in Minty's Yard, New Street. That was actually six years after the foundation of the world's first microbrewery, Selby of North Yorkshire, established by Martyn Sykes. Martyn was also a founding member of CAMRA's national executive and helped many newcomers get started; but Peter eclipsed him in proselytising zeal and earned the Father of Microbrewing accolade by becoming as much a consultant as a brewer, pretty much leaving the running of Ringwood to David Welsh.

"PETER WAS THE APOSTLE OF MICROBREWING, EARNING REVERENCE FROM CASK ALE DRINKERS"

David, whose background was in the City, was very much the business dynamo of the two. Although Ringwood never had any pubs of its own, by 1986 sales of its beers, especially its two strong ales – Fortyniner (4.9% ABV) and Old Thumper (originally 5.6% ABV) – were such that the brewery had to move into today's rather grander premises. This featured a large yard and handsome brick buildings that was purely coincidentally the site of Tunk's Brewery, which closed in 1821. The beers' rich, strong, toffee-ish character perhaps betrayed Peter's northern experience but it did them no harm in the south: the brewhouse has had to be expanded twice to cope with increasing levels of production. In 1988 Old Thumper became the second-ever microbrewery product to win CAMRA's Champion Beer of Britain award, the first having been Pitfield Brewery's Dark Star the previous year.

Meanwhile Peter was the Apostle of Microbrewing, earning reverence from cask ale drinkers and even grudging respect from the big brewers. As well as founding and chairing the Small Independent Brewers' Association in 1980, he helped establish 40 microbreweries in the UK and a further 100 around the world over the course of a decade. His first venture in consultancy – perhaps his most memorable but sadly his least successful – was helping *Monty Python* star Terry Jones set up a microbrewery in Penrhos Court, Herefordshire, which sadly lasted only from 1977 until 1983. His impact in the USA was, by contrast, immense: he helped found 74 breweries there and was one of the leading figures behind the country's microbrewing revolution.

After Peter sold his share of Ringwood to David to pursue consultancy more vigorously, the brewery became the first of its kind to be sold to a much bigger mainstream rival: Marston's (page 128) bought it for more than £19 million in 2007. You might therefore argue that the current brewery is not really a memorial to Peter (he died in 2014 aged 92), but we reckon you won't be saying that if you actually make your pilgrimage.

> **THE BEER** Try Old Thumper 5.15 ABV, fruity and hoppy, Circadian 4.5% ABV, packed with American hops giving you a citrus and pine flavour, or Razor Back 3.85% ABV, malty with a toffee finish.

5 BOMBAY SAPPHIRE DISTILLERY

NOT QUITE NEW WINE IN OLD BOTTLES, BUT A VERY NEW DISTILLERY IN A VERY OLD BUILDING.

✉ Laverstoke Mill, London Rd, Whitchurch RG28 7NR ✆ 01256 890090 ⌖ distillery.bombaysapphire. com ⏱ 10.00–20.00 daily, last admission 18.00; tickets must be bought in advance, self-guided & hosted tours are available.

Visually and in every other way, this is going to be one of the most astonishing places you will see on your odyssey around the distilleries, breweries, cider mills and wineries of Great Britain. This early Georgian papermill, which in Victorian times made banknote paper for both the Bank of England and the Raj, ceased production in 1963 and was selected to be the home of Bombay Sapphire in 2010. The four-year transformation project that ensued boggles the mind.

The brand itself had had a confused background involving many changes of ownership in the musical-chairs world of global corporations. Suffice it to say that Bombay Dry was originally Greenall Whitley's Dry repackaged for the US market in 1960. By 1987 it had run out of steam, but rather than quietly drop it, its owners at the time, International Distillers & Vintners, decided on a truly Protean upgrade. A new name, a new bottle (blue, like the name), a new botanical grist including cubeb and grains of paradise and a new rectification regime using Carterhead stills all created a radically different gin: softer, richer, rounder and fatter than London dry brands and the first of a new generation of superbrands.

Bombay Sapphire didn't set the world alight from the word go, but then superbrands don't need to sell huge volumes to make solid profits – that's the whole point. It changed hands very quickly in the continuing corporate shuffle, first in 1997 when IDV was sold to United Distillers to form Diageo and again in 1998 when Diageo

"THE REDEVELOPMENT HAS BEEN A MODEL OF AESTHETIC AND ENVIRONMENTAL SENSITIVITY"

had to divest some of its brands to satisfy the competition authorities. New owner Bacardi wasn't entirely pleased that its star brand was still being made by Greenall's in Warrington and eventually found a new home here, literally straddling the River Test in deepest Hampshire.

It was an inspired choice of site, which has been treated with the utmost care and respect. The Test is one of the purest chalk streams in Britain, legendary among anglers for its brown trout and home to otters and a plethora of birdlife including heron and kingfisher. The redevelopment has been a model of aesthetic and environmental sensitivity.

▲ *Futuristic glasshouses at Bombay Sapphire Distillery*

Some of the old mill buildings stood over the river: they were carefully taken down, their bricks and tiles being reclaimed for use in new buildings, and in their place are the extraordinary glasshouses, their fluid organic lines complementing the formal angularity of the existing architecture.

A turbine in the river helps power the distillery, as do solar panels and a biomass boiler that burns locally sourced woodchips. The distilling process, necessitating as it does an awful lot of heating stuff up and then cooling it back down, uses a colossal amount of water, but Bombay Sapphire takes none from the River Test: instead the distillery harvests rainwater and uses flow-restricted equipment. All this is as important as the gin itself: there are other distillers — Adnams (page 156) and Roseisle spring to mind — that are equally environmentally conscious.

THE GIN Three distinct styles: Bombay Sapphire 40% ABV, the classic giving you a peppery finish, Star of Bombay 47.5% ABV, with added botanicals of bergamot and ambrette seeds, and Bombay Dry Gin 40% ABV, that puts the juniper first.

BEER STYLES

TODAY'S CRAFT BREWERS LOVE TO RING THE CHANGES. AND THEY OWE IT ALL TO MICHAEL JACKSON.

All beer was much the same, or at least most people thought it was, until 1989 when the late great Michael Jackson's documentary series *The Beer Hunter* was first aired on Channel 4 and the Discovery Channel. (The Michael Jackson from Leeds, not the one from Neverland.)

Suddenly the world knew that there was more to beer than bitter, lager, Guinness and, if you were very old, mild. In those benighted years BC (Before Craft), Michael's discovery that foreign lands had beer too and it wasn't very like ours came as news to the average British drinker, but it didn't provoke much of a reaction beyond an eye-roll and a tut. A few specialist beer importers found it a little easier to keep up with their mortgage repayments, but outside a tiny niche of enthusiasts 'foreign' continued to mean Danish lager from Northampton and Irish stout all the way from London NW10.

The microbrewers of the time proved far more amenable to trying new ideas or reinventing old ones than their mainstream competitors. The first microbrewer to win the Campaign for Real Ale's Champion Beer of Britain award was Pitfield of East London, which operated from a former, ahem, leather goods warehouse in Hoxton long before former, ahem, leather goods warehouses in Hoxton became the most desirable real estate in all Bohemia. Its competition winner in 1987 was Dark Star, a recreation of the kind of old ales last

produced in the 1940s when many brewers would blend the ullage, or sour beer and dregs returned by publicans, with dark mild to produce a sharp, tangy ale much loved (apparently) by East End OAPs.

"THEN CAME CRAFT, AND A HECTIC DECADE WHEN THE NUMBER OF BREWERIES IN BRITAIN ROSE FROM 600 TO MORE THAN 2,000"

Meanwhile other microbrewers simultaneously invented a bitter/lager hybrid, golden ale, a mid-strength very pale bitter overloaded (by the standards of the times) with aroma hops and intended to maintain the loyalty of bitter drinkers through the summer months when many of them defected to lager – the hope being that the hop flavour would survive the extreme chilling demanded by lager drinkers. Many of these golden ales also contained a proportion of wheat to provide a depth and roundness that would counter the tongue-numbing effects of refrigeration.

It has to be admitted that with a few outstanding exceptions – Woodforde's Wherry and Titanic Plum Porter being obvious exceptions – few of these beers really broke through, although many retained a cult following. The same was true in the lager world, where the pursuit of quality rather than innovation made national brands of Budweiser

Budvar and Pilsner Urquell from the Czech Republic but the big brands continued to dominate in terms of sales.

Then came Craft, and a hectic decade when the number of breweries in Britain rose from 600 to more than 2,000 fuelled by the increasingly eclectic taste of a new generation of affluent and cosmopolitan young professionals. Craft brewing is American in inspiration and if there's one thing Americans are keen on, it's minute categorisation. The Champion Beer of Britain competition has 14 classes, and here they are: Mild, Bitter, Best Bitter, Strong Bitter, Premium Bitter, Special Bitter, Golden Ale, Speciality Beer, Strong Ale, Old Ale, Barley Wine, Stout & Porter, New Brewery Beer and Bottle-Conditioned Beer. The last two aren't actually beer styles; stouts and porters are run together; and 'speciality beers' is a catch-all that covers everything from Mango Kölsch to Earl Grey Pale Ale (if such confections exist, that is). Judging at the Great American Beer Festival, by contrast, has 102 classes, of which 39 are sub-divided – although, to be fair, GABF embraces reproductions of European beer styles such as alt and saison, which the Champion Beer of Britain competition doesn't. However, American expertise in hair-splitting has also produced nonsenses such as Black IPA (the P stands for Pale!); so perhaps from the beer drinker's point of view a broader-brush approach to beer styles makes more sense.

ISLE OF WIGHT

GIN DISTILLERY

7 ISLE OF WIGHT DISTILLERY

⌂ Pondwell Hill, Ryde PO33 1PX ✐ 01983 613653 ⌖ isleofwightdistillery.com ⏱ 11.00–23.00 daily (summer). Check website for winter opening times. Co-founded in 2014 by Conrad Gauntlett of Rosemary Vineyard (see opposite) and Xavier Baker of Goddard's Brewery, this is – as far as records tell – the only distillery in the island's history. The building in which it is housed used to be a pub called The Wishing Well, now closed, whose sunny terrace overlooked the vineyard. Reopened as The Mermaid in January 2018, the stills are separated from the stone-flagged bar only by a glass screen, so tours are a little redundant, but there are regular short talks followed by free tastings. Their core Mermaid gin delivers a smooth but complex blend of fresh organic lemon zest and peppery notes, with a hint of sea air from locally foraged rock samphire. Their other products include a single malt whisky, a navy-strength dark rum, a dry gin, a pink gin, a navy-strength gin and a barrel-aged gin.

▲ *Adgestone Vineyard*

VINEYARDS

8 ADGESTONE VINEYARD

✉ Upper Rd, Brading PO36 0ES ✆ 01983 402882
 adgestonevineyard.co.uk ⏱ 10.00–17.30
Mon–Sat, 11.00–17.30 Sun (summer); see
website for winter opening hours. Planted in 1986,
Adgestone is one of the forerunners of the English
wine revival. Its table wines – Blush, Full-bodied
red, Dry Wight and Oaked White – are blended
from old favourites such as Bacchus, Schoenburger,
Rondo, Regent, Seyval Blanc and Orion; the
sparkling Something Blue makes good use of
Adgestone's Pinot Noir and Phoenix. Country wines
and liqueurs come from the fruit of the vineyard's
hedgerows. As well as the local produce shop and
café there are hour-long audio tours followed by
tutored tastings – no need to book. New plantings
include 120 vines at Brading Roman Villa 200yds
down the road, just as a reminder that there's
nothing new...

9 ROSEMARY VINEYARD

✉ Smallbrook Ln, Ryde PO33 4BE ✆ 01983
811084  rosemaryvineyard.co.uk ⏱see the
website for opening times & tour details;

audio-guided tours & tastings are free; group & private tours must be booked in advance. First planted in 1986, Rosemary Vineyard has grown to 30 acres over the years, making it one of the country's bigger growers. It hasn't just grown in size, either: the range has expanded from a core of two whites, a red and a rosé table wine to include a rosé and a white sparkler, still country wines, liqueurs, sparkling elderflower and cider. Also on sale is Mermaid Gin made by the Isle of Wight Distillery (page 62). The café and shop open on to an attractive courtyard surrounded by shady pergolas with a view of vines and wooded slopes.

OXFORDSHIRE

BREWERY

10 HOOK NORTON
See page 66.

VINEYARD

11 CHILTERN VALLEY WINERY & BREWERY
⌂ Old Luxters, Hambleden RG9 6JW
✆ 01491 638830 ⌕ chilternvalley.co.uk ⊙ shop 09.00–17.00 Mon–Fri, 11.00–17.00 Sat–Sun; evening group tours must be booked in advance. The first vines were planted at this former pig farm in 1982 by solicitor and wine buff David Ealand and the business just grew. When David retired from law in 1990 he converted the woodshed into a brewery specialising in bottle-fermented ales

to accompany the winery's wide range of still and sparkling wines. The farmhouse was later converted into a luxury B&B to accommodate visitors who didn't want to go home after their tours, while a 17th-century barn became one of the area's most sought-after wedding venues. The latest addition is a cookery and wine-pairing school.

WILTSHIRE

BREWERIES

12 ARKELLS
⌂ Kingsdown Brewery, Hyde Rd, Swindon SN2 7RU ✆ 01793 833966 ⌕ arkells.com ⊙ 09.00–17.00 Mon–Sat. Arkells is one of the many breweries established by a farmer and maltster who decided to take his business to the next level. In this case the guilty party was one John Arkell and the year of foundation was 1843, the very year in which Isambard Kingdom Brunel opened the Great Western Railway that transformed Swindon from country town to industrial hub. Arkells grew rapidly and in 1861 commissioned the rather handsome tower brewery you see today. Sadly it doesn't do tours (except virtual ones), but the visitor centre opened in 2018 by the Duchess of Cornwall houses not only a heritage centre and archive but a truly lavish shop. Grape & Grain is not just a brewery store but is the retail outlet of the brewery's wines and spirits wholesaling division, so the choice on offer is truly astonishing.

13 RAMSBURY ESTATE BREWING & DISTILLING

⌂ Stockclose Farm, Aldbourne, Marlborough SN8 2NN ✆ 01672 541407 ⌚ ramsburyestates. co.uk ⌛ 09.00–17.00 Mon–Fri, 09.00–13.00 Sat. On his 19,000-acre estate in North Wiltshire, H&M magnate Stefan Persson is emulating the processes that led John Arkell and John Carter to make their fortunes – except that Persson already had a fortune when he set up Ramsbury Brewery in 2004. But the evolution of food and drink production on the estate with its 27 farms might show how other farmers can go about harvesting profits in a post-EU era. The Ramsbury Distillery (opened in 2014), the Ramsbury Smokehouse, the shop and more recently the cold press all exist to make full use of the estate's produce and resources. Even the juniper for the gin (whose base spirit is made here from the estate's own wheat rather than being bought in) and some of the hops are locally grown.

14 WADWORTH

See page 68.

VINEYARD

15 A'BECKETT'S

⌂ High St, Littleton Panell, Devizes SN10 4EN ✆ 01380 816669 ⌚ abecketts.co.uk ⌛ 11.00–16.00 Wed–Sat; tours with tastings can be arranged for groups of 10–30, but nibbles are extra. Founded by Paul and Lynne Langham in 2001, the site has since grown to 12 acres, making it Wiltshire's biggest vineyard. The focus is on Chardonnay and Pinot Noir for the white and rosé sparklers, but the range of still wines includes single-varietal Pinot Auxerrois and Seyval Blanc too. The Langhams also restored an old table-fruit orchard and extended it to nine acres with cider varieties and perry pears. Barnstormer cider is fermented with Champagne yeast, and while the pear trees come to full bearing the Langhams produce a naturally fretting cider–perry hybrid. A'Beckett's offer a vine leasing scheme where you can rent 10, 25 or 50 vines over a year and have your own wine made.

▼ Chiltern Valley Winery & Brewery

10 HOOK NORTON

YOU MAY THINK IT'S A COUNTRY BREWERY, BUT HOOKIE WAS FOUNDED ON THE THIRST OF NAVVIES AND MINERS.

✉ Brewery Ln, Hook Norton OX15 5NY ☏ 01608 730384 ⌨ hooky.co.uk ⏰ 09.00–17.00 Mon–Sat, 10.00–16.00 Sun.

Not so very long ago – within living memory if you're over 70, in fact – most of Britain got its beer from local breweries much like this one: of modest size, family-owned, built as a tower to let gravity do the heavy work and selling most of its output via a compact bloc of tied houses. Precious few of them survived the corporate takeover binge that started in the 1960s, but one of the most precious that did is Hook Norton.

This was a 52-acre farm and maltings when John Harris bought it in 1849 and, as so many of his contemporaries did, he soon saw the sense of adding value to the malt he produced by turning it into beer. Brewing started in 1856 and in 1872 business was strong enough for Harris to commission the magnificent seven-storey tower brewery you see today. And have you noticed what it's built of? Locally quarried ironstone, that's what; and when in 1887 (the year of the founder's death) tests revealed that the iron content of the stone was much higher than had been previously thought, the sleepy Cotswold village suddenly became a hive of very lucrative activity.

First, hundreds of thirsty and well-paid navvies arrived to build a railway to carry all that ore to distant steelworks, as well as smaller tramways

to connect the railway to the individual workings. Then local men were recruited off the farms and from surrounding areas to dig away thousands of tons of overburden by hand and lift the ironstone by wheelbarrow to the tramlines. Vast kilns were built to calcine the stone before it was loaded on

▲ The classic 1899 steam engine
◄ The brewery designed by William Bradford

to the trains to make it lighter and more friable. All those men were well paid, and all those men were thirsty. By 1897 Hook Norton needed more capacity and hired the celebrated brewery architect William Bradford to add a new and much bigger brewhouse to the 1872 building. As you can see, Bradford was very fond of embellishment and decoration.

"ALL THOSE MEN WERE WELL PAID, AND ALL THOSE MEN WERE THIRSTY"

It all ended in 1948 when the last ironstone was lifted from the soil. How was Hook Norton to survive the corporate predators? When would Watneys come calling? Well, it undoubtedly helped that Harris had left the property to a trust and not to his actual heirs. Trustees have less to gain than shareholders from selling, and can be hard to convince. And although it's a fairly big brewery, it only had a handful of pubs – even today it's as many as 36 – and that made it a less attractive takeover target. So its beers were never barbarised and it still produces a range that if anything errs on the malty side. That means that its Dark Mild is astonishingly tasty for a beer of only 2.8% ABV; its session and strong bitters – Hooky and Old Hooky – are world classics; and its Hooky Gold makes lager redundant.

Because it's quite a big site, it's a longish tour – two hours from top to bottom, ending with a tasting in the cellars. You get to see an engineer's dream en route: the 1899 steam engine installed to hoist the malt, drive the pulleys, power the pumps and so forth, all of which functions uniquely and can still perform. You also get to meet the shires, which still deliver beer to the three village pubs – The Pear Tree, The Sun and The Gate Hangs High. The old maltings has been converted into a visitor centre with a shop, bar-restaurant and museum.

THE BEER Hooky 3.5% ABV, amber bitter, Old Hooky 4.6% ABV, fruity and full bodied, and Hooky Gold 4.1% ABV, fruity, zesty and with a citrus finish. You could also try their Original cider 4.8% ABV, medium dry.

67

14 WADWORTH

HEY, GOOD LOOKING! WHAT YA GOT COOKING? BEER, ACTUALLY. AND PIES.

⌂ 41–45 Northgate St, Devizes SN10 6QW ✆ 01380 732277 ⊘ wadworth.co.uk ⏱ 09.00–17.00
Mon–Sat; tours & tastings must be booked.

Devizes in Wiltshire is often voted one of the country's best places to live, and if looks are anything to judge by, its market square and high street make as fine a townscape as any in the land. There's the grand old Bear Hotel fronting the marketplace, with the elegant portico of the Corn Exchange right beside it, the no less grand Black Swan on the high street and closing off this panorama of civic dignity the six-storey Victorian red-brick colossus that is Wadworth & Co. Brewery. You'd be surprised and probably not best pleased to see a modern factory disfigure such a setting, but in the olden days they even built factories to impress.

Wadworth was founded by brothers-in-law H A Wadworth and J S Bartholomew in 1875 and the splendidly preserved tower brewery you wonder at today was built ten years later. Don't be fooled by its antique solemnity, though: inside, the Steinecker brewhouse is a marvel of modernity installed in 2008. That says a lot about Wadworth: it's very proud of its roots and heritage, but it's not afraid to modernise. Next to the Steinecker stands the original copper, which can still be fired up if required. As with Hook Norton, a horse-drawn dray is still used for local deliveries and the old steam engine is still oiled and polished and ready

for action. It seems they just don't throw things away here: they give them a dust down and stick them in the Brewseum (for which they make no apologies). Sadly, though, the celebrated cooperage had to close only a few years ago when the last cooper retired. Apparently new coopers are hard to find: the only place they grow them these days is Scotland, and it seems they don't grow any spares.

"A HORSE-DRAWN DRAY IS STILL USED FOR LOCAL DELIVERIES"

Wadworth don't throw their beer recipes away either. They've been making 6X here since 1923, and apart from the fact that its alcoholic strength had to be cut from 6% ABV to a more sessionable 4.1% ABV during the war because of malt rationing, its formula has never changed. It's an old-school malty best bitter, hoppy enough but not too hoppy, that became a national brand in the 1990s when Whitbread adopted it as its house best bitter. Another interesting beer produced here is Bishop's Tipple, a low-strength barley wine (it's low-strength for barley wine, that is!) actually produced by another brewer, Gibbs Mew of Salisbury, to celebrate the enthronement

of a new bishop in 1973. Gibbs Mew closed in 1998 and Usher's of Trowbridge brewed it for a couple of years until it too closed. Those were the days, eh? Wadworth took up the baton, brewing the Tipple at 5% ABV (cask) and 5.5% ABV (bottle-conditioned) as a strong bitter in its range. However, Wadworth also has an in-house microbrewery that produces up-to-the-minute craft beers, seasonal specials and limited editions. So everything from craft stout to old-style best bitter under one roof!

The visitor centre is new, purpose-built in 2007 and includes the Harness Room Bar where your post-tour tasting will be held, the brewery shop with another small bar and seating area and the aforementioned Brewseum with interactive displays. There's also a rather unusual light catering operation that consists entirely of pies. Nothing else, just pies. But very good pies.

▲ *The bottle-store at Wadworth c1950*
◄ *Wadworth's fortress-like brewery*

THE BEER Wadworth 6X 4.1% ABV, the absolute classic malt and fruit bitter, Henry's IPA 3.6% ABV, light in colour with delicate malt aromas, or if you are feeling adventurous try Swordfish 5% ABV, a blend of Wadworth Beer and Pusser's Navy Rum. Bishop's Tipple 5.5% ABV, good and strong.

HONEY

DESPITE MITES AND PESTICIDES, WORLD HONEY PRODUCTION IS RISING AND MEAD IS MAKING A COMEBACK TOO!

Honey is among the candidates for the earliest fermentable material used by humankind in its quest for a good night out. Not necessarily *the* earliest – various tree saps were also readily available sources of sugar for our technically unsophisticated ancestors – but honey has always had the advantage of being sweeter than any of its rivals. Of course, tree saps don't come with swarms of angry defenders to keep intruders at bay but, long before beekeepers started dressing like Imperial Stormtroopers', honey and wax were reckoned to be well worth a few stings to collect.

Honey is such an ideal candidate for fermentation that it's well worth asking why there isn't far more mead about. For starters, honey is 80% sugar or more and it doesn't need any sort of processing. Just add water! That doesn't mean that mead is sweet, despite a widespread misconception: the strength and sweetness of the finished product depends on the ratio of honey to water and the alcohol-tolerance of the yeast strain. The standard addition is three parts water to one part honey, which if you have a sufficiently tolerant yeast will come out at 16% ABV, so slightly stronger than standard table wine. A larger amount of honey will either give you an even stronger or an even sweeter drink – again, depending on the yeast. It may have been mead's alcoholic strength that gave it its reputation among Celts, Anglo-Saxons and Vikings as a shaman's little helper, inducing divine trances and hallucinations. An ABV of 16% was more than twice as strong as the ale of the time: taken on an empty stomach... well, a trance and a stupor are pretty much indistinguishable to the casual observer.

"THE STRENGTH AND SWEETNESS OF THE FINISHED PRODUCT DEPENDS ON THE RATIO OF HONEY TO WATER AND THE ALCOHOL-TOLERANCE OF THE YEAST STRAIN"

The alcohol content gave mead great keeping and maturing qualities and also made it the best available solvent for the therapeutic alkoloids found in medicinal herbs and spices: here's the grist from just one of the 101 recipes given in *The Closet of Sir Kenelm Digby Opened*, published in 1669:

Bugloss, Borage, Hyssop, Organ, Sweet-marjoram, Rosemary, French-cowslip, Coltsfoot, Thyme, Burnet, Self-heal, Sanicle, Betony, Blew-buttons, Harts-tongue, Meadowssweet, Liverwort, Coriander, Bistort, Saint John's wort, Liquorish, Carraways, Yellow-saunders, Balm, Bugle, Ginger, Cloves, Agrimony, Tormentil-roots, Cumfrey, Fennel-roots, Clowns-all-heal, Maiden-hair, Wall-rew, Spleen-wort, Sweet-oak, Pauls-betony, Mouse ear.

What could such a concoction have failed to cure, and what must it have tasted like! Well, herein perhaps lies one of the reasons why you can't get draught mead in every pub and bag-in-box mead in any supermarket: it never became an industrial product. That sonorous roll-call of herbs comes from a rich man's kitchen garden or a leisured lady's country walk, not an open field. Honey was in plentiful supply as a kitchen ingredient – one of Sir Kenelm's recipes calls for 42lb of it – but beekeeping techniques remained very primitive. Normally the beekeeper had to smash open the 'skep' or hive – no more than an upside-down basket – and kill all the bees to get at the honey within; for most large households the wax was actually a far more important commodity than the honey. It wasn't until 1770 and the invention of the moveable comb that apiculture started to be a controllable and commercial venture, but by then it was too late. Enclosure and deforestation reduced apiculture almost to a sideline; and a much cheaper and more effective vector had been popularised for herbs and spices such as cardamom and juniper – gin.

Despite the threat posed by neonicotinoids and varroa destructor mites, world honey production shot up from 1,225,000 tonnes in 2014 to 1,860,000 in 2018. If you're visiting a meadery, take notes and when you get home buy a fermenting bucket, fill it a quarter full of honey, top it up with warm water, lob in some Champagne yeast and wait...

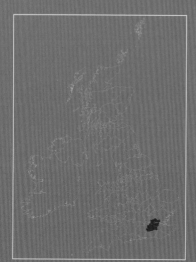

CHAPTER FOUR
GREATER
LONDON

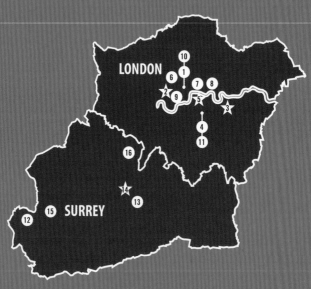

LONDON

BREWERIES

1 CAMDEN TOWN

⌂ 55–59 Wilkin St Mews, NW5 3NN ✆ 020 7485 1671 ⊕ camdentownbrewery.com ⏲ bar open 13.00–22.00 daily (23.00 Fri); tours must be booked. Founded in 2010 in North London railway arches, Camden Town scored early success with its hugely popular Hells lager. It still brews at its original site but has a new and much bigger plant in Enfield. The arches themselves are now glassed in to form a big and very trendy bar.

2 FULLER, SMITH & TURNER

See page 76.

3 MEANTIME

See page 78.

CIDER MILL

4 HAWKES CIDERY & TAPROOM

⌂ 92–96 Druid St, SE1 2HQ ✆ 020 3903 8387 ⊕ wearehawkes.com ⏲ taproom 16.00–23.00 Wed–Fri, 11.00–23.00 Sat, 11.00–18.00 Sun; tours by appointment. Cider enthusiast Simon Wright founded Hawkes Urban Cider in 2012 in Forest Gate using both found and donated fruit, and more recently set up the Hawkes Cidery & Taproom on Bermondsey's Beer Mile. It's the only place in London where you can see cider being made, much of it still pressed from apples brought

in by customers. Simon and cidermaker Roberto Basilico aren't worried about the varieties of apples they get because, they say, the secret lies in the blending.

DISTILLERIES

5 BEEFEATER

See page 82.

6 BIMBER

⌂ 56 Sunbeam Rd, Park Royal, NW10 6JQ ✆ 020 3602 9980 ⊕ bimberdistillery.co.uk ⏲ bar, tours & tastings 09.00–17.00 Mon–Fri, 09.00–14.00 Sat. Tours must be booked in advance. Founded in 2015 by Polish émigré Dariusz Plazewski, who had learned the art of distilling at his grandfather's knee, Bimber distillery laid down its first single malt whisky in May 2016 and also produces vodka, rum and tea-infused gin.

7 CITY OF LONDON DISTILLERY

⌂ 22–24 St Bride's Ln, EC4 8DT ✆ 020 7936 3636 ⊕ cityoflondondistillery.com ⏲ bar 16.00–23.00 Mon–Sat; tours, tastings & the gin experience must be booked in advance. Just off Fleet Street and close to the famous 'wedding cake' of St Bride's Church, you'll find the City of London Distillery, opened in 2012 as the Square Mile's first for nearly 200 years. From the bar you can look down on the three gleaming copper Carterhead stills, designed to create a particularly smooth spirit, where London Dry, Square Mile and Christopher Wren gins are produced.

8 EAST LONDON LIQUOR COMPANY

221 Grove Rd, E3 5SN 020 3011 0980
eastlondonliquorcompany.com shop,
bar & restaurant 10.00–17.00 Mon (shop only),
17.00–23.00 Tue–Thu, 17.00–00.30 Fri, 12.00–
00.30 Sat, 12.00–23.00 Sun; tours & tastings
by appointment. Founded in 2014, East London
Liquor Company released its limited-edition rye
whisky (the first London-made whisky to go on
sale since 1904) in early 2019 and also makes
three gins, a wheat vodka and a Demerara rum.
The company imports abstruse craft spirits which
are stocked in its on-site shop. The stills are visible
from the bare-brick and stripped-floor cocktail bar
and Italian-inspired restaurant.

9 THE GINSTITUTE

186 Portobello Rd, W11 1LA 020 3034 2234
theginstitute.com bar 16.00–01.00 Mon–
Tue, 12.00–01.00 Wed–Sat, 12.00–midnight,
Sun; restaurant 16.00–midnight Mon–Sat,
11.00–23.00 Sun; gin experience by appointment
only. The Ginstitute in the former Colville Hotel
on the corner of Talbot Road offers not only a
restaurant and cocktail bar but also a shop, a small
museum and three letting rooms. The basement
is home to Portobello Road Gin's two stills and
the tasting room that hosts a three-hour Gin
Experience course in selecting and blending the
botanicals to make your own. You get a free bottle
and can order more.

▲ *East London Liquor Company, with the still clearly visible from the bar*

2 FULLER, SMITH & TURNER

LONDON'S VERY LAST LOCAL BREWERY.

⌂ Griffin Brewery, Chiswick Ln South, W4 2QA ✆ 020 8996 2085 ⌗ fullers.co.uk ◷ 10.00–20.00
Mon–Fri , 11.00–18.00 Sat; tours start 11.00, 12.00, 14.00, 15.00 Mon–Sat (+16.00 on Fri) – book ahead.

It has to be admitted that from the street, London's oldest brewery is not especially prepossessing – it's one of those random accretions of industrial brick buildings you used to see everywhere. Mind you, the street itself is not especially prepossessing either – it's the howling madness of the A4 spewing its automotive breath over the wilderness of the Hogarth Roundabout.

But take a few steps down Chiswick Lane South and all is suddenly transformed in that unexpected way that makes London so enchanting, for Fuller's is sandwiched between the awful Great West Road and the most beautiful half-mile on London's riverfront: the exquisite Georgian and Regency confection of Chiswick Mall. Behind us the traffic was deafening; here the tranquillity is equally so.

The brewery complex itself also includes a number of fine houses that in the days when men of business lived above the shop were home to senior brewery staff and their families. They are now offices but one of them, originally the head brewer's house, is host to England's oldest wisteria, planted in 1816. Time your tour for early summer when it's in full flower and you may need a little sit-down, for it will take your breath away.

Fuller's only acquired its 'London's oldest' status in 2006 when Young's, whose recorded roots are a century older, found it impossible to operate from central Wandsworth so slipped its moorings and sailed away to Bedford. Brewing on the Fuller's site was first recorded in the mid-17th century, when there was a pub with its own brewery there and a private brewhouse nearby. Eventually they merged and over the years changed hands through sale and inheritance until 1845 when the partnership of Mr Fuller, Mr Smith and Mr Turner was established.

"FULLER'S IS SANDWICHED BETWEEN THE AWFUL GREAT WEST ROAD AND THE MOST BEAUTIFUL HALF-MILE ON LONDON'S RIVERFRONT"

During the decades of mergers, takeovers and closures that followed World War II Fuller's and Young's doggedly held on to their independence, emerging as London's last two local breweries, strong on their home turf but hardly represented elsewhere. It was the high quality of their respective beers (and the poor quality of their competitors) that widened their appeal: Fuller's ESB won four of the Campaign for Real Ale's first five Champion Beer of Britain awards in 1978, 1979, 1980 and 1982. For much the same reason

▲ *Heavy horses with the Fuller's dray*

Fuller's London Pride, luscious and biscuity thanks to its high crystal malt content, went from ubiquity on its own small manor to near-ubiquity across the whole country.

More recently Fuller's has invested in opening itself up to its fans. Its showcase has long been the Mawson Arms, which stands right beside the brewery gate and has acted both as brewery tap and departure point for brewery tours. In 2018 the company opened a visitor centre including a beer shop and deli, a small pilot brewery, and a 'growler bar' where you can buy draught ale to take home to round off the whole experience.

THE BEER Fuller's bottled beers -- London Porter 5.4% ABV, 1845 6.3% ABV and Vintage Ale 8.5% ABV -- and a true favourite of beer-lovers London Pride 4.1% ABV, giving you sweet raisin, biscuit and dried fruit notes.

3 MEANTIME

LEARN FROM THE EXPERIENCE OF ONE OF BRITAIN'S MOST ACCOMPLISHED BREWERS.

✉ 118 Blackwall Ln, SE10 0AR 📞 020 3384 0582 🖉 meantimebrewing.com 🕑 Tours start 17.00, 19.00 Mon–Fri, 11.00, 14.00, 18.00 Sat, 16.00 Sun.

A few miles downriver from Fuller's (page 76) stately pile – at the opposite end of town, you might say – Meantime Brewery could hardly be more different. The only similarity between the two is that Blackwall Lane is as unlovely as the Great West Road. True, Meantime is also a stone's throw from the Thames, but the waterfront here – well, it's nothing like Chiswick.

"IN ALL THESE VENTURES, ONE THING SET HOOK APART FROM HIS MICROBREWING CONTEMPORARIES: NO REAL ALE"

The austere, even perfunctory brewery building is the brainchild of one of the great technicians of craft brewing, Alastair Hook. He had the beer world's equivalent of a Rhodes scholarship: a degree from the brewing school at Heriot-Watt University, Edinburgh, followed by post-graduate studies at Weihenstephan, the Brewing Technology faculty at the University of Munich. When he came down from the mountain he didn't join the mainstream industry. Instead he set up a German-style brewhouse at the Packhorse in Ashford, Kent, making mainly pilsner and other German-style beers. In 1994 he founded one of London's most

progressive microbreweries, Freedom, opposite the legendary White Horse in Parson's Green. After that he moved to Manchester, co-founding the Mash & Air boutique brewbar before returning to London in 1999 to found Meantime.

In all these ventures, one thing set Hook apart from his microbrewing contemporaries: no real ale. He had experience of drinking cultures where serving draught beer full of sediment and open to the elements was unthinkable, and where the beer had to be filtered to purity and swaddled with CO_2 to reach the customer in exactly the condition the brewer intended. This earned the opprobrium of real ale enthusiasts who never accepted that it wasn't CO_2 that made bad beer bad and good beer good – it was the liquid that mattered, not the dispense. But Hook, along with a couple of others, persisted and can rightly be regarded as one of the founders of craft brewing.

Meantime didn't stay in its shed for long: the £7 million state-of-the-art brewery you see before you was custom-built in 2010 and fitted with the most modern kit Germany's engineers could manufacture. And although the dull brushed steel pipes and tanks might look serene, they're all hard at work: Meantime is close to its capacity of 120,000hl a year and before long there may be a few additions to its 78 giant vessels. And what a variety of styles those vats allow the erudite Hook to produce! Coffee porter, chocolate porter, Bohemian dark, citrus wit, helles, kikku, zwickelbier, raspberry wheat, saison, hefeweizen, red ale and barrel-aged old ale. For this is a true beer academy where people come to learn as well as to enjoy and where regular events include beer and food matching sessions, 'The Knowledge' beer appreciation masterclasses and workshops and private previews of limited edition beers.

THE BEER London Pale Ale 4.3% ABV is packed with citrus flavour, London Lager 4.5% ABV gives you a strong bitter, and Helles Lager 4.2% ABV is a crisp lager with a malt body and light bitterness – a 19th-century classic.

▲ *Meantime's sampling bar*
◀ *One of the maturation vessels*

BOTANICALS

THE DISTINCTIVE FLAVOUR OF GIN COMES FROM LOCAL FORAGING.

An opinion you will often hear regarding the origin of gin is that juniper and other flavourings were intended to mask the taste of the raw spirit. Don't believe it: the opposite is true. The flavourings were the whole point – the spirit was merely a solvent to extract the therapeutic alkaloids from herbs and spices and create, as the song says, medicinal compounds most efficacious in every case.

"ONE BOTANICAL COMMON IN THE 18TH CENTURY THAT RAISES MODERN EYEBROWS WAS TURPENTINE, WHICH WAS MADE FROM CONCENTRATED PINE RESIN"

Every culture had its favourite medicinal herbs. Akvavit was commonly infused with caraway, vodka with bison grass, arrack and other Mediterranean spirits with aniseed. 'Aniseed water', according to Daniel Defoe, was also the best-selling spirit in 17th-century London, but once William III ascended the throne in 1690 it was farewell aniseed and hello juniper, the favourite cure-all of the Dutch for two centuries and the heart of their national spirit. But it wasn't taken up so quickly just to flatter the new king and his Dutch entourage: the sticky little berry – actually a miniature pine cone – is delicious. Crush a few and you release a wonderfully clean, pungent aroma that has been

used as an alternative to pepper for centuries. The oil has been a staple in cosmetics since the time of the pharaohs and juniper twigs thrown on the barbecue fill the air with fresh piney vapours.

This is because the cone is packed with terpenes (the hydrocarbons that give fruit and flowers their scents and flavours), dominated by pinenes both alpha (which is water-soluble) and beta (which is only soluble in ethanol), hence gin's pungency. Its other terpenes are also mostly at the sharp end of the spectrum: borneol, a component of camphor; myrcene, present in cardamom, hops and verbena; sabinene, found in black pepper, tea-tree and nutmeg; and limonene. Farnesene, whose warm floral aroma is also found in lavender and bergamot, adds depth and fullness.

Juniper was only one of a number of 'botanicals' with which early gin was flavoured. Others included the roots of angelica, an umbellifer with similar therapeutic properties to juniper; liquorice, good for respiratory ailments; and iris, dried and ground to create a dark floral background. One botanical common in the 18th century that raises modern eyebrows was turpentine. This is not to be confused with today's synthetic paint thinner: it was concentrated pine resin (as used in the making of retsina) stuffed with alpha and beta pinenes, camphene, carene, linalool and geraniol, the fresh, clean, outdoorsy terpenes found in some hop

varieties. It has been used by doctors from Hippocrates to the makers of Vick's to treat cystitis, neuralgia, rheumatism, nephritis, pulmonary infections, bronchitis and blocked noses.

These ingredients were available locally, but the more exotic spices that gin drinkers craved were harder to come by. In the 15th century the Mongols had cut the spice road and the Ottomans had captured Constantinople, the principal entrepôt for Oriental trade. The sea routes to the spice isles were in the hands of the Portuguese, who mercilessly exploited their monopoly; therefore the Dutch sent their own fleets to the East Indies to establish a regular supply of cloves, cinnamon, coriander seed, cardamom and other exotics. This is how the Dutch Empire was founded, in part, on gin.

For centuries gin distillers were fairly conservative in the palette of botanicals they drew on. But now we are in the throes of the 'ginaissance',

and modern rectifiers are as profligate and as playful as craft brewers in their madcap selection of aromatics. There's baobab fruit in Whitley Neill and cucumber and rose in G&J's Bloom. However, these are tame by comparison with some of the exotics that now scent the world's little copper pots: the peel of distinctive citrus varieties, naturally, not just lemon and lime but also mandarin, grapefruit, pomelo, bergamot, kuzu, calamansi and kaffir lime (leaves rather than peel). Then there's almond, apricot kernel, blue butterfly pea, bog myrtle, buchu, chocolate, clove, clover, coconut, dandelion leaves, dragon eye, elderflower, galangal, ginseng, hibiscus, honeysuckle, hops, Kampot pepper, lavender, lotus leaf, nettles, olives, pomegranate, poppy leaf, quince, raspberry, rhubarb, rose root, rowanberry, saffron, savory, seaweed, shamrock, spruce tips, tarragon, tea, thyme, truffle, vanilla... oh, and elephant dung. And ants. Take care.

5 BEEFEATER

LAST OF THE OLD GUARD GETS AN EYE-CATCHING MAKEOVER.

⌂ 20 Montford Pl, SE11 5DE ✆ 020 7587 0034 ✎ beefeaterdistillery.com ⏲ 10.00–18.30 Mon–Sat; 90min tours start on the hour 11.00–15.00 & must be booked in advance.

The James Burrough Beefeater distillery is one of a trio of historic attractions in Kennington, sitting snugly at the side of the Oval and just down Kennington Road from the Imperial War Museum. It's the last of the great London gin distillers to have stayed loyal to the capital, the others all having been tempted away after the war to the overspill towns where their bombed-out workforces had been relocated.

But there is, in one sense at least, less than meets the eye to James Burrough: nothing about it is really old. It was only founded in 1862 when Burrough, a pharmacist by trade, bought the old Chelsea distillery. A compulsive experimenter, he hit the jackpot in 1876 with Beefeater, a clean London Dry with a markedly full body thanks to liquorice, orris and angelica roots, pronounced citrus notes from lemon and Seville orange peel, and a herby character conferred by angelica seed. The botanicals are steeped in spirit for 24 hours before rectification, a novel technique back then that emphasises and intensifies the flavours.

The gin's distinctive quality and branding made it a hit, and in 1908 it had to move from its original home in Chelsea across the river to a bigger purpose-built distillery in Lambeth. Half a century later, following success in the USA where it was touted as the perfect gin for a Martini, it had to move once again, this time to the old Hayward's Pickle factory in Kennington. To the rather drab stock-brick Edwardian factory was added a dramatically brutal concrete still house; although neither building is of any merit, side by side they make a very striking ensemble. It has just been made even more striking by the addition of an ultra-modern atrium clad with copper vanes that houses the visitor centre and museum and allows tourists to view the working areas without interrupting the process.

"IT'S THE LAST OF THE GREAT LONDON GIN DISTILLERS TO HAVE STAYED LOYAL TO THE CAPITAL"

Tours start with a self-guided trip round the museum helped by an iPad and interactive exhibits. One curio of particular interest is the puss-mew machine, supposedly an early vending machine, in the form of a cat. This was allegedly used during the late 1730s when gin was all but prohibited. It was fixed into the window of a shebeen: passers-by would put twopence into its mouth and a server indoors would pour a measure of gin down a spout through the cat's paw into

GREATER LONDON: BEEFEATER

▲ *Museum displays and Carterhead stills*

the customer's own glass. A more nonsensical story would be hard to imagine, although nobody knows what the contraption really is.

As well as its smart new visitor centre, Beefeater has some very on-trend brand extensions founded on its original botanicals. Pink is infused with strawberries, and there's also a blood orange version. The Oriental-inspired 24 has Japanese and China teas added to the botanicals, while London Garden includes thyme and lemon verbena from the Chelsea Physic Garden in memory of Beefeater's original home.

THE GIN London Dry Gin 50% ABV, Beefeater Pink 37.5% ABV, with that strawberry finish, Beefeater 24 45% ABV, brilliant for cocktails, Burrough's Reserve 43% ABV, floral spice notes with vanilla, and Blood Orange 38% ABV, especially refreshing with ginger ale.

▲ *Hog's Back Brewery*

10 HALF HITCH

✉ West Yard, Camden Lock Pl, NW1 8AF ✆ 020 3096 3027 🖰 halfhitch.london 🕓 sessions start 10.00 & 17.30 Mon, Tue, Thu, 10.00 & 18.30 Wed, 10.00 & 17.00 Fri; shop 11.30–16.30 daily. Half Hitch microdistillery occupies a tiny corner of what was the enormous Gilbey's Gin HQ from 1871 to 1967 – not only a vast distillery but also the bonded warehouses that held the firm's spirits (it owned three Scotch distilleries as well) and the majestic quantities of wine it imported. Half Hitch consciously evokes the history of the Lock – its name is that of a bargee's knot, and its exotic botanicals echo the days when the Lock was a hub of Empire-wide trade. Half Hitch has a shop and also offers twice-daily hour-long gin-making sessions.

11 LONDON DISTILLERY COMPANY

✉ 58 Druid St, SE1 2EZ ✆ 020 7403 8533 🖰 londondistillery.com 🕓 tours & workshops by appointment. Established in a Victorian dairy almost at the foot of Tower Bridge in 2011, London Distillery Company has established a reputation for diversity, including a rye whisky, a triple sec, an Old Tom gin, a range of organic gins and a horseradish vodka, formulated in collaboration with Kew Gardens.

SURREY

BREWERY

12 HOG'S BACK BREWERY

⌂ Manor Farm, The Street, Tongham GU10 1DE
✆ 01252 783000/784495 ⏚ hogsback.co.uk
☉ tours by appointment, check website for
details. Established in the picturesque red-brick
outbuildings of an 18th-century farm in 1992,
Hog's Back's main visitor attraction was for many
years its fantastically well-stocked beer shop. More
recently it has been joined by an 8½-acre hop
garden, which is the first in these parts for more
than a century. Beers include TEA, Ripstar, Hogstar
Lager and Montezuma Chocolate Lager.

GIN DISTILLERY

13 THE GIN KITCHEN

⌂ Goldenlands Farm, Punchbowl Ln, Dorking
RH5 4DX ✆ 01306 889598 ⏚ gin.kitchen
☉ 10.00–17.00 Mon–Fri, 10.00–19.00 Sat,
10.00–16.00 Sun. Founded in a pub outbuilding
in Dorking by gin-loving best friends Kate Gregory
and Helen Muncie, the Gin Kitchen produced its
first Gutsy Monkey Winter Gin in November 2016
and added Dancing Dragontail Summer Gin the
following year. They offer a cocktail bar and
buffet, shop, talks, tastings, tours, workshops
and cocktail suppers, and they must be doing
something right – in 2018 they had to move to
a much bigger picturesque Victorian barn in the
Surrey Hills.

VINEYARDS

14 DENBIES WINE ESTATE

See page 86.

15 GREYFRIARS VINEYARD

⌂ Hog's Back, Puttenham GU3 1AG ✆ 01483
813712 ⏚ greyfriarsvineyard.co.uk ☉ shop
open 10.00–17.00 Tue–Sat; tours & tastings on
Sat; booking is essential. They also run open days
through the growing season, check the website for
details. A 50-acre vineyard in a stunning location
on the southern slope of the Hog's Back in the
North Downs. Greyfriars specialises in bottle-
fermented sparkling wines made from classic
Champagne varieties.

16 PAINSHILL PARK VINEYARD

⌂ Portsmouth Rd, Cobham KT11 1JE ✆ 0932
868113 ⏚ painshill.co.uk ☉ 10.00–18.00 daily;
entry as part of admission to gardens. Tiny
(1.8 acres) vineyard set in spectacular
158-acre 18th-century landscaped gardens
complete with folly and grotto in the Surrey
Hills Area of Outstanding Natural Beauty. The
vines were planted as a restoration project in
1981, and the range includes a bottle-fermented
sparkling rosé made from Pinot Noir and
Chardonnay and a white from Seyval Blanc. A
registered charity, Painshill Park Trust is committed
to restoring and maintaining the historic
landscape at Painshill, so it can continue
to be enjoyed for many future generations to
come. The vineyard relies entirely, at harvest
time, on volunteer pickers.

14 DENBIES WINE ESTATE

AMBITIOUS PLANS HAVE LED TO BRITAIN'S LARGEST VINEYARD.

✉ London Rd, Dorking RH5 6AA ✆ 01306 876616 ⌖ denbies.co.uk ⏲ Apr–Oct 09.30–17.30 daily, Nov–Mar 09.30–17.00 daily.

Denbies Wine Estate on the edge of Dorking is a place of superlatives. It wasn't among the pioneers of the English wine revival, as the first vines were planted in 1986, by which time there were more than 300 working vineyards in England and Wales. But it was certainly among the most ambitious: that first planting totalled 30 acres, which was ten times more than a lot of established operations. And now it's far and away the largest in the UK, with 265 acres of vines on the estate's total of 627 acres. And it must be one of the most beautiful as well. Set in the dramatic landscape of the Surrey Hills, classified as an Area of Outstanding Natural Beauty, the Denbies Estate includes 200 acres of woodland criss-crossed by seven miles of public footpaths. The vineyards themselves are mostly set on south-facing chalky slopes enjoying pretty much the same aspect, soil and climate as their opposite numbers in the Champagne region of France.

Denbies takes its name from the 100-room Italianate mansion designed and built in 1854 by the great developer Thomas Cubitt, but demolished a century later after successive rounds of death duties reduced the 6,000-acre estate to its present dimensions. What the visitor sees is entirely modern and is a testament to the vision of the wine estate's founder, water treatment entrepreneur Keith White, who from the moment he bought it in 1984, understood that a place like this has to be shared.

"SET IN THE DRAMATIC LANDSCAPE OF THE SURREY HILLS, CLASSIFIED AS AN AREA OF OUTSTANDING NATURAL BEAUTY"

The great visitor centre, built from scratch at a cost of £3.3 million and reminiscent of Cubitt's demolished palace, demonstrates just how serious he was about sharing. The centre is the base for tours both of the vineyards and of the winery, which opened in 1993. Built around two courtyards, the centre's star attraction is the third-floor Gallery Restaurant with its sweeping views over the hills. There's a second restaurant, the Conservatory, occupying one of the courtyards, but that's just the beginning. There's a wine and gift shop, of course, but also a farm shop because much of the estate is still run as a working concern and because there are dozens of artisan food producers in the surrounding area whose efforts deserve such a grand showcase. There's even a microbrewery on the site: Surrey Hills Brewery occupies a building just behind the visitor centre

▲ *Sampling cellar at Denbies*

and you're welcome to poke your head round the door as well as buy beer from their shop.

As well as things to see there are things to do and places to do them in. The Pavilion is a favourite venue locally for weddings and there are six indoor function/meeting rooms catering for parties of 175 guests to just 16. Other attractions include a gallery and exhibition spaces used by local artists and events as different as wedding fairs, food fairs and the Denbies Bacchus Marathon. It almost takes you back to the mid-18th century when the estate belonged to London impresario Jonathan Tyer, owner of the Spring Gardens in Vauxhall where every (legal) pleasure was on offer.

Oh yes – they also make wine here, including sparkling wines that regularly beat Champagne itself in international tastings and competitions. The grape varieties planted are principally cold-climate varieties including Bacchus, Ortega, Reichensteiner and Rondo.

THE WINE There are up to 19 wines in the range, including seven still white wines, two dessert wines, a rosé, three red wines and seven bottle-fermented sparkling white wines. Try Surrey Gold 11.5% ABV, a blend of Müller-Thurgau, Ortega and Bacchus giving you a herbal, fruity citric quality.

ORCHARDS

RETURN TO EDEN – AND FEEL FREE TO EAT THE FRUIT.

Everyone has their own heaven on Earth. For some it's a wild, rugged place, maybe a mountain, a jungle or the angry rapids of a tumbling river, where they can pit mind and body against the elements at their most fierce. For others the elements would be kinder – the caressing warmth of a tropical sun on the gleaming white sand of a palm-fringed beach. For any civilised person, however, heaven on Earth is an orchard.

An orchard is nothing more unusual or spectacular than some trees in a field; but like any field of trees it's full of life. You cannot be alone in an orchard, and everything in it changes all the time. It is impossible to be bored in an orchard.

In high summer you can set up your picnic table or just spread a blanket in the dappled shade of an apple tree and have a lazy glass or two of cider. The tree will have been pruned in late winter to allow all the fruits a glimpse of the sun and a kiss of the breeze, so when you look up you will see clear sky through the dancing mesh of leaves.

For company you might well have a *corps de ballet* of gamboling lambs, separated after weaning to finish in the orchard's lush grass, which is planted with antibiotic and antifungal herbs and flowers – burdock and buttercup, dandelion and dill, lemon balm and marigold, tarragon and thyme – to keep them well and fatten them up naturally. In return, they'll nitrogenate the soil with their dung and urine, making for heavier fruit and a healthier fermentation; and they'll nibble the shooting brambles, making the harvest easier.

And there will be bees, too, for without bees there is no orchard. In the spring they will have feasted on the apple blossom's nectar, spreading the pollen that makes the fruit; in the summer they will be browsing among the meadow herbs and on the summer flowers – dog roses, poppies,

mallows – that stud the hedges. Less welcome but equally necessary, wasps scavenge the first-fallen apples and in due time will infest the windfalls. This orchard is unsprayed, so fritillaries and speckled wood butterflies and buff-tip moths flutter ceaselessly between the trees; the birds and bats that feed on them are equally prolific.

The orchard is a place of labour as well as leisure, where nature can thrive only because industry thrives alongside it. We've already mentioned the bees, and bees make honey. (And wax, too.) Mistletoe's a pest if allowed to grow freely, but at Christmastime the trimmings go to market, to the florist's and to restaurants, pub dining-rooms and function suites across the district. It's only a trickle of cash, but it comes when you most need it. Even the late winter prunings from the orchard, normally raked up and burned, can be a cash-crop: fed through a chipper (along with the Christmas tree!), they make wood-pellets for the boiler or charcoal for summer's barbecues. And the hedges that shelter the orchards from the worst of the wind have their bounty, too: sloes, damsons, hazelnuts, crab apples and elder, with mushrooms sprouting in their shade.

Finally comes the apple harvest itself. In commercial orchards they use a vibrating clamp to shake the apples loose from the tree without harming the roots. Ancient rustic wisdom says that nature knows when an apple's ready, so wait for nature to do her thing and, as the fruit falls, pile it up in little heaps or tumps for a few days to soften, dry out a little and to let it finish ripening.

Much of orcharding is hard work in uncomfortable conditions. The winter pruning in particular is cold, wet and actually quite dangerous. But as a visitor, you get to pass on all that and hopefully experience it at its best.

CHAPTER FIVE
SOUTHEAST

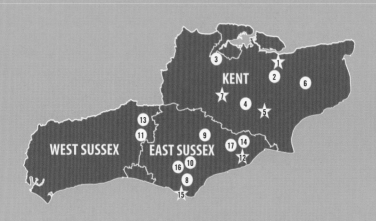

KENT

WEST SUSSEX

EAST SUSSEX

KENT

1 SHEPHERD NEAME

SO MANY OLD-ESTABLISHED TOWN-CENTRE BREWERIES HAVE BEEN TURNED INTO A TESCO. THIS ISN'T ONE OF THEM!

✉ 17 Court St, Faversham ME13 7AX 🖉 01795 542016 🖉 shepherdneame.co.uk ⏰ shop, visitor centre 10.30–16.30 Mon–Fri; tours & tastings must be booked in advance.

There was a time when every town in the country had an old-established brewery more or less in the middle of it and bursting out of its confines. The nostalgist remembers with a sigh Usher's of Trowbridge, Phipps of Northampton, Morland of Abingdon, even Young's of Wandsworth… dozens of them, most strangled by the constrictions of their age-old locations.

There are survivors, of course, and among them are Marston's, Banks's, Adnams, Robinson's, Cameron's and Shepherd Neame, the last

distinguished as being comfortably the oldest brewery, or at least brewery site, in the country. In 1147 an abbey was founded nearby, and wherever there was an abbey there was ale. In this case, however, the brewery survived the Dissolution of the Monasteries in 1536. In the abbey's dying days, the abbot's nephew was the contemporary equivalent of a beer wholesaler – perhaps trafficking the surplus product of a brewhouse that was by now far too big for the dwindling population of monks. After the abbey was finally dissolved the

brewery survived, moving to its present premises in Court Street, Faversham, in 1570.

Over the centuries the enterprise changed hands many times and for many reasons, gradually expanding in output and in the size of its estate as it did so, until the current dynasty arrived in 1864. The first Neame — the present head being Jonathan Neame of the fifth generation — promptly planted a brand new up-to-the-minute brewhouse plumb in the heart of the six-acre site, where it remains to this day. What gives the complex its character for the visitor is the way it has expanded within those six acres as the years have gone by: it's completely ad hoc and a total jungle at first sight.

"AND ONE OF THE MANY FACTORS IN ITS SUCCESS HAS BEEN ITS EXCELLENCE AS A BREWER"

Shepherd Neame has been one of the most extraordinarily successful regional breweries as the very fact of its continued independence demonstrates, and one of the many factors in its success has been its excellence as a brewer. Being in the heart of hop-growing country, its brewers might be excused for going crazy with hops, for producing Kentish-themed beers that taste overwhelmingly of nettles, or lemon or blackberries, and damn the malt. But they don't. They believe in balance: if anything, Shep's most celebrated beers — Spitfire, launched to mark the 50th anniversary of the Battle of Britain;

◀ *Shepherd Neame brewery complex*

Bishop's Finger, named after the fingerboard signposts that pointed pilgrims to Canterbury; 1698, commemorating a change of dynasty in the company history — err on the malty side. But Shep's real expertise lies in yeast and fermentation: in 1968 it became the first British regional to brew a continental lager under licence, and not just any lager either but Hürlimann, from a Swiss brewer which specialised in yeast and fermentation research and development.

Given the chaotic (to the outsider) nature of the brewery's expansion into a labyrinth of alleys and passageways connecting brooding buildings of uncertain purpose, towering slender chimneys and vast metal silos, it might not have been the most obvious candidate for a tourist attraction. However, the nakedly functional character of much of it is part of its appeal as not only a maker of superb beer but also a site of importance in industrial archaeology; and where facilities have been designed especially for tourists, such as the visitor centre and the Old Brewery Store venue — well, the awards keep coming.

THE BEER Bear Island Triple Hopped Lager 4.6% ABV, and Bear Island East Coast Pale Ale 4.8% ABV. Under licence from the USA, Samuel Adams Lager 4.8% ABV, and using only Kent barley, Master Brew 3.7% ABV, with a distinctive hoppy aroma. For those who like a stronger beer, try Bishops Finger 5.45% ABV, one of Britain's oldest beers, dating back to 1958.

CIDER MILL

2 BROGDALE NATIONAL FRUIT COLLECTIONS

✉ Brogdale Farm, Brogdale Rd, ME13 8XZ
✆ 01795 536250 🖉 brogdalecollections.org ⏱
Apr–Oct 10.00–16.00 daily; guided tours 11.00,
13.00, 14.30 – no need to book. The 140-acre
Brogdale Farm has been home to the National
Fruit Collections for 70 years and has amassed a
collection of 2,200 apple and 550 pear varieties
from all over the world, as well as cherries, plums,
quinces, medlars and cobnuts. The roots go back a
bit further, though: in 1533 Henry VIII established
a similar venture at Teynham, two miles away, to
supply growers with new varieties from abroad.
There are guided tours, self-guided and children's
trails, courses in country crafts and garden skills,
tractor trails, shops, garden centre, café and of
course cider made from Brogdale's own fruit.

GIN DISTILLERY

3 COPPER RIVET

✉ Pumphouse No.5, Leviathan Way, Chatham
Historic Dockyard ME4 4LP ✆ 01634 931122
🖉 copperrivetdistillery.com ⏱ 10.00–17.00
Mon–Sat, 12.00–17.00 Sun. Brothers Bob, Matt
and Stephen Russell had scoured the UK for a site
for their dream distillery when Pumphouse No.5,
built in the 1870s to drain the yard's dry docks,
became available. Crucially the cavernous hall
could accommodate their three towering stills and

▲ *Apple varieties at Brogdale*
▶ *The award-winning Biddenden Ortega*

▲ *Copper Rivet Distillery*

also had space to brew the basic wash, making this one of the few artisan distilleries where you can see the entire process under one roof. Commissioned in 2016, the stills make Dockyard Dry, a classic gin; Vela, a very pure vodka; and Son of a Gun, a grain spirit.

VINEYARDS

4 BIDDENDEN VINEYARDS

Gribble Bridge Ln, Biddenden TN27 8DF
01580 291726 biddendenvineyards.com
shop/café 10.00–17.00 Mon–Sat, 11.00–17.00 Sun. Marked trails. Open tours Apr–Sep every Sat, private tours can be booked in advance. Kent's first commercial vineyard was a 40-acre orchard on the edge of the High Weald AONB when falling apple prices persuaded the Barnes family to diversify. The first third of an acre was planted with vines in 1969 and the first wine was bottled three years later. Today there are 23 acres of 11 grape varieties, mostly the German hybrid Ortega, producing 80,000 bottles of red, white, rosé and

sparkling wines a year. 'Bid' is also locally renowned for its eastern-style ciders. The latest uses a Swiss apple that produces a natural red juice.

5 CHAPEL DOWN
See page 96.

6 ELHAM VALLEY

Elham Valley Rd, Breach, Barham CT4 6LN
01227 831052 fifthtrust.co.uk 09.00–17.00 daily. Founded in 1985, the Elham Valley complex includes the vineyard, café, garden centre and a workshop that makes garden furniture and accessories from trees felled by Canterbury Council's parks and gardens department. It belongs to the Fifth Trust, which employs and trains adults with learning difficulties. Set in the beautiful Kent Hills between Dover and Canterbury, the vineyard is known for the quality of its sparkling wines.

7 HUSH HEATH ESTATE
See page 100.

5 CHAPEL DOWN

ENGLAND'S BIGGEST WINEMAKER, CHAPEL DOWN IS THE BRIGHTEST STAR IN ITS CONSTELLATION.

⌂ Small Hythe, Tenterden TN30 7NG ✎ 01580 766111/763033 ⊘ chapeldown.com ◯ shop, gardens, vineyard walks 10.00–17.00 daily; guided tours by appointment Apr–Nov; see website for opening hours of Swan restaurant.

Tenterden Vineyard Park, home to the Chapel Down Group's headquarters and main vineyard, has a special place in the history of English wine: it was first planted in 1977 by one of the industry's living legends. Stephen Skelton had spent two years training and working in Germany and, like many of his contemporaries in the early microbrewing scene, devoted as much time and energy to training others, to mentoring start-ups, to writing and to running industry associations as he did to making a success of his own business.

Mr Skelton, who is still active in the industry today, sold Tenterden to Chapel Down in 1995. In 2001 it made history yet again when it merged with several other English vineyards, the best-known of them probably being Lamberhurst, and changed direction completely. The new and highly experienced owners decided to switch their focus from the German-style grapes and wines for which Rock Lodge (as the vineyard was originally called) was known for to Champagne-style bottle-fermented sparkling wines. At the same time they planned on attracting investment that would hugely expand production while putting the Tenterden site itself on the tourist map.

Both strategies paid off handsomely and within a few years sparkling wine production increased tenfold. They used grapes both from the company's own vineyards such as Boxley and Kits Coty and also bought in from other growers across the South East, who had been encouraged to plant the traditional Champagne varieties – Pinot Blanc, Pinot Noir and Chardonnay. They are absolutely single-minded about quality.

Chapel Down has been one of the most powerful driving forces behind the irresistible rise of English sparkling wines, and the reward for its past investment along with hundreds of acres of new plantings will soon be sales of more than a million bottles a year.

> **"CHAPEL DOWN HAS BEEN ONE OF THE MOST POWERFUL DRIVING FORCES BEHIND THE IRRESISTIBLE RISE OF ENGLISH SPARKLING WINES"**

Throwing open its doors to you, its public, has also been an area of serious focus and investment. The visitor centre, incorporating the Swan pub and restaurant, is a converted oasthouse that has been clad with oak boards intended to evoke wine barrels but which also recall the traditional clapboard barns and fishing sheds so characteristic of the county. Indeed the adjoining Wine Sanctuary tasting suite, with its terrace overlooking the vineyards, is actually a former farm building that has been totally and magically transformed.

The large herb garden is also an extremely popular feature because the vineyard has now become a venue for weddings, with full catering included.

Chapel Down may be best-known for its bubbles, but there's more to it than that. The different vineyards scattered across Kent and Sussex give the winemakers plenty to play with, and the range of table wines they conjure up is extensive and varied. But there's more still! For years, Chapel Down has commissioned a range of beers under the Curious Brew label. Now they've brought production in-house at a brand-new facility in Ashford. There's also an unusual range of spirits based on a marc made from the winery's spent grapes. Meanwhile the group's London restaurant, Ginworks in that unexpectedly pleasant quarter behind King's Cross, has a new member of the family: Helga, a little copper still that will be called on from time to time to produce limited editions of small-batch artisan spirits.

> **THE WINE** Try the sparkling Bacchus 2018 12% ABV, or Pinot Blanc 2016 12.5% ABV, a crisp refreshing white wine giving a nose of pears with greengage and floral aromas.

▲ *The vineyards*

◄ *Shop and winery*

BRANDY & RUM

SAILORS, SQUIRES AND SMUGGLERS – THEY ALL LOVED THEIR BRANDY AND RUM.

Two things you're unlikely to see in your tour of *Britain in a Bottle* are a rum distillery and a brandy distillery. Not that they don't exist, but those that do are very small and not really suited to accommodate visitors such as your good self. Perhaps this circumstance echoes their history as the only imported spirits that had much significance in the British market.

> **"ENGLISH WORKERS DRANK EITHER RUM FROM NEWLY CONQUERED JAMAICA OR NATIVE 'STRONG WATERS', OFTEN FLAVOURED WITH ANISEED"**

In the late 16th century, Dutch merchants were after a source of cheap wine to sate the bourgeoisie of their country's fast-growing towns; but at the same time they were paying the price of their recently won independence from Spain – ie: no cheap Spanish wine. Instead they started shipping the thin, acidic wines of the Charente Maritime through their base at Protestant-held La Rochelle in West France; and to save money they invested in the expansion of a fledgling distilling industry that was already exporting a small volume of eau de vie to London. They reasoned that concentrating the wine by distillation would save shipping costs and that the brandewijn could be rehydrated before sale back home. It tended not to be, though: very

watery eau de vie is not quite the same as the wine from which it was originally distilled. Besides, the time the spirit had spent in oak, both in warehouses and at sea, had transformed it from firewater to something much, much better: Cognac.

War with France in 1672 disrupted the trade, so the distillers of the Charente had to find another market. They found it in England. Spirit-drinking was just beginning to take off; English workers drank either rum from newly conquered Jamaica or native 'strong waters', often flavoured with aniseed. But Cognac was expensive and French – just the right kind of prestige beverage for the courtiers of the Francophile Charles II and those who aped them. And when the Franco-Dutch war was expanded to embrace England too, English shippers discovered that just about every wine-growing region bordering the Mediterranean now had its own brandy industry too. Hence, among other drinks, port and sherry. And hence, too, the smugglers who infested Britain's porous coastline and their constant war with the excisemen: British distillers had neither the vines to make their own brandy nor a convincing artificial substitute.

However, British distillers could and sometimes did work with molasses. The sticky black residue of the ludicrously inefficient method of extracting sugar from cane by beating and milling had almost as many uses as the sugar itself; and after the

▲ *Sugar cane field*

accidental taking of Jamaica from the Spanish in 1655 (by a flotilla of Cromwell's navy, which had been sent to take Santo Domingo but had been beaten off), both sugar and molasses became plentiful in Britain – and so did rum.

It is quite possible that the Dutch had a hand here too. The origin of the word 'rum', first recorded in 1654 and thought to be a contraction of 'rumbullion', is hotly disputed, but the Dutch – who had been active in the Caribbean for more than 70 years at that time – made great use of a large all-purpose short-stemmed drinking glass called a rummer. The 'bullion' element could be a version of the French 'bouillon' or hot drink or 'firewater'. So it

may well be that rum was first made by the Dutch imperialists who plundered the sugar plantations of Brazil in the early 17th century.

As British power in the region spread, so did sugar planting and rum distilling; but although molasses was sometimes used to make up a shortfall in grain, rum was rarely made in Britain. Only Glasgow had a significant rum distillery, long razed so sadly there's nowhere to visit. And it was not part of the Royal Navy's official rations. From the 17th century until 31 July 1970 – Black Tot Day – the official ration was beer, and rum was (on paper) only a substitute on stations where beer was not available.

7 HUSH HEATH ESTATE

AT HUSH HEATH THE WEALD IS YOUR OYSTER – AND IT'S GOT A SECRET PEARL AT ITS HEART.

⌂ Five Oaks Ln, Staplehurst TN12 0HT ✆ 01622 832794 ☍ hushheath.com ◷ 11.00–17.00 daily; drop-in trail; see website for details of guided tours – booking required; private tours by arrangement.

Hush Hall dates back to 1503 but was substantially remodelled about a century later. It's an absolute orgy of exquisite Tudor joinery inside and out, replete with spandrels and bressumers and other such chiselled goodies, and is set in 400 acres of almost unrivalled variety and beauty.

> **"THE MICROCLIMATE WAS JUDGED TO BE PERFECT FOR THE CLASSIC CHAMPAGNE VARIETIES"**

The Hall and its 1930s ornamental garden is the private home of the Balfour-Lynn family and therefore out of bounds, but the endless rolling green of the Kentish Weald with its oak forests and wildflower meadows are there to explore. These oak forests, some ancient, some restored, are a feature of particular delight, and as they amount to 200 acres you might well say that Hush Heath is a wood with some wine rather than a vineyard with a bit of forestry. Trees that are not thriving are systematically felled to give the stronger trees room and to open up the canopy, allowing sunlight to reach the forest floor and wildlife of all shapes, sizes and degrees of creepiness to flourish.

The felled trees are left where they lie, blocks of flats for fungi, bugs, lichen, mosses and other vital players in the circle of life.

Hotel du Vin and Malmaison entrepreneur Richard Balfour-Lynn and his family bought Hush Heath in the 1980s, and after major restoration they set about adding to the estate, first planting 20 acres of orchards and then gradually buying more and more farmland and woodland. The first vines were planted in 2002, and as the soil – deep Wealden clay – and the microclimate was judged

to be perfect for the classic Champagne varieties, there are now 50 acres of Chardonnay, Pinot Noir and Pinot Meunier all in their neat rows.

The state-of-the art visitor centre and winery, built in a rather Scandinavian style in 2010, is designed around the *méthode champenoise* or, as we must call it, the traditional method of putting bubbles into wine. It is best known for the Hush Heath speciality, Balfour Brut Rosé, but it has other strings to its bow: Balfour Blanc de Blancs is all Chardonnay; 1503 is all Pinot Noir; and Leslie's Reserve – named after Mrs Balfour-Lynn – is a blend. Oh, two more strings: bottle-fermented sparkling apple wines, both blends of russets, bramleys and coxes, one white, one rosé.

While we're in the orchard, Hush Heath also produces a range of fresh-pressed apple

juices named after number-one son Luke and a blended cider named after junior Jake (who is also co-owner of the brewery that produces Hush Heath's saffron lager). So, what with four naturally sparkling bubblies, two *méthode champenoise* apple wines, a cider, a beer and still wines named after Luke (red Pinot Noir), daughters Nanette (rosé blend) and Skye (white, Pinot Noir and Chardonnay) and dog Liberty (Bacchus) to browse, here we are in the tasting room aptly named The View, watching the sun set over the woods we've just spent hours tramping through, and… well, who's going home?

No chance…

THE WINE Balfour Liberty's Bacchus 11.5% ABV, a grassy nose with citrus spice and long finish, or Springfield Chardonnay 2018 12% ABV, fresh with hints of grapefruit, green apple and cinnamon.

▲ *The visitor centre*
◀ *The bottling plant*

EAST & WEST SUSSEX

CIDER MILLS

8 ENGLISH FARM CIDER CENTRE

⌂ Middle Farm, West Firle, Lewes, East Sussex BN8 6LJ T ✆ 01323 811411 ⌖ middlefarm. com ◷ 09.30–17.00 daily. Southern England is scattered with picturesque old farms whose original buildings aren't quite up to the job any more and have been converted to retail or office use, but Middle Farm is the best because as well as the produce shop, the gift shop, the open farm, the tea room and the plant sales it's got the English Farm Cider Centre, a shop so large its stock qualifies as a National Collection. Some 200 traditional ciders and perries, bottled and draught, rub shoulders with meads, country wines, fruit liqueurs, apple brandy, gin, eau de vie and even a selection of beers. Not so much a shop, more a way of life. Middle Farm is also the home of Pookhill Cider.

9 PERRYHILL ORCHARDS

⌂ Edenbridge Rd, Hartfield, East Sussex TN7 4JJ ✆ 01892 770595 ⌖ perryhillorchards.co.uk ◷ shop 09.30–17.00 daily; tea room 09.30–16.30 daily; butcher 10.00–17.00 Tue, 09.00–17.00 Wed, 09.00–16.00 Thu, 09.00–17.00 Sat–Sun. Another splendid example of the farm that has everything, Perryhill, on the edge of the Ashdown Forest, has been a commercial apple producer since 1966, making sweet, medium and dry ciders as well as single-varietal juices. On top of

that it has a farm shop stocking regional produce (including wines, ciders and beers), a tea room/ restaurant, a craft centre and an artisan butcher.

VINEYARDS

10 BLUEBELL VINEYARD

⌂ Glenmore Farm, Furner's Green, Uckfield, East Sussex TN22 3RU ✆ 01825 791561 ⌖ bluebellvineyard.org ◷ 10.00–16.00 Mon– Sat, 11.00–16.00 Sun. The first Chardonnay, Seyval Blanc, Pinot Noir and Pinot Meunier grapevines were planted at this former piggery in 2005 and it has since expanded to 70 acres, producing the well-known Hindleap range of bottle-fermented sparkling wines. Vineyard and winery tours with tastings are conducted by appointment throughout the week but there are also woodland and vineyard trails and a picnic terrace overlooking the estate.

11 BOLNEY ESTATE

⌂ Foxhole Ln, Bolney, West Sussex RH17 5NB ✆ 01222 881575 ⌖ bolneywineestate.com ◷ 09.00–17.00 Sat–Thu, 18.00–22.30 Fri, 10.00–17.00 Sun. Tours and tastings should be booked; there are also extensive trails and evening events, as well as a grand gourmet lunch and afternoon tea. If you have time then why not try their vineyard trail, where where you can explore their 18 acres. Founded in 1972, Bolney is one of England's oldest commercial vineyards and is

going through a phase of immense expansion. A merger with neighbouring Pookchurch has seen the acreage under vines double to 104; a new visitor centre with enlarged café and shop opened in 2018; and a new winery with a capacity of 500,000 bottles is under construction. It also has its pomace distilled by Foxhole Spirits to make gin.

12 CARR TAYLOR
See page 104.

▲ *Try catching the Bluebell Line and alighting at Kingscote station for the Kingscote Estate*

13 KINGSCOTE ESTATE
🏠 Mill Place Farm, Vowell's Ln, East Grinstead, West Sussex RH19 4LG ✐ 01342 327535 ✐ kingscoteestate.com ⊙ shop 10.00—17.30 daily; the range of tours must be booked in advance. Extensive trails. The 150-acre Kingscote Estate produces cider from its own orchards as well as still and sparkling wines from its vineyards. It also offers country sports including angling and clay pigeon shooting and has converted a 15th-century tithe barn into a wedding venue and function suite. Kingscote has its own stop on the Bluebell Line preserved steam railway, so you can arrive in style!

12 CARR TAYLOR

YOU DON'T NEED TO IMITATE TO GET THE TOP PRIZES.

⌂ Wheel Ln, Westfield, Hastings, East Sussex TN35 4SG ✆ 01424 752501 ✎ carr-taylor.co.uk
◷ 10.00–17.00 daily; no booking required for self-guided trails.

When you arrive at Carr Taylor the protocol requires you to get down on your hands and knees and kiss the soil. That's because this soil is sacred. This is where David and Linda Carr Taylor came to the conclusion that English wine didn't have to be imitation German. And this, just a few miles inland of Hastings, is where the fightback against the French began in earnest...

When David, managing director of an engineering firm, and Linda, who had trained as a pianist and flautist at the Royal College of

Music in London, planted the first vines at their farm, guess what they chose? Yup, it was 1971 and English growers still believed that our soil and climate were so like the Rhineland's that German varieties would do best here, so that's the direction they took. Their first commercial bottling was in 1976 and by the following year they had finished planting their 21 acres. Soon the prizes started rolling in – the 1981 Gutenborner won a silver medal in the 1983 International Wine & Spirit Competition, the 1982 Kerner Huxel took

Bronze in the English Wine of the Year and the 1982 Schönburger scored a Médaille d'Or in the Challenge International de Vin.

At that time people were beginning to agree with pre-war pioneer George Ordish, who had written on the similarity between the climates and soils of southeastern England and the Champagne region. From as early as 1966 some growers were trying their hands at making Champagne-style bottle-fermented sparkling wines using German varieties, and in 1980 Hambledon Vineyard in Hampshire planted 1,000 Chardonnay vines. Lamberhurst Vineyard, where Carr Taylor had

> ## "IN 1987, THEY ENTERED THE 1988 CONCOURS EUROPÉEN DES GRANDS VIN… AND WON GOLD"

its grapes vinified before its own winery was completed, also experimented with bottle fermentation. But it was David and Linda who got there first. From a bumper 1984 harvest, and with the century-old farm buildings now converted into the winery, warehouse and public spaces you see today, they made their first sparkler for release in 1987, entered it in the 1988 Concours Européen des Grands Vin… and won gold. Of course it was only a modest affair back then with a trifling 1,800 challengers. The next time Carr Taylor scooped that same gold in 1999 there were 4,300!

The wine world takes its competitions very seriously, so the French were understandably

interlopers and wrote the wine off as a fluke. However, as the awards piled up – not just for the Carr Taylors but for the many English makers who followed their lead – it was clear that the English wine industry had made the transition from (in the eyes of cynics) a bunch of middle-class eccentrics with more money than sense growing whatever they could persuade to sprout from their patch of freezing English mud, into serious competition. And it started here. Right here where you're standing now.

There are a range of tours, starting with a self-guided tour where you can just turn up without any booking and be given a map showing the vineyard trail; dogs are very welcome. Or you can book a group tour where you have your own dedicated guide which concludes with a wine-tasting session. They also offer a full wedding service with marquee and pergola.

> **THE WINE** A choice of sparkling Carr Taylor Brut 12% ABV, still Carr Taylor Cannonball 10.5% ABV, and fruit Carr Taylor Elderberry 11.5% ABV.

▲ *The vineyard*
◀ *Take in the bluebells on a self-guided tour in spring*

105

14 OXNEY ORGANIC ESTATE

✉ Hobbs Ln, Beckley, East Sussex TN31 6TU
✎ 01797 260137 ✐ oxneyestate.com ◯ farm shop Apr–Nov 10.00–16.00 Mon–Fri, 12.00–16.00 Sat; tours followed by tastings Apr–Oct start 10.30 Fri–Sat, must be booked in advance. Post-tour picnic hampers available. At 850 acres, Oxney claims to the biggest sustainably farmed organic estate in the country. It includes 35 acres of Chardonnay, Pinot Noir, Pinot Meunier, Pinot Précoce and Seyval Blanc planted between 2012 and 2018, and it produces both still and sparkling wines in a brand-new winery sited in a converted oasthouse. Several old barns have also been converted into comfortable holiday cottages.

15 RATHFINNY WINE ESTATE

See page 108.

▲ Sedlescombe Organic Vineyard
▶ Kingston near Lewes on the South Downs, East Sussex

16 RIDGEVIEW WINE ESTATE

✉ Fragbarrow Ln, Ditchling Common, East Sussex BN6 8TP ✎ 01444 242040 ✐ ridgeview. co.uk ◯ shop 11.00–16.00 daily; vineyard & winery tours & tastings must be booked in advance. Hampers available for picnics in the Wine Garden. Established in 1995 in the beautiful prehistoric landscape of the South Downs in Sussex and now in the hands of the second generation of the founding family, Ridgeview was one of the vineyards that pioneered the production of English sparkling wine. With a string of international awards under its belt it also helped British Bubbles earn their worldwide reputation for quality. To get more involved you can join their wine club OurView for special invitations to bespoke events.

17 SEDLESCOMBE ORGANIC VINEYARD

✉ Hawkshurst Rd, Sedlescombe, Robertsbridge, East Sussex TN32 5SA ✎ 01580 830715 ✐ englishorganicwine.co.uk ◯ shop 10.00–18.00 Wed–Sun, barn bar/café 10.30–17.30; drop-in self-guided vineyard & woodland trails. Guided tours must be booked in advance. Founded in 1979 by self-sufficiency enthusiasts Roy and Irma Cook, Sedlescombe was England's first organic vineyard and produced the country's first organic bottle-fermented sparkling wine in 1990. Since 2010 it has been fully biodynamic. As well as a wide range of white, red, rosé and sparkling wines it also makes fruit wines and highly regarded ciders. It is situated in the picturesque High Weald Area of Outstanding Natural Beauty.

15 RATHFINNY WINE ESTATE

FEELING JADED? A STAY AT RATHFINNY GUARANTEES TOTAL IMMERSION IN EVERYTHING SOOTHING.

⌂ White Way, Polegate, East Sussex BN6 5TU ✆ 01323 870022 ✎ rathfinnyestate.com ⏲ 10.00–17.00 Wed–Thu, Sun, 10.00–22.30 Fri–Sat.

If any single enterprise could be said to sum up the way the English wine industry has shifted gear in recent years, Rathfinny would be a good avatar. In its early days English winemaking was almost tentative, lacking both investment and identity. Bit by bit the pioneers were discovering what the English soil and climate could achieve, but it was only when the South East's suitability for the Champagne grape cohort – Chardonnay and the various Pinots – was firmly established that English wine decided what it was: Champagne, only better.

> **"THE DRIVERS HAVE DEVOTED CONSIDERABLE EFFORT TO ENCOURAGE WILDLIFE THROUGH HABITAT RESTORATION"**

With that discovery has come a new confidence and a new dynamism, epitomised here on 600 acres of downland no more than a crow's mile from the sea near Alfriston in East Sussex. When Sarah and Mark Driver – she a solicitor, he a hedge fund manager – bought the derelict farmstead in 2010 they had big plans, and they had the professionalism, the experience, the acumen

and the access to funding to get the wheels turning. Planting started with 50 acres in 2012, with a programme intended to create 400 acres of vineyard capable of exceeding a million bottles a year. While the planting progressed under the watchful eye of experienced vineyard manager Cameron Roucher from New Zealand, work started on developing the estate buildings.

A ramshackle set of modern but very run-down sheds disappeared under a new winery. The original 1860s farmstead, left derelict after the 1987 hurricane, was not so much restored as rebuilt. The original flint and brick barn with its enormous wagon door has become an architectural landmark: in the pruning and picking seasons it's a ten-room hostel capable

of putting up 45 workers in comfortable and stylish accommodation. For the rest of the year it's a highly praised B&B. The Tasting Room fine dining restaurant and Cellar Door shop are just as distinguished, sculpted and shaped to meld into the landscape with a terrace commanding superb views of the Downs and the Channel beyond. The whole complex, even the 16,000 sq ft office building, scooped the commercial category awards at the 2015 Sussex Heritage Trust awards. Of course it is all designed to be as environmentally friendly as possible.

Grand though the scale and scope of the buildings are, Mark Driver's vision is broader still. It was instrumental in gaining coveted Protected Designation of Origin for Sussex Sparkling Wine – in fact, Mark's is the signature on the application document – guaranteeing not only that all the grapes come from Sussex but also that demanding standards in production are rigorously adhered to. To ensure that Rathfinny meets these standards

the Drivers have put Champagne winemaker Jonathan Médard in charge. The first releases, a Blanc de Blancs, a Blanc de Noirs and a rosé, went on sale in 2018. The spent pomace is not wasted: a small pot still converts it into marc that's blended with grain spirit and botanicals to make Seven Sisters Gin, while the Seven Sisters Vermouth is the estate's own wine suitably fortified and aromatised.

The estate is criss-crossed with footpaths that anyone is free to wander: the Drivers have devoted considerable effort to encourage wildlife through habitat restoration, so don't forget to bring your copy of the *Observer Book of Butterflies* with you. Alternatively, book a guided tour, followed by lunch and tastings or just dinner in the Tasting Room.

THE WINE Blanc de Blancs 12.5% ABV, delivers creamy apricot and acacia notes on the nose, Rosé 12.5% ABV, wild strawberries and mandarin zest, and Blanc de Noirs 2015 12.5% ABV, raspberries and toasted almonds with a red-apple finish.

▲ *Courtyard seating*

◀ *The Tasting Room restaurant*

109

OTHER FRUIT

CAN YOU PASS A BLACKTHORN HEDGE WITHOUT THINKING OF SLOE GIN? NO? WHY WOULD YOU.

Home winemaking, using either grape concentrate or preferably fruit gathered from garden or hedgerow, is one of Britain's favourite hobbies… and one of the most quickly abandoned once the novice discovers how difficult it is to produce a drink that's actually drinkable. But if making fruit wine is hard, so is buying it. Hardly anybody makes it commercially; even fewer retailers sell it; and, because it pays the same tax as grape wine, it's expensive. Which is sad because although we laughed at Tom Good's peapod burgundy, it is perfectly possible to produce exquisite wines from the most unlikely of vegetals.

You'd have thought that thrifty peasants down the ages would have made the best use they could of whatever bounty nature proffered, but there is no ancient tradition of country winemaking in Britain. In the Middle Ages orchard fruits were widely grown and fermented for cider and perry, but soft and wild fruits were such a chore to pick (especially as they ripen while the hay harvest is on) that it was a task left to children and the aged. Whatever they picked couldn't be vinified because they weren't sweet enough to ferment without added sugar… of which there was none. Or there was, but it was in short supply and therefore so fabulously expensive that it was used only to make sugar sculptures, crystallised exotic fruits and other such confections for the wealthy to blacken their teeth on.

Then in 1655 Cromwell captured Jamaica, simultaneously founding the Empire and conquering some huge sugar plantations. American colonists also started plantations, and in a remarkably short time sugar became an affordable commodity. Fruit wines – known as 'sweets' – joined a long list of novel beverages that Britain was trying out at the time: tea, coffee, chocolate, rum, flavoured eau de vie (known as 'waters') and gin. By 1707 production of sweets was significant enough to attract a duty of £3 a barrel. Some 30 years later it was cut to 12/-, but still yielded enough to secure £500,000 credit.

"FORTUNATELY THE CURRENT EXCITEMENT ABOUT FRUIT AND OTHER NATURAL FLAVOURS HAS NOT PASSED THE ENGLISH WINE INDUSTRY BY"

Proper fruit wine gradually died out because it was easier and cheaper to concoct a cordial of fruit juice, grape wine and sugar, or a compound of fruit, neutral spirit and sugar, than it was to fiddle about with fermentation. Homemade country wines were still popular, especially among women who could pretend they were for medicinal use only – held to be good against headaches and hysteria. But compounds were more popular still because the same dainty measure held four times the alcohol.

Cordials and compounds in turn gradually lost popularity to fortified wines, but a handful remain in production, ginger wine representing the cordials and sloe and damson gin the compounds. Some makers of 'British' wines – ie: imported grape concentrate, rehydrated and fermented over here – have also marketed versions dosed with fruit juices.

But only one really traditional fruit wine (apart from cider and perry) has survived the centuries: jerkum, the fiendishly strong plum liquor traditionally made in the Vale of Evesham. In the 1660s the cidermaker John Beale recorded: 'I could also give some account of cherry-wine and wine of plums. Their vast store in some places, under a penny the pound, and their expedite growth makes it cheap enough... the large English or Dutch sharp cherry, and the full black, tawny Plum, as big as a walnut... make the wine.' Cherry wine, once common in Kent, gave way to cherry brandy, but jerkum is still reputedly being made in the sheds and garages of Worcestershire today.

Fortunately the current excitement about fruit and other natural flavours has not passed the English wine industry by. Like craft brewers with their exotic hops and artisan distillers with their unexpected botanicals, winemakers are increasingly investigating the potential of fruit wines and liqueurs. Spurred on by the possibility of creating their own artisan spirits, firms like Bramley & Gage are now producing products such as Elderflower liqueur, Organic sloe gin and even an English Vermouth. Other compamnies such as Lyme Bay and Lurgashall are exploring their kitchen gardens to find new delights under old cloches.

CHAPTER SIX
MIDLANDS

DERBYSHIRE

① ②

LINCOLNSHIRE
☆

STAFFORDSHIRE

⑨
⑧

⑩

SHROPSHIRE

☆☆

●

⑥

LEICESTERSHIRE

HEREFORDSHIRE ⑤

③ ☆

WARWICKSHIRE

☆

DERBYSHIRE

BREWERY

1 PEAK ALES

⌂ The Barn Brewery, Bakewell DE45 1EX
✆ 01246 583737 ◷ peakales.co.uk ◔ 09.00–
16.00 Mon–Fri, 11.00–16.00 Sat–Sun. It is best
to ring in advance to find out when it is possible
to visit. By rights, Peak Ales ought to be one
of the most visited breweries in the country.
Located in an old barn on the Chatsworth Estate,
it's got Chatsworth House itself just up the road
in one direction and Bakewell in the other, with
Tideswell, Miller's Dale and the heart of the Peak
District not much further. In summer the whole
district swarms with day-trippers from Sheffield,
Chesterfield, Nottingham and Derby and more
serious tourists from all over the world. The
brewery was planned by Robert and Debra Evans
in 2003, using grants from the Estate and the
National Park Authority to bring a very attractive
but totally derelict stone byre and cattleyard,
called Cunnery Barn, back into use. It proved to be
quite a job: the barn was near to collapse and the
yard was choked with head-high brambles. After
two years' work, when the repairs and restoration
were finally completed and dignitaries from all
the various authorities involved were gathered
to inspect what they'd paid for, two barn owls
emerged to see what all the fuss was about. That
put an end to the work for three months until
their chicks had fledged – a reminder of a very
similar event at the opening of the Isle of Arran

distillery (page 228) 19 years earlier, only the birds
in Arran's case were golden eagles. The owls now
inhabit one of the most luxurious bird boxes in
the Peak District. Robert and Debra judged their
market well and flourished by presenting a range
of solidly traditional ales, using mainly good old
English hop varieties such as Fuggles, Goldings
and Brambling Cross. By 2012 they had outgrown
Cunnery Barn and had to transfer production to a
much bigger site in nearby Ashford in the Water;
but rather than give up the barn altogether they
decided to capitalise on its attractiveness and
location by creating a visitor centre with a shop,
a bar (or sampling room, as they prefer to call it,
although it's fully licensed and you're more than
welcome to drop by for a casual pint if you happen
to be passing) and a 2½-barrel pilot brewery.
The visitor centre is self-guided, or rather self-
navigated, by the use of placards and leaflets as
it's too small for guided tours. However, at 13.00
every day there's a talk that you are welcome to
listen in on; you are advised to phone ahead in
early or late summer as Robert and Debra haven't
finalised yet when the high season and low season
start and end.

VINEYARD

2 RENISHAW HALL

⌂ Renishaw Park, Chesterfield S21 3WB
✆ 01246 432310 ◷ renishaw-hall.co.uk
◔ 10.30–16.30 Wed–Sun. Renishaw Park has
been the home of the Sitwell family since 1625,
and the massive late Georgian mansion you see
today attests to their wealth and power. There are

▲ *Diagrammatic explanation of Chase Distillery*

HEREFORDSHIRE

CIDER MILLS

3 HEREFORD CIDER MUSEUM
See page 116.

. . . .

4 WESTONS
See page 118.

GIN DISTILLERY

5 CHASE DISTILLERY
✉ Rosemaund Dr, Preston Wynn HR13PG
✆ 01432 820455 ⬦ chasedistillery.co.uk
🕐 10.00–15.30 Mon–Sat. Will Chase had been
growing potatoes for supermarkets for 20 years
when in 2002 he decided that turning them
into top-end crisps would be more profitable.
Tyrrell Crisps was born; and because the brand
was distinctive when all around was Walker's the
venture blossomed. Then while on a trip to the
US, Will came across a distillery that was making
vodka from potatoes, which seemed even more
profitable than frying them. So in 2008 he sold
Tyrrell's and installed a distillery instead. Cider-
based gin followed potato vodka later that year,
sparking the whole craft gin revolution. Since
then new products have virtually cascaded from
the rather unlovely barn that houses the still. This
is no delicious old half-timbered Herefordshire
farmstead but, if you want to know how the spirit
world was turned on its head, this is where you
have to come.

occasional guided tours of the magnificent interior
but the park's chief glory is the seven-acre formal
Italianate garden, laid out in 1895 by Sir George
Sitwell just in time to host the childhood romps
(and what strange romps they must have been!)
of those darlings of early 20th-century art and
literature, Edith, Osbert and Sacheverell. The
gardens are all you could want, an Eden of topiary
and follies. In 1973 the then Sitwell, Sir Reresby,
father of the current Sitwell, realised that they
needed a vineyard and planted one. It was until
1986 the most northerly in the world, producing
a white, a red, a rosé and a sparkler that you may
enjoy in the café and can buy in the shop. Vineyard
tours with tasting must be booked in advance.

3 HEREFORD CIDER MUSEUM

IN LOVING AND LIVING MEMORY OF CIDERTOWN'S LOST GREATNESS.

✉ 21 Ryelands St, Hereford HR4 0EF ✆ 01432 354207 ✆ cidermuseum.co.uk ⏰ 10.30–16.30 Mon–Sat.

▲ *Antique bottling equipment and cider press*

Like the Louvre or Schönbrunn, the museum in Ryelands Street is a monument to cider in a city where cider is no longer king. Oh, the Bulmer factory is still there, or parts of it, but since Scottish & Newcastle Breweries bought the company in 2003 it's no longer the HQ but merely an outlying production unit, much of whose heritage – especially its fermenting hall, a labyrinth of vast oak vats packed so close that an overweight man could hardly squeeze between them – has gone.

A little sad, perhaps; but the Hereford Cider Museum is no relic. It's Arts Council-accredited, and despite being a little off the beaten track it gets 12,000 walk-in visitors annually, as well as thousands of attendees at the exhibitions and other events it hosts. It used to be the Bulmers' company offices and boardroom, and the bottling hall and the cold cellars where once the *pupîtres* and other paraphernalia were situated to make the Pomagne.

Its conversion into the museum was the work of Bertram Bulmer, retired MD of Bulmers; Norman Weston of Westons; and John Hudson of the sadly defunct Long Ashton Research Station. The three men saw and rued (even though they were responsible for it) the speed at which the cider industry was changing and feared the irrevocable loss of its heritage. In 1973 they banded together to start collections of literature and art, and in 1981 they moved the lot into a spare corner of the Bulmer factory along with a huge assortment of antique kit and memorabilia: horse-powered trough mills, flatbed presses of various types, oak vats and barrels, costrels (coopered flagons) and heat-formed cowhorn cups. That wasn't enough, though. Mr Bulmer wanted a still, even though distilling cider to make apple brandy had died out in the 1820s and had had its heyday a century before that. But a still he wanted and a still he got from France, where the practice of wheeling alembics ambulants from farm to farm in spring to distil last autumn's vintage had not yet passed into folklore.

▲ *Apple identification at Hereford Cider Museum*

"THE BULMER COLLECTION OF EARLY 18TH-CENTURY LEAD-CRYSTAL CIDER GOBLETS, IS TRULY EXQUISITE"

Now that he had his still he wanted a licence to operate it. Customs were unsure: the only licences they had granted within living memory were to allow established firms such as Gilbey's to move their operations out of London to sites in new locations. Being naturally risk-averse naysayers, they thought they could fob Mr Bulmer off with procrastination and excuses. However, in the end, he got his licence, and the King Offa Distillery functioned at the museum from 1987 to 1998, by which time Mr Bulmer had been safely in his grave for five years. The still is still there, as are a few casks of the brandy itself. You would have to bribe the museum director very handsomely to get any.

The prize exhibit here in purely aesthetic terms is not oak but glass. The Bulmer collection of early 18th-century lead-crystal cider goblets, donated when S&N consigned Bulmers to history, is truly exquisite, among the finest glassware on Earth, made when cider was as prized as French wine. Pointless to try to describe them – you must see them and then wonder how you might contrive to steal them. Even the tea room is charming in a cosy, chintzy way, and the gift shop sells more than 150 brands of craft cider and the bottle openers to open them.

4 WESTONS

REG, PRINCE, ROSIE, PIP, SQUEAK AND WILFRED – COME ON DOWN AND MEET THE GANG!

✉ The Bounds, Much Marcle HR8 2NQ ✐ 01531 660233 ⊘ westons-cider.co.uk ⊙ for restaurant, shop & tour times, visit the website; book in advance.

▲ *The Bounds, Westons Cider*

There is little to rival the view of the Malvern Hills from the car park at Westons Cider. Mind you, if you turn round, the view of the old farmhouse – 17th century, refronted in the early 19th century in assorted brick and stone – against a backdrop of rolling pasture studded with great parkland perry pear trees reputedly dating back to Queen Anne, isn't too shabby either.

Commercial cidermaking at The Bounds goes back to 1880 when the tenant, Henry Weston, decided to diversify from the fruit growing and sheep and cattle rearing that had been his main business and replaced his horse-powered cider mill and hand-turned screw-presses with steam. It speaks volumes about perceptions of cider at the time that his first product was draught Westons

Rough, widely sold in local pubs but also after the 1887 Truck Act to neighbouring farmers who were giving up making their own. And as luck would have it, the station at Dymock some 3½ miles away between Greenway Halt and Four Oaks Halt on the Daffodil Line opened for passengers and freight in 1885, giving the company's products national reach. By 1924 Westons was profitable enough to afford to buy out The Bounds along with two other farms from the Homme House Estate, which was sorely afflicted by death duties.

"THE STATION AT DYMOCK ON THE DAFFODIL LINE OPENED FOR PASSENGERS AND FREIGHT IN 1885, GIVING THE COMPANY'S PRODUCTS NATIONAL REACH"

Staying true to its roots served Westons well through the 1950s and 60s and into the real ale revolution. Bulmers and Taunton both sold traditional ciders, uncarbonated and on handpump, but only in their home regions. Westons alone maintained national distribution – it even owned a pub in London – so if an inn outside Herefordshire or Somerset had a market for scrumpy, it had to be Westons. They were also alone in distributing a genuine perry – unless you count Babycham, that is! The same positive attitude to tradition underpins its current range: Stowford Press is keg but all-juice, and the only keg cider most aficionados will drink. Old Rosie, named after the 1921 Aveling & Porter steamroller enjoying a peaceful retirement at The Bounds, is still and cloudy, almost the only one of its kind nationally distributed. Henry Westons Vintage

reserve is carbonated but beautifully deep and tannic and probably too much like cider for most of today's cider drinkers.

In recent years Westons has shed its natural rustic reticence and opened itself wholeheartedly to visitors. The place is a veritable garden of delights and a joy to visit. The shire horses Reg and Prince no longer have to toil at the mill as their forebears did, but are much-loved ambassadors for the company at agricultural shows, village fêtes and weddings. In the fermentation hall you will be awed by the ranks of huge oak maturation vats, some of them originally porter tuns bought secondhand from George's Brewery of Bristol. They are named Pip, Squeak and Wilfred after the children's cartoon published in the *Daily Mirror* from 1919 to 1956. Take the orchard walk in late March or early April when all the trees are bare, but the giant perry pears are in full and prolific blossom and look like schooners under sail. All this and the excellent Scrumpy House restaurant in a 17th-century barn, the Orchard tea room, a well-stocked shop, a play and picnic area... and of course the picturesque Malverns.

THE CIDER Henry Westons Vintage Cider 8.3% ABV, dry, rich and full of fruit. If you like a fruit flavour, Rosie's Pig, which comes in rhubarb, raspberry or strawberry, all at 4.2% ABV. For a cloudy cider then try Old Rosie 6.8% ABV, bittersweet apples, haybarns and honey. For organic, Wyld Wood 6% ABV, oak and honey flavour giving a rich and very well-balanced finish.

LEICESTERSHIRE

BREWERY

6 BELVOIR

✉ Crown Park, Station Rd, Old Dalby LE14 3NQ
✆ 01664 823455 ☞ belvoirbrewery.co.uk
🕐 08.00–16.00 Mon–Fri. There are daily brewery tours, but the brewhouse can be seen without having to stir from The Sample Cellar via large viewing windows. Founded in 1995 by ex-Shipstone and Theakston brewer Colin Brown, Belvoir Brewery moved from its original home in the middle of the village to a rather handsome purpose-built site in 2007. The Alehouse visitor centre comprises the fully licensed Sample Cellar bar-restaurant, which serves locally sourced food throughout the day as well as Belvoir's wide and eclectic range of ales (one, Blue Brew, incorporates whey from Stilton cheese). There's a shop also selling local produce, and the room is heavily ornamented with Colin's collection of brewing memorabilia from other now-defunct breweries, including such gems as the mash tun and copper from Boddingtons of Manchester.

LINCOLNSHIRE

BREWERY

7 BATEMANS
See page 122.

SHROPSHIRE

BREWERY

8 LUDLOW BREWING COMPANY

✉ The Railway Shed, Station Dr, Ludlow SY8 2PQ ✆ 01584 873291 ⏀ theludlowbrewingcompany. co.uk ⏰ 10.00–17.00 Mon–Sat (18.00 Fri), 13.00–16.00 Sun; tours at 15.00 Mon–Fri & 14.00 Sat should be booked; the whole venue is available for evening hire. Like many a small market town, Ludlow in south Shropshire had managed without its own brewery since the 1930s but, once the town had become foodie capital of the Marches with the opening of Shaun Hill's Merchant House restaurant in 1995, it just had to have one. To the rescue, in 2006 (the year after the Merchant House closed) came Gary and Alison Walters, who opened their brewery in an old maltings in Corve Street. It soon proved far too small for their needs and, in 2011, after three years' planning, the brewery moved to a much bigger and grander site in a cavernous Victorian red-brick railway shed. Alongside the towering 20-barrel plant (did we say the place was cavernous?) they installed a cheery slate-floored bar and shop selling its range from Best at 3.7% ABV to Stairway to Paradise at 5% ABV and pork pies to soak it all up. During the designing of the brewery every opportunity was taken to ensure that an environmentally friendly and low carbon facility was established. They

reclaim a substantial amount of heat during the brewing process which is used to power the underfloor heating, recycle rainwater, have low carbon insulation, use low energy lighting and have installed solar panels.

VINEYARD

9 WROXETER ROMAN VINEYARD

✉ Wroxeter SY5 6PQ ✆ 01743 761888 ⏀ wroxetervineyard.co.uk ⏰ 09.00–17.00 Mon–Sat, 10.30–16.30 Sun. That eerily quiet stretch of country between Shrewsbury and Telford is made all the more otherworldly by the remains of the dead Roman city of Viroconium, marooned there in the wrong century, its surface exposed as if by scratching dogs. Beside it since 1991, there has been an apt memorial to at least one aspect of its former life – a vineyard, founded by agricultural consultant David Millington after a business trip to California. A revered member of the Great British Awkward Squad, Mr Millington spent eight years fighting the council's ruling that winemaking, bottling and retailing were industrial activities requiring planning permission. As the Awkward Squad so often does, he won. The vineyard has passed to his son Martin and is celebrated for its blended table wines – no *dégorgement* here! – as well as for its long and informative tours, which include complimentary bottles and lunch as well as the customary tasting that unsurprisingly must be booked in advance. If you really want to get involved then take part in their 'adopt a vine' scheme or you can buy this experience for a real wine enthusiast.

◀ *The visitor centre at Batemans, housed in an 18th- century windmill*

7 BATEMANS

THE FAMILY THAT BREWS TOGETHER STAYS TOGETHER.

⊠ Salem Bridge Brewery, Mill Ln, Wainfleet All Saints PE24 4JE ✐ 01754 880317 ⊘ bateman.co.uk
⊙ 09.00–17.00 Mon–Fri.

The A52 is far too spindly a thoroughfare to connect Skegness to the rest of the world: it only takes a single tractor to slow the traffic to an agonising crawl. But there's never a single tractor, of course: there's always half a dozen. By the time you get to Wainfleet All Saints, all thoughts of Skegness will have fled. But look! That windmill! That's the Batemans Brewery trademark, isn't it? Skeggie can wait.

Batemans is a small-to-medium family brewery with a big family history. It was founded in 1874 by farmers and home brewers George and Susannah Bateman who decided to concentrate on the brewing side of their business, supplying other farmers who still paid their labourers partly in beer but no longer wanted to make it themselves. In 1880 the Batemans moved from their original home to the larger Salem House, and after paying wages in kind was outlawed in 1887 they were brewing enough to supply the village pubs where farmworkers now had to get their ale.

The firm has descended in direct line ever since, first to Harry, then to George II and his queen Patricia, and then to siblings Stuart and Jacqui. The status of family brewery is much vaunted as

a marker of tradition, of continuity, of reassurance and of comfortable certitude. Of course the reality isn't necessarily that cosy, especially when the value of individual holdings among the non-brewing arms of the family has become diluted down the generations. When a takeover bid comes along, relations with no particular ties to the brewery are usually advised to accept the offer – more often than not, they do. So when a bid came knocking at the various doors of the extended Bateman family home in the 1980s, it was the sad assumption of every beer-lover that another light in the dimming constellation of family brewers was about to flicker out.

But to George and Patricia, Batemans-in-chief at the time, their funny-looking brewery with its almost random collection of buildings on the banks of the little River Steeping meant more than

> ## "XXXB HAS ENDURED BECAUSE IT'S JUST SO GOOD"

a livelihood or a sheaf of share certificates. It meant George's grandfather. It meant his father Harry. It meant their children, for whose future they were prepared to fight, however hard the contest. And it was hard. Few banks were

AT LUNCH

we all agree that

beer is best

MALT · HOPS · SUGAR · YEAST

interested in putting up funds for a stubborn old couple who didn't know which side their bread was buttered on. But sleepless nights and frantic days and looming deadlines notwithstanding, George and Patricia managed to raise the money. As a result Batemans at least is one light that never flickered out.

There is an aura of family values around Batemans, and if that sounds like romantic twaddle it's actually quite real in practical, pragmatic terms: it means that everything is done for more than just money

but for love as well. What it boils down to for the beer drinker is a portfolio of beers that George and Susannah would be proud of: some of them incredibly wild and imaginative, as Batemans was a very early adopter of unorthodox limited editions such as strawberry and the revolutionary mixed-grain Combined Harvest, long prefiguring

the mangomaniac craft brewers of today but always formulated and brewed with the customary skill and care. Its flagship, XXXB (always pronounced, Triple XB), dates to 1978, when many keg brewers were coming back to cask beer, but XXXB has endured because it's just so good. More recently, Batemans opened an in-house microbrewery just to produce the small-batch limited-edition beers for which it had become famous.

For the visitor, Batemans' devotion to family is attested by the many reminders of previous generations. The museum in the windmill is dubbed Harry's Artefact

Room because it was Harry who bought and incorporated the 100-year-old cornmill next door to Salem House when it closed in 1920. The visitor centre bar is dubbed Mr George's Bar, and visitors can enjoy lunch from 12.00 to 14.30 every day in the Patricia Room bistro (closed Oct–Dec Mon–Tue). Tours followed by tastings start at 11.00 and 14.00 every day; booking is strongly recommended to avoid disappointment.

THE BEER The classics Yella Belly Gold 3.9% ABV, made with American hops, Batemans XB 3.7% ABV, an amber pale ale, or XXXB 4.8% ABV, an award-winning strong bitter, deliciously spicy, fruity and biscuity flavour.

CIDER TRADITION & FOLKLORE

THEY SAY THAT IN THE OLDEN DAYS... BUT THEY'RE WRONG.

At the bottom of every mug of cider there lurks a paradox. On the one hand it is the only major category of alcoholic beverage that can't be made without a piece of seriously engineered mechanical equipment beyond a simple mill, which makes it at least proto – if not actually – industrial. On the other, since cidermaking only started moving off the farm and into the factory in 1887 (when Bulmers was founded) an aura of rusticity still clings to it. And with rusticity, naturally, comes that most timeless of double-acts, Folklore and Tradition. Let's deal with a couple of choice examples.

"CIDERMAKING ONLY STARTED MOVING OFF THE FARM AND INTO THE FACTORY IN 1887 WHEN BULMER'S WAS FOUNDED"

As everyone knows, wassailing is the ancient, even pre-Christian ritual of frightening away the devil or other demons with a particular animus towards apples by rushing out into the orchards at midnight on Old Twelfth Night (17 January) firing shotguns and banging pots and pans together, all to the accompaniment of wassailing carols sung fortissimo. The participants then apologise to the understandably disgruntled trees by pouring cider over their roots and putting slices of cider-sodden toast in their boughs. As one antiquarian website solemnly informs us: 'Rev Ian Bradley makes the excellent point that the tradition of wassailers going door to door, singing and drinking to the health of those whom they visit, goes back to pre-Christian fertility rites where the villagers went through orchards at mid-winter singing and shouting loudly to drive out evil spirits, and pouring cider on the roots of trees to encourage fertility.' Complete tosh, sadly. As a toast, 'washail' ('your health!') is first recorded in Geoffrey of Monmouth's *History of the Kings of Britain*, written in 1135–40. The salutation occurs again in songs and carols of the late Middle Ages but the practice of wassailing as a drunken frolic is first described only in 1585 in Kent. It wasn't specific to orchards but also, at different times and places, to beehives and livestock. To Shakespeare the word just meant a party, as in: 'He is wit's peddler, and retails his wares/At wakes and wassels, meetings, markets, fairs,' (*Love's Labour's Lost*, 1596) and 'The king doth wake to-night, and... Keeps wassel.' (*Hamlet*, 1603). A century later, Aubrey records oxen being wassailed, and it's only comparatively recently that wassailing has become specific to cider orchards. The whole family of door-to-door rowdyism probably dates to the Protestant Revolution of 1547–53, when Popish customs such as mystery plays, mummers and guild and fraternity celebrations and processions were driven out of churches and their practitioners took to the streets as waits, carollers, guisers, first-footers and wassailers.

▲ *Trough mills like this were in everyday use well into modern times to crush cider apples before pressing*

The Church — in this case the Methodist and Baptist variants — also played a part in the death of another much older tradition: the part-payment of wages in ciderkin, a weak beverage made by rehydrating spent pomace, then pressing it again and fermenting the watery juice. This went right back to the Middle Ages, when tenants paid their rent in labour. It was customary for the lord to provide them with basic food and drink; and as labour service gave way to all-money rent the bread and cheese and ale or cider came to be reckoned as part of the labourers' wages. But it's not true, as fable has it, that they were happy with this and drifted from farm to farm seeking the best cidermaker to work for.

In fact having been excluded from the 1831 Truck Act that abolished part-payment of wages in the employer's produce or vouchers redeemable in the employer's shop, they spent more than 50 years in a campaign to overturn the exemption, led by trade unionists with the invaluable practical support of pastors and ministers. Only in 1887 was their exemption lifted, although it long remained common for farmers to allow their labourers a ration of cider on top of their wages but by then fortunately workers were much better off.

One last myth to debunk: whatever anyone tells you, cider and cyder have always had exactly the same meaning, just like tiger and tyger. The difference is entirely orthographical.

STAFFORDSHIRE

BREWERIES

10 BANKS'S

Park Brewery, Brewery Rd, Wolverhampton WV1 4JT 01902 329653 bankssbeer.co.uk you must book in advance. Banks's is a great monument not only to brewing – and it produces a surprising number of very different brews, including Britain's best-selling dark mild at 3.1% ABV giving you a malty with a touch of bitterness taste – but also to Black Country industrial and cultural heritage. Founded in 1875, as soon as it had found its feet it embarked on the relentless and single-minded pursuit of growth through acquisition and merger, which climaxed when it took over Marston's (page 128) of Burton in 1999.

11 MARSTON, THOMPSON & EVERSHED

See page 128.

12 NATIONAL BREWERY CENTRE

See page 130.

WARWICKSHIRE

WHISKY DISTILLERY

13 COTSWOLDS DISTILLERY

See page 132.

▶ *Heavy horse and dray at the National Brewery Centre*

The Bre

11 MARSTON, THOMPSON & EVERSHED

MARSTON'S — A BREWER OF SOME PEDIGREE. WELL, QUITE A LOT OF IT ACTUALLY.

⌂ Albion Brewery, Shobnall Rd, Burton upon Trent DE14 2BG ✆ 01283 531131 🖰 marstonsbrewery.co.uk ⊙ for opening times & tour details, see the website; must be booked in advance.

If Burton upon Trent is Britain's brewing capital then Marston's is its Tower of London, for it guards one of the brewing world's great historic treasures. The company was formed by the merger in 1898 of two older breweries, John Marston and John Thompson, which both deserted their former homes and moved into the much larger Albion Brewery together. Here they settled down in a fecund harmony and produced 100,000 barrels of beer a year; the happy couple became today's *ménage à trois* in 1905 with the acquisition of another Burton brewer, Sydney Evershed.

The move was important not only because it gave the new regional superpower the production capacity to expand its pub empire across the Midlands and into North Wales but also because it included a Burton Union set (a wood barrel fermentation system) that helped give Burton ales their reputation for clarity and flavour. Burton brewers had a head start thanks to the town's gypsum-rich artesian wells and, thanks to regional deforestation, its maltsters were early adopters of coke in their drying kilns. The Burton Union system gave them a further advantage.

A Union set — or, more accurately, *the* Union set, since this is the last in existence — is a row of XXL oak barrels linked by a pipe, each with a swan-neck rising from its top and positioned over a slightly sloping trough. The beer starts its first fermentation in a conventional vessel, but as soon as it's really frothing it's released via a reservoir into the connecting pipe until all the barrels in the row are full. As the ferment becomes more and more furious, thick barm is forced up the swan-necks and into the trough. The barm itself

"PEDIGREE'S POPULARITY WAS AN IMPORTANT FACTOR IN THE PRESERVATION OF CASK-CONDITIONED HAND-PULLED BEER IN THE KEG AGE"

is collected for future brews, and any liquid mixed with it runs down the trough, into the reservoir and back through the barrels. This constant circulation can go on for an entire week until the beer calms down and is drawn off for a little lie-down; in the meantime it has been thoroughly purged of yeast and, through prolonged contact with oak, has acquired a pleasing depth of flavour.

The process proved particularly successful when applied to the John Marston flagship pale ale, known simply as P until 1952 when it was

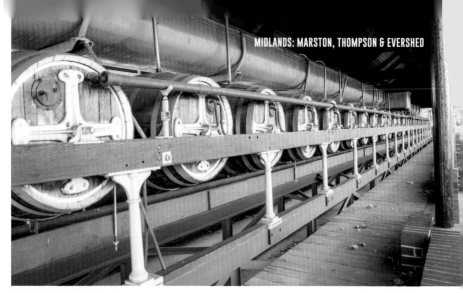

▲ *A Burton Union set*

dignified with the formal adoption of its full name, Pedigree. Pedigree's popularity was an important factor in the preservation of cask-conditioned hand-pulled beer in the keg age: across the northern and western Midlands none of Marston's regional competitors – chiefly Banks's (page 126), Greenall Whitley and Ansells – ever went all-keg because they felt they had to offer a cask alternative to Pedigree and, of course, Draught Bass, neither of which were kegged.

And, what's more, this is the only place in the world where you can see a Burton Union set – and a relatively new one at that: Marston's spent £1,000 a barrel on a 120-barrel set in 1992.

Bass gave up its Unions in the 1980s: they were considered too expensive to clean and maintain and were far more labour-intensive than any modern finance director would consider sustainable. Ironically, all the corporate shenanigans that have shaken the brewing world since then saw production of Draught Bass itself transferred to Marston's in 2005; but sadly, it's not fermented on the Union sets here.

Tours start and end at the newly refurbished visitor centre, housed since the 1980s in a rather forbidding red-brick warehouse from the 1870s that now contains a tiny two-barrel pilot plant or nanobrewery named D14, as well as a small shop, a bar and a permanent display of artefacts and memorabilia.

THE BEER A large portfolio of different brands. The classic Pedigree 4.5% ABV, biscuity malt, spicy hops and light fruitiness. Old Empire IPA 5.7% ABV, a citrus hop aroma with a bittersweet finish.

129

12 NATIONAL BREWERY CENTRE

BURTON UPON TRENT…BRITAIN'S BREWING CAPITAL.

✉ Horninglow St, Burton upon Trent DE14 1NG ✆ 01283 532880 ✇ nationalbrewerycentre.co.uk
🕑 year-round, see website.

▲ *The steam engine that originally powered the Bass Brewery*

Every industry deserves its museum, and in the case of the British brewing industry this is it – appropriately enough, almost in the geographic heart of our 'brewing capital'. But until quite recently this wasn't a national museum at all. It was founded by, funded by and stocked with exhibits by the brewery that was Burton and Britain's biggest, Bass. It was also dedicated to magnifying, and lauding not British brewing as a whole but the glory that was Bass.

The Bass Museum was set up in 1977, when Bass was pretty much at its peak, in a mid-Victorian building on the company's Horninglow Street site. Not only was it packed to the rafters with memorabilia great and small – steam engines, horse-drawn drays (complete with

horses), vintage lorries, promotional bottle vans, brewing vats of one type and another, mash paddles, enamel signs, Edwardian bar-fittings and beer-pumps and everything the most fevered breweriana fanatic could dream of – but in 1995 it was given a marvellous addition: a five-barrel microbrewery all of its very own. This too was antique – a late Victorian pilot brewery, in fact – and it was used to recreate lost ales recorded in brewers' books from all over the galaxy of Bass-owned breweries, as well as many more recently delisted. Among them was Bass No.1, the first beer ever to be sold as 'barley wine' and to many the best.

In 2002 at the height of the corporate *danse macabre* that laid low so many once-great

▲ *Vintage three-wheel motor dray*

brewing names, Bass was sold and split up. Its museum ended up in the hands of Coors and was rechristened the Coors Visitor Centre; but soon Coors bridled at the £1 million annual running cost and in 2008 closed it down. From its distant Colorado eyrie Coors perhaps didn't realise the significance of what it thought was a purely local institution, and the depth of feeling its loss would arouse. However, petitions and helpful political interventions – the Department of Culture, Media and Sport actively bringing brewers together to discuss funding – persuaded it to reconsider.

"THE MUSEUM BREWERY HAS BEEN GIVEN AN UPGRADE: THE VICTORIAN PILOT PLANT HAS BECOME AN EXHIBIT IN ITS OWN RIGHT"

Two years later after much deliberation, the museum reopened more or less as you see it now: not just a collection of historic artefacts, however entrancing they might be to brewing, engineering and industrial archaeology buffs, but full of interactive displays, touch screens, automata, machinery that actually works and things to keep the kids happy while dad gawps at all the ironmongery. For the place is run commercially now, with only a small grant from the industry itself, and it works very hard for its living. It hosts all kinds of functions and is an active live entertainments venue most evenings. A very pleasant café with gift shop, a big, bright, airy pub-style restaurant and bar, the Brewery Tap, and a beer boutique stocking 150 brands from near and far complete the picture. And perhaps best of all, the Museum Brewery has been given an upgrade: the Victorian pilot plant has become an exhibit in its own right, and the new William Worthington Brewery that has replaced it is a brand spanking new gleaming steel behemoth of 25 barrels capacity. So, P2 Stout all round!

131

13 COTSWOLDS DISTILLERY

THEY'VE GOT THE WATER, THEY'VE GOT THE BARLEY, SO HOW COME THEY HAVEN'T GOT THE WHISKY? OH – THEY HAVE!

✉ Whichford, Stourton, Shipston-on-Stour CV36 5HG ✆ 01608 238533 ✎ cotswoldsdistillery.com
🕐 09.00–17.00 Mon–Sat, 10.30–17.00 Sun; tours must be booked in advance.

Cotswolds Distillery is, as the name suggests, a distillery in the Cotswolds that doesn't feel like a distillery and isn't even all that Cotswoldy. The buildings, for a start, have a Scandinavian feel about them. They're constructed of the appropriate stone, of course, but they're clean-cut, unfussy and as untwee as they can be. And, although the northern Cotswolds are pretty enough, they're much more workaday than the showpiece towns and villages further south, where even the pedal-cars are 4x4 and the cleaners have to be bussed in from Swindon.

▲ *Reception and shop*

Even so, there's something a bit unreal about the fact that there's a distillery here at all. For a start, its principal product is malt whisky (although it produces gins and liqueurs as well), and it's probably safe to say that North Oxfordshire has no great tradition of whisky-making… until Dan Szor decided to create one. New Yorker Dan spent 26 years as a currency trader in Paris and London before his eureka moment on a trip to Bruichladdich in 2013. Ten years earlier he'd bought a cask to lay down and was on his annual pilgrimage to visit it when he mentioned to manager Jim McEwan that he'd been thinking

about opening a distillery of his own. Jim simply told him to get on with it; and a mere 14 months later Dan was able to fire up his 500l Holstein gin still while his two pot stills – a 2,400l wash still and a 1,600l spirit still – had only to be connected to the gas before his first batch of new make dripped from the condenser.

Luck, it must be said, played its part in the breakneck pace of developments. Exactly the right premises in the form of a newly built house and barn, empty as the result of a planning wrangle, came on the market just five miles away from Dan's country home. The house was perfect for

▲ *The new visitor centre*

the laboratory, offices and shop, while the barn has become possibly the most spacious new-build still house in the land. The last pieces fell into place when Warminster Maltings boss Chris Garrett mentioned a local farmer with 2,000 acres of

"IT'S PROBABLY SAFE TO SAY THAT NORTH OXFORDSHIRE HAS NO GREAT TRADITION OF WHISKY-MAKING... UNTIL DAN SZOR DECIDED TO CREATE ONE"

organic Odyssey barley and when Dan was able to reopen the Malvern Mineral Water spring, closed three years earlier. So the barley and the water are genuinely local, and Cotswolds Distillery can proclaim its whisky to be as true to its terroir as any Scottish single malt.

Soon after opening Dan started running guided tours and tastings. In 2015 he and his team escorted 7,000 trippers round the place, and before long the number rose to 30,000. But there was scarcely any space for the tastings, let alone a post-tour cuppa, so the distillery now has a purpose-built visitor centre with comfortable tasting rooms more like the foyer of a well-appointed hotel, a terrace, a shop stocked with all manner of local produce and a café that offers simple but top-notch snacks and light meals.

THE WHISKY The single malt 46% ABV matured in ex-Bourbon casks, giving you a rich fruity finish. Also try the peated version 59.3% ABV.
THE GIN Cotswolds Dry Gin 46% ABV, a blend of nine botanicals including local lavender.

133

PEARS

PERRY WAS RATED ENGLAND'S FINEST NATIVE DRINK
IN ITS GOLDEN AGE. AND TO THOSE IN THE KNOW IT STILL IS.

Spotted recently on the website of an online drinks retailer: 'Babycham Sparkling Perry Pear Cider'. What? You'd think a drinks trade professional would know better than to perpetrate such a gear-grindingly irritating tautology (although perhaps not quite as irritating as '10-year anniversary'!); but listen – for future reference, perry is pear cider and pear cider is perry. And if the sweet-toothed youngsters who suck on a synthetic 'pear cider' – fruit-flavoured ciders being the alcopops of our times – have forgotten that, it just goes to show how far Babycham has fallen from grace. For not so very long ago Babycham's subtitle – originally 'the genuine champagne perry', succeeded by the less contentious 'sparkling perry' – was so well known that pretty much the entire general public of Great Britain knew what perry was.

But perhaps it's a blessing in disguise that the very word perry has all but slipped from the public mind, for it dissociates one of the finest of native English drinks from its synthetic successors. For perry at its best can rival some of the world's great white wines – but perry at its best is often hard to find.

"THE RESURGENCE OF PERRY IS A KEY THEME IN ARTISAN CIDERMAKING"

Both the tree and the fruit are problematic. The traditional perry pear tree is a very different plant from the apple tree. It is towering and long-lived, but slow growing – some of the trees at Westons (page 118) in Much Marcle, Herefordshire, were planted in the reign of Queen Anne (1702–07). One of the tallest of parkland trees, it is also one that stands out from others thanks to its very early blossom – a characteristic that in itself can be a headache, as it makes the buds very susceptible to frost damage. The height of these old trees makes them impossible to pick: you have to wait for the fruit to fall and pray it's not too damaged. Their very size is the orchardist's equivalent of having

all eggs in one basket: if a tree succumbs to the rot and canker to which they are prone, that's an awful lot of pears written off, and you'll never see the fruit of the tree you plant to replace it for, as it is said that he who plants pears plants for his heirs. Once these majestic trees were ubiquitous in the Three Counties – Herefordshire, Worcestershire and Gloucestershire – but they're a less common sight now. Showerings provided the answer: in 1954, three years after its launch, Babycham proved so popular that it ran out of juice. The company had to resort to laying in two years' supply of concentrate as an emergency measure but also planted 3,000 acres of pears grafted on to quick-growing quince stock, pioneering work that eventually led to a longer-term restoration of supplies.

The fruit itself can be something of a handful. In medieval times pears were harvested so hard that they were inedible without lengthy boiling, and even as recently as 1962 Elizabeth David in *French Provincial Cooking* prescribed poaching in red wine for five to seven hours! Having said that, the opposite problem is that once ripe they soften very quickly and can turn to an unpressable paste in the mill. Perry pears are also sources of sorbitol, a natural low-calorie sweetener that is suitable for diabetics and has a smooth, clean character that can mask excess astringency and acidity. A warning, though: it also has a marked laxative effect!

It's a lasting shame that Showerings' 3,000 acres of perry pears were all grubbed up years ago, but the resurgence of perry is a key theme in artisan cidermaking and you'll be glad to know that even as we speak – and all for love, for there's precious little money in it – enthusiasts are busily scouring the twisty lanes and neglected hedgerows of the Welsh Marches to track down long-lost varieties, taking cuttings to bear home triumphantly and graft on to quince or wilding stock. An antique jewel casket rediscovered!

CHAPTER SEVEN
EAST ANGLIA

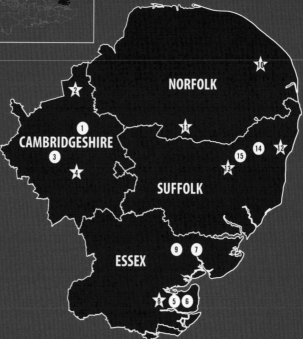

NORFOLK

CAMBRIDGESHIRE

SUFFOLK

ESSEX

CAMBRIDGESHIRE

BREWERIES

1 DOJIMA SAKE BREWERY

✉ Fordham Abbey, Newmarket Rd, Fordham CB7 5LL 🖉 01638 721695 🖰 fordhamabbey. co.uk 🕓 ring in advance to check opening hours. Quite possibly the last thing you would expect to come across attached to a Georgian mansion in the Cambridgeshire countryside is a sake brewery and Japanese cultural centre. But here it is, and actually the set-up is not as outlandish as you may think. Yoshihide Hashimoto's Kotobuki Shuzo brewery in Osaka has been making rice beer since the 1820s. In recent years Cambridge-educated Yoshihide has been in charge of an offshoot setting up craft breweries across the Far East; his thoughts were already turning westward when Fordham Abbey came on the market. The sake is made in a purpose-built, Japanese-style brewery opened in 2018, and there are tours and tastings by appointment. Sake is made in a similar way to beer but instead of barley it's made from fermented rice. It's non-carbonated, has a sweet flavour and normally comes in at about 18% ABV. There are also 75 acres of gardens and pasture to explore, while a café and visitor centre were scheduled to open in early 2020. Ring before your visit to check on progress.

2 ELGOOD'S
See page 140.

GIN DISTILLERY

3 CAMBRIDGE GIN LABORATORY

✉ 10 Green St, CB2 3JU 🖉 01223 751146 🖰 cambridgedistillery.co.uk 🕓 10.00–18.00 Mon–Thu, 10.00–19.00 Fri–Sat, 11.00–17.00 Sun. Just what you'd expect to find in Cambridge – a blend-your-own gin lesson in a workshop known as The Classroom where you get a serious talk before settling down to experiment with botanicals gathered from the city's many wildflower meadows, each distilled individually to capture its distinctive flavour and character. Gonville & Caius College is less than 200yds away and it seems the brainwaves are radiating! Founded in 2015 to make bespoke gins for Cambridge's many high-class bars and restaurants, the company opened this very handsome city-centre shop and venue two years later as a multi-functional space that can do anything from capturing the angel's share (ie: the portion lost to evaporation) to make a gin costing £2,200 a bottle to hosting poetry readings. Blend your own gin and they'll keep the recipe to make you another batch to order. A wide variety of gins are available in the shop including their classic dry gin and a Japanese gin where all the botanicals used are local to Japan. You need to book everything except the shop.

VINEYARD

4 CHILFORD HALL
See page 142.

▶ *The Japanese-styled Dojima Sake Brewery*

ESSEX

VINEYARDS

5 CLAYHILL

⌂ Lower Burnham Rd, Latchingdon CM3 6HF
✆ 07771 995460 🖱 clayhillvineyard.co.uk
🕐 10.00–16.00 Fri–Mon; closed Jan. First
planted in 2006, Clayhill has an unrivalled position
on a south-facing slope between the rivers Crouch
and Blackwell, where a cool winter and a hot, dry
summer guarantee ideal growing conditions for
its Chardonnay, Pinot Noir, Bacchus and Auxerrois
vines. Still wines are made on site, as are grape
and apple juice; sparklers are made at nearby New
Hall. A newly opened café, shop and tasting room
have a grandstand view of the slope down to the
Crouch and the vines ranked along it.

6 CROUCH RIDGE VINEYARD

⌂ Fambridge Rd, Althorne CM3 6BZ ✆ 07970
527892 🖱 crouchridge.com 🕐 10.00–18.00 Sat–
Sun (Wine Barn); check website for tour times.
Crouch Ridge enjoys a very similar soil, situation
and mesoclimate to Clayhill vineyard only a couple
of miles away. The long, dry growing season, low
rainfall and – thanks to its maritime location – a
low risk of frosts are all perfect for growing high-
yielding Chardonnay and Pinot Noir with exactly
the right sugar and acidity for top-notch bubbles.
The first 2½ acres were planted by fifth-generation
farmers Ross and Samantha Lonergan in 2012,
with more plantings in 2015 and 2016; the Wine
Barn bar and café is only open at weekends but
for the rest of the week it is the base for a wide
range of tours and tastings. Perhaps the next step
is to reopen the oyster shack that once stood on
Althorne Creek…

2 ELGOOD'S

NEVER MIND THE BEER – SMELL THE ROSES.

✉ 72 North Brink, Wisbech PE13 1LW ✆ 01945 583160 🖥 elgoods-brewery.co.uk 🕘 09.00–17.00
Mon–Fri, 12.00–16.00 Sun; garden 10.30–16.00 Wed–Fri, 12.00–16.00 Sun.

Once a prosperous inland port, Wisbech has crept further and further away from the sea thanks to land reclamation, and the big ships don't come this far up the Nene any more. But, although the town has seen wealthier days, it's still peppered with architectural memories of those times. One such monument is Elgood's brewery, whose disciplined brick façade dating from 1795 is one of many fine Georgian fronts overlooking the Nene. The brewery was built on the site of a much earlier tidal oilseed mill with granary and orchards and changed hands several times in the ensuing decades, finally ending up with maltster-turned-brewer John Elgood in 1877. It's now owned by the fifth generation of the family.

The brewery tours hold more for the enthusiast than the casual nomad: not often seen is a pair of coolships (one of many Dutch survivals in the vocabulary of brewing) – shallow open pans in which the hot mash was allowed to cool overnight before being run off into the fermenting vessels. The very air itself in this part of the brewery is full of natural yeasts and other microorganisms of the uncultivated and souring variety (like the

▶ The four-acre formal gardens
▶ Tea and cake are available in the café

vat of dark mild and let it mature – or rather ripen – for a while. The old fenmen loved it, he said; and since the Flemish relish a similar concoction to this very day, who's to say he was romancing? Anyway, it may very well be that Black Dog had its origins not as a mild, but as an old ale.

"ITS FOUR ACRES OF FORMAL GARDENS ARE SPECTACULAR"

For the visitor, though, Elgood's has much more to offer than just beer. Its four acres of formal gardens are spectacular, and it's telling that the visitor centre, shop, café and bar are to be found in the garden rather than in the brewery itself. A maze shaped like a yard of ale, a lake and many other water features, a laburnum walk and wisteria bower, specimen trees brought back from distant climes by 19th-century plantsmen – the garden is a tourist attraction in and of itself and is also a cultural hub, hosting events ranging from beer festivals to craft and plant shows to live jazz. (And speaking of delicious gardens, the National Trust-owned Peckover House is a few doors up the road.)

brettanomyces that turns perfectly good beer into lambic in Flanders), which would sniff out the presence of all that defenceless sugar and dive in, delivering either a pleasing astringency or a vile stockyard tang, depending on your taste.

Hardy & Hanson's in Nottingham and the Crown Brewery in Pontyclun used to have these same archaisms in place, but they're long closed, making Elgood's the only British brewery that can make an authentic lambic. Which from time to time it does, with great success. In the old days tart dark beers like this, known as old ales, used to be very popular in the east, albeit at a higher gravity; one old-time brewer from the region confessed that in his pupillage the brewery used to tip all the ullage – the gallon or two of unsold beer in every barrel returned to the brewery from 'outdoors' – into a

THE BEER Enthusiasts might detect a faint whiff of the past in one of Elgood's flagship beers, Black Dog Mild. At 3.6% ABV it's strong for a dark mild, but it also has an interesting grist that includes a dash of biscuit, toffee-ish crystal malt and a soupçon of unmalted roasted barley with its burnt-wood astringency.

4 CHILFORD HALL

ART, SCULPTURE, FINE ART PRINTING – WHAT ARE THEY WITHOUT WINE?

⌂ Balsham Rd, Linton CB21 4LE ✆ 01223 895600 ⌂ chilfordhall.co.uk ⏲ Mar–Oct 09.00–17.00 Sat–Sun, from Jun also Thu–Fri; booking advisable.

Sam Alper was one of those colourful working-class entrepreneurs who, by his example, made the 1960s a decade of hope and aspiration for so many. Son of a North London hairdresser, he served as an aircraft electrician in the Fleet Air Arm and then went to work at his brother's caravan-building business. Here he designed the hugely successful Sprite range just as car ownership was becoming almost nationwide; and with his knowledge of motor touring in 1950s Britain he was inspired to found the Little Chef chain of roadside restaurants in 1958.

"OPERA AND FINE WINES WERE AMONG ALPER'S OTHER PASSIONS"

In 1965 he treated himself to Chilford Hall, an early Victorian farmhouse in the South Cambridgeshire Downs with extensive flint-built farm buildings and a working estate of rolling chalkland. It wasn't merely an indulgence, though: the practical aim was to establish a prestige conference and function venue and, as a cultured man, Alper also established a collection of sculpture and architectural salvage (including a pediment and pillars from Waterloo station), founded an art gallery and created a new home

and study centre for the Curwen Press, a historic firm of fine art printers threatened with eviction from its London studio.

Opera and fine wines were among Alper's other passions and although he didn't establish a rival to Glyndebourne here he did plant 18 acres of vines in 1972, later expanded to more than 20. (The story is that he was asked if he would let some land to a would-be winemaker and declined, but thought that he'd give it a go himself!) The ten varieties of grape are principally old-style Rhine/Alsace types, although Pinot Noir has long been one of them and Bacchus is a newcomer to the vineyard. Given that the terroir is free-draining flint over chalk, Chilford Hall is yet another strong English challenger to Champagne's dominance of the sparkling wine scene. Unusually, the 18,000 bottles of white, red and rosé still and sparkling wines the estate produces are all vintage, even the blends. The half-timbered winery itself originally stood in Linton, but was threatened with demolition and in 1976 was dismantled beam by beam and brick by brick and re-erected to start its new life here.

Alper died in 2002 at the age of 78, but Chilford Hall is still family-owned and continues to go from strength to strength. Since 1994 when weddings

▲ *The shop and visitor centre*

were first permitted in approved premises other than churches, chapels and register offices, its barns have been among the country's most spectacular wedding venues. They were burnt down by arsonists in 2012, causing damage of £5 million to buildings and artworks (the objects destroyed included one of Alper's own sculptures); but they were replaced almost immediately by today's Garden Room, and heaven alone knows how many young couples have started their journeys together here in a blur of fairy lights and bubbles!

The visitor centre in the old farmyard includes a café (set lunches are provided for visitors taking the tour) and a shop that sells Chilford's own wines as well as a wide selection of food and drink from other local producers.

THE WINE Bacchus 13% ABV, Chalk Ridge 11% ABV, Graduate Sparkling Wine 12% ABV. In exceptional years such as 2018 they are able to produce their Granta Valley Red 11% ABV.

143

▲ *The Reichensteiner vines at New Hall Vineyard*

7 DEDHAM VALE

✉ Green Ln, Boxted CO4 5TS ✆ 01206 271136 ✇ dedhamvalevineyard.com ⏱ 11.00–17.00 Wed–Fri (shop & tasting barn). Originally known as Carter's, the seven-acre vineyard on this sprawling and delightful 40-acre leisure estate was established in 1990 by international viticulturalist and wine judge Mary Mudd, and was run by the Bunting family until it was sold in 2018. Set in Constable Country, the estate offers many public rights of way where you can wander at will through orchards, woods and meadows, taking in two huge artificial lakes on the way. The vineyards produce white, red and rosé still blends, a highly regarded brut cuvée and a sparkling rosé. As well as the newly refurbished and highly acclaimed tasting barn and winery shop, the complex is home to a seasonal local produce shop.

8 NEW HALL VINEYARD

See page 146.

9 WEST STREET VINEYARD

✉ West St, Coggeshall CO6 1NS ✆ 01376 563303 ✇ weststreetvineyard.co.uk ⏱ 09.00–23.00 Fri–Sat, 09.00–17.00 Sun, Wed, Thu. Coggeshall may be best known for its astonishing collection of late medieval and Tudor buildings, but since 2013 a big two-storey flat-pack building imported from Germany and erected in four days has been something of a talking-point too. It houses the high-end restaurant, cellar door and tasting room that are the public face of West Street Vineyard, originally established back in the 1970s but greatly expanded since Stephen and Jane Mohan bought it in 2009. The restaurant and its terrace now overlook some 4,000 vines, mainly Pinot Noir and Chardonnay, on six acres sloping down to the River Blackwater. The still and sparkling white and rosé wines are made and bottled at New Hall. Tours and tastings can be booked.

▶ *Woodforde's brewery shop*

NORFOLK

BREWERY

10 WOODFORDE'S
See page 150.

WHISKY DISTILLERY

11 ENGLISH WHISKY COMPANY
See page 152.

8 NEW HALL VINEYARD

TRY A DOUBLE DOSE OF HISTORY AT A VINEYARD WITH DEEP, DEEP ROOTS.

⌂ Chelmsford Rd, Purleigh CM3 6PN ✆ 01621 828343 🖉 newhallwines.co.uk
🕔 09.00–16.00 Mon–Fri, 10.00–14.00 Sat.

According to local records, the first vineyard in Purleigh was planted in 1120 when Henry I was on the throne, only 500yds from where New Hall Vineyard is today, and it covered three acres on a south-facing slope near the church. It's reputed that Purleigh wine was drunk during the sealing of the Magna Carta in 1215.

Viticulture returned to Purleigh in 1969 when Bill and Sheila Greenwood planted the first 850 Reichensteiner vines at New Hall Farm on trellises improvised from hundreds of railway sleepers.

The Greenwoods had bought the 500-acre farm in 1962, having previously bred and raised chickens, rabbits and chinchilla, and grown soft fruit for jam. The farm had been put down to pasture and hay and the Greenwoods started diversifying into fruit and veg. The decision to add vines to the mix may have been opportunistic, but it seemed like a logical one and was certainly in keeping with the times. In 1970 they followed up with 2,800 Huxelrebe and Müller-Thurgau vines, which they had to hoe by hand more or less continually because self-seeding potatoes continued to keep growing uncontrollably between the rows.

The first vintage was made in the kitchen by Mrs Greenwood in 1971. She used 30kg of fruit to make a magnificent 18 bottles; but the first commercial harvest the following year told a rather different story. It yielded over three tonnes, which had to be vinified and bottled by Jack Ward at Merrydown in Sussex, and the cellars at New Hall House had to be extended to fit not 18 but 40,000 bottles. And things didn't stop there: in 1976 New Hall got a press and winery of its own, big enough to process a harvest of 30 tonnes.

"THE FIRST VINTAGE WAS MADE IN THE KITCHEN BY MRS GREENWOOD IN 1971. SHE USED 30KG OF FRUIT TO MAKE A MAGNIFICENT 18 BOTTLES"

In 1983 Bill and Sheila's son Piers took a forward-thinking step by having New Hall's Pinot Noir and Chardonnay bottle-fermented at Lamberhurst in Kent. Carr Taylor (page 104) was the first English grower to bring a bottle-fermented wine to market when it had a glut year's crop of Reichensteiner vinified by the *méthode champenoise*, also at Lamberhurst. This went on sale in 1984, pipping New Hall to the post; but it might be argued that New Hall was the more truly pioneering because of its use of Champagne grape varieties. Be that as it may, the work of the 1980s innovators transformed

the English wine industry: more than two-thirds of English output is now of the mushroom-and-cage persuasion (the cork and wire used to seal most sparkling wines), and 350,000 of the four million bottles we drink per annum come from New Hall.

Having long been a working farm before its rebirth as a spring of beautiful bubbles, New Hall is a fairly prosaic if cheerful place. Its centrepiece is a red-brick hay barn called the Railway Barn, presumably because the double-height doors originally intended to accommodate fully laden haycarts make it rather resemble a Victorian loco shed. What New Hall does have is an engrossing vineyard trail: the farm now has more than 100 acres under vines, and while the marked trail itself is quite short – 30 minutes if you're just strolling – you're free to roam; and doing justice to 100 acres calls for more walking than you might think. But do bring a picnic – New Hall has no café or restaurant. Call in at the Cellar Shop for a self-guided tour followed by a tasting or to book a place on a guided tour. (Ring ahead if all you want is a walk and they'll warn you if and where they've been spraying!)

THE WINE White Hart 2017 10.5% ABV, a combination of Schönburg and Chardonnay, gives you a really dry wine with delicate jasmine aromas, complimented by bold flavours of pineapple and ripe stone fruit.

◀ *The winery*

▶ *Bill and Sheila Greenwood – the founders*

147

THE BREWING PROCESS

HOW YOUR BEER REACHES YOUR GLASS — IT'S A TALE OF HUMAN INGENUITY… AND BUCKETS.

Given that 60% of adult Britons enjoy a beer from time to time, it's surprising how little they know about the drink. It's an everyday commodity you take for granted, really, like tea or flour, and to ask too many questions about something so common-or-garden can make you look a little odd – obsessive, even – if taken to extremes.

So it's possible that as you venture forth upon your first ever brewery tour you won't have much idea of what you're about to see, and when you do see it you won't know what it is or what it's meant to do. Let us enlighten you, therefore, and as the tour guide explains what everything is and what happens inside it (because most things in breweries are, at heart, just giant buckets or, as Dr Johnson described them, 'a parcel of boilers and vats'), you may allow yourself a smirk. Because you already know.

First, an outline of what's going to happen. Beer is an incredibly complicated mixture of chemicals of one sort or another, all of which are created from only a handful of ingredients during what looks like a set of pretty straightforward processes. But there's a lot more to it than meets the eye – literally so, since most of the reactions that turn barley into beer are caused by microscopic biochemicals. Anyway, here we go.

Grains of barley, having been persuaded to start the process of converting their insoluble starches into sugar by soaking and drying, are ground to the consistency of coarse flour and mashed in hot water to dissolve the newly formed maltose. The water must not be boiling, or the diastatic enzyme that completes the conversion will not function. The resulting syrup will then be boiled with the dried flowers of the hop bine and dosed with yeast, a microscopic variety of fungus. This will first reproduce rapidly, producing a thick, dark foam, and will then start digesting the sugars in the syrup, producing equal volumes of CO_2 and ethanol. Once the yeast has poisoned itself with its own toxins, both ethanol and CO_2 being pretty lethal, the residual proteins and other solids will be precipitated by the addition of fish-derived collagen. Some will be poured into a glass for you to drink. Tastes better than it sounds, believe me.

"THE MASH TUN IS REALLY JUST A GIANT PORRIDGE POT WITH A STIRRER INSTALLED TO STOP ALL THAT FLOURY MALT FORMING INTO GREAT STICKY CLUMPS"

Now, about the buckets. The tour guide will tell you that the first one is called the mash tun, and is really just a giant porridge pot with an electric stirrer installed to stop all that floury malt forming into great sticky clumps. The lumps may be the best bit of gravy, but not of beer! After a couple of

▲ *Hops being added to the mash tun*

hours the sweet syrup or wort (might as well get to know the jargon) is strained off into a big copper cauldron, and the remaining mash is sprayed with more hot water to extract the last of the maltose. This is called sparging, from the Latin *aspergere*, to sprinkle. In the cauldron or copper it's all brought to a nice rolling boil, and in go the hops. Hops are wonderful things. Drab-looking creatures, but they're packed with all sorts of biochemicals including the bitter-tasting antibacterial tannins that help protect the beer from hungry microbes, and the various 'terpenes' – natural chemicals that

create the beer's aroma and flavour (and which also give fruit and flowers their characteristic tastes and smells). After a good long boil the hopped wort will be sieved off via a bucket called a hop back into the fermenting vessel, which is pretty much the last of the buckets and the most amusing to watch. A tip here to sort the novices from the old hands: if the fermenter is an open one, or if it has a hatch open, DO NOT lean over it and breathe deeply of its heady vapours. It will not smell of beer. In fact it will burn your eyes, mouth and nose most unpleasantly. Carbon dioxide really hurts!

149

10 WOODFORDE'S

THERE'S SOME BOOTIFUL BEER IN THE BROADS AND A BOOTIFUL BREWERY TOO.

✉ Slad Ln, Woodbastwick NR13 6SW ✆ 01603 720353 ⊘ woodfordes.com ⏱ 09.00–17.00 Mon–Fri, 10.00–17.00 Sat, 11.00–17.00 Sun.

Set up in 1981 by inveterate homebrewers Ray Ashworth and David Crease, Woodforde's was named after the 18th-century Norfolk parson, diarist and lover of good (and plentiful) food and drink James Woodforde and has become one of the most successful British microbrewers because its beer is so very good.

The microbrewers of the 1970s and 80s were a bunch of heavy-duty beer guerrillas whom no obstacle could deter. And there were some pretty big obstacles, too, principally that the established brewers had the pub trade almost completely tied and precious few publicans were allowed to stock the newcomers' beer. Woodforde's, though, struck it lucky. Its first home was in an industrial unit in Norwich that proved completely unsuitable, so in 1983 Ray and David shifted kit and caboodle into a stableblock at the picturesque (well, fairly) Spread Eagle at Erpingham in the Norfolk countryside.

Those stables did good service during the hard years of the 1980s while their beers slowly won the exposure they deserved. From Mardler's Mild to Norfolk Nog to Headcracker, its quality was demonstrated. By 1989 it was time to move again, this time to a set of attractive brick-built barns, some of them listed, with a couple of cute thatched cottages on the Woodbastwick Hall Estate. Woodforde's promptly moved in and has been there ever since.

In 1990 when guest beer legislation finally allowed microbrewers to pitch their products to tied publicans, Woodforde's bitter – Wherry – came into its own. Wherry fell into a then-undefined but now mainstream category of golden ales. Lighter in both colour and body than old-school bitters and milds (often thanks to the use of a pinch of wheat), golden ales were designed to deter real ale drinkers from straying to lager during the summer. One of their defining characteristics was much heavier use of aromatic hops than was traditional, creating all sorts of floral and citric scents and savours that even many non-beer drinkers adored. And Wherry was (and still is) one of the best of them, as was proved that year when it won the national award for new breweries in the Campaign for Real Ale's Champion Beer of Britain competition.

It was lift-off time for Woodforde's. Guest ales were appearing in tied tenancies up and down the country and often the spare wicket bore the Wherry pumpclip. National recognition brought customers to the brewery door asking for a look

▲ *The Fur & Feather, Woodbastwick, home of Woodforde's*

round. That pair of cute cottages was extended and converted into the Fur & Feather in 1992 so that all those visitors could enjoy a beer and something to eat; a shop and visitor centre were incorporated in 1995; and then in 1996 Wherry

"THOSE STABLES DID GOOD SERVICE DURING THE HARD YEARS OF THE 1980S WHILE THEIR BEERS SLOWLY WON THE EXPOSURE THEY DESERVED"

grabbed the Champion Beer of Britain spotlight again by winning the overall unqualified top-dog national title. Woodforde's has changed owners twice since then, but the rule of quality in the brewhouse hasn't altered, which would be suicide

for a set-up like this. So after you've pulled into that attractive courtyard, enjoyed a guided tour (18.30 Thu, 14.00 w/ends; make sure you book in advance), had a poke round the artefacts on show in the visitor centre, bought yourself a polypin of Headcracker (careful now) in the shop and ordered your dinner at the bar of the Fur & Feather, you can sit yourself down with a pint of the very best.

THE BEER The classic Wherry 3.8% ABV, rich amber ale with floods of flavours, as sweet malts clash with grapefruit hops and big floral aromas. Norfolk Nog 4.6% ABV, dark chocolatey taste with liquorice and treacle.

151

11 ENGLISH WHISKY COMPANY

ENGLISH WHISKY: A TRADITION REBORN. OR BORN. WHATEVER.

✉ St George's Distillery, Harling Rd, Roudham NR16 2QW ✆ 01953 717939 🖊 englishwhisky.co.uk
🕐 09.00–17.30 daily.

No-one can proclaim themselves whisky-lovers until they have visited St George's Distillery: it's the place where a non-existent tradition of whisky distilling in England was reborn.

It's part of the mythology now that when international farming consultant James Nelstrop and his son Andrew produced their first 29 barrels of new make in December 2009, it was the first to be made in England since the Lea Valley Distillery in Stratford, East London, closed in 1903. That much is true. The journalist Alfred Barnard in his 1887 odyssey *The Whisky Distilleries of the United Kingdom* listed four in England: Lea Valley, two in Liverpool and one in Bristol. They were not, however, part of any bucolic tradition on the Scottish or Irish pattern but were all large, modern and extremely well-equipped plants. Mostly they made 'plain' or neutral base spirit for the gin industry, but by maturing some of it in oak (thus qualifying it as grain whisky) they could sell it to the burgeoning Irish and Scottish blenders. Only Lea Valley made any malt whisky, says Barnard, then contradicts himself by saying that Bank Hall in Liverpool made a little too. Tempting as it is, therefore, to fancy Nelstrop *père et fils* as the revivers of long-departed rustic arts, that wasn't their motive. Nelstrop Sr, as is so often

▲ *The visitor centre shop*

the case with high-powered technologists and businesspeople, had retired too early at the age of 60. He still had more than enough vim and vigour in him, and he just fancied making whisky. And so he did.

The Nelstrops could hardly have found a better place for it: East Anglia's barley is renowned for its quality. And as Elizabeth I proudly told the Spanish Ambassador, Hertfordshire malt made liquor as fine as any grape. Perhaps as a tribute to the region's barley the distillery entrance is topped by a mock pagoda, just like one you'd find on a real maltings; and in a nod to East Anglian architectural tradition the upper storey is weatherboarded. The first release for sale from the imposing and

▲ *The Kitchen restaurant*

actually rather handsome set of buildings came in 2009 and was noted for its delicate pale colour. Since then St George's has turned out peated and unpeated malts, matured and finished in a great variety of casks and bottled at either cask proof or 46% ABV, all to huge acclaim.

"PERHAPS AS A TRIBUTE TO THE REGION'S BARLEY THE DISTILLERY ENTRANCE IS TOPPED BY A MOCK PAGODA, JUST LIKE ONE YOU'D FIND ON A REAL MALTINGS"

The distillery was always planned with you, the visitor, in mind. There are, of course, tours that you can book including the St George's Tour on the hour, every hour, seven days a week, with the optional extra of a two-course meal. There's also the more expensive World Whisky tour and Ultimate Tasting experience. But if you just happen to be tootling along the A11 with nothing booked and no particular place to go, a swift detour down

the B1111 will lead you straight to the distillery door where you can pop in unannounced for lunch or just a cuppa in The Kitchen, stretch your legs with a stroll along the River Thet and through the two acres of gardens, then load your car boot with plunder from the shop where more than 200 varieties of whisky are to be had.

Sadly, James Nelstrop died in 2014. By that time, though, many other splendid English whisky distilleries had sprung out of nowhere, and yet more have done so since. So if he didn't actually revive a tradition, you could say he founded one.

THE WHISKY The English Original 43% ABV, unpeated and aged in ex Bourbon casks, The English Smokey 43% ABV, giving you 45ppm for those who like smoke on the palate, or for a single grain whisky, try The Norfolk Farmers 45% ABV, using eight different grains – giving chocolate and pear notes.

153

SUFFOLK

BREWERIES

12 ADNAMS

See page 156.

13 GREENE KING

See page 158.

14 ST PETER'S BREWERY

St Peter's Hall, St Peter South Elmham NR35 1NQ 01986 782322 stpetersbrewery.co.uk 09.00–17.00 Tue–Fri, 11.00–19.00 w/ends; brewery tours Easter–end Dec 11.00, 12.30, 14.00 w/ends, booking advisable. St Peter's Brewery was founded in 1996 on a derelict farm in the depths of the Suffolk countryside by Interbrand tycoon John Murphy. The plan was to produce bottled beers mainly for export, all packaged in a distinctive green flagon-shaped bottle based on an 18th-century original from Philadelphia. However, these bottles have also become a familiar sight in UK supermarkets, and St Peter's produces a huge range of quirky and original beers. The brewing takes place in the old farm buildings that have their own borehole, but the star of the show is the breathtaking pub/restaurant and brewery shop (now under separate management) in the medieval moated farmhouse, St Peter's Hall. The hall was embellished in 1539 with architectural salvage from the dissolved Flixton Priory.
St Peter's also has a London pub, the Jerusalem Tavern, in Clerkenwell.

▲ *Wyken Hall Vineyard*

VINEYARD

15 WYKEN HALL

Wyken Rd, Stanton IP31 2DW 01359 250287 wykenvineyards.co.uk 10.00–18.00 Sun–Fri, 09.00–18.00 Sat. This is the farm that does everything. It grows the barley that goes into its beer, Good Dog Ale. It raises the Red Poll cattle and the Hebridean sheep you might enjoy in the Leaping Hare café-restaurant (*Good Food Guide* and *Michelin* for over 20 years). It runs a sophisticated country crafts shop and a weekly farmers' market. The red-washed Tudor manor house itself is the private home of former MP Sir Kenneth Carlisle and his wife, journalist and author Carla Carlisle, but the exquisite and varied gardens are open six afternoons a week. There are woodland walks and seven acres of vineyards producing two whites, a sparkler and an intriguing dark rosé blended from two Alsatian heritage varieties, Triomphe d'Alsace and Léon Millot. Sounds like the future of farming – and a great day out to boot!

▶ *St Peter's Brewery*

12 ADNAMS

GRANNY TAKES A TRIP – PAY HER A VISIT AND SHE'LL POUR YOU A GIN.

✉ Sole Bay Brewery, Southwold IP18 6JW ✆ 01502 727225 ⌀ adnams.co.uk ◷ 10.00–15.00 daily.

Adnams is one of the most respected names in British brewing. It has always had something of the genteel about it, perhaps by association with its home town which is as genteel a seaside resort as you'll find. One thinks more of doilies than beer-mats. But in the late 1990s, Adnams was hurtling towards extinction and something had to change.

The dear old maiden aunt of a brewery was rescued by a remarkable double act: Simon Loftus, the chairman (a Cambridge-educated earring-wearing food, wine and travel writer), and Jonathan Adnams (the managing director, school dropout, trawlerman and lifeboatman), who succeeded the older generation in 1996 and set about reinventing, reengineering and rethinking. The brewery was almost rebuilt from the inside, not just replacing old kit with new but adopting technical innovations that saved time, money, water and energy, and allowed absolutely perfect consistency and quality control. At the same time the management's structures, protocols and operating procedures were reviewed to energise the whole company, and new beers such as Regatta, Ghost Ship, Lighthouse and Explorer that appealed to more modern tastes were rolled out under the 'Beers from the Coast' banner. (Having said that, the old range – including Southwold

Bitter and the very wonderful Tally Ho barley wine – have not been neglected.)

All these initiatives brought Adnams into the spotlight again, and output climbed from 56,000 barrels a year to 92,000. However, it was in 2006, the year Simon Loftus relinquished the chair and Jonathan Adnams took over, that The Amazing Thing happened. Stuffy old Adnams moved all of its distribution and haulage operations out of Southwold, sparing the town centre 50 lorry movements a day, and into a new building actually inside an old gravel pit a few miles away that was – and is – an ecologist's dream of green. Lime and hemp walls. Sedum grass roof. Rainwater management. Solar power. Sunlight management. Naturally constant temperature... and zero emissions. All this technology was already out there waiting to be put together. It was the fact that it took a 130-year-old British family brewery to do it that made the world gasp. One of their other

innovations was to start opening their own stores – from the very first one in Southwold in 1987 to now 13 in operation – and these are in addition to their own pubs, some of which offer accommodation. You can see full details of these on their website.

"STUFFY OLD ADNAMS MOVED ALL OF ITS DISTRIBUTION AND HAULAGE OPERATIONS OUT OF SOUTHWOLD, SPARING THE TOWN CENTRE 50 LORRY MOVEMENTS A DAY"

But Adnams wasn't finished with us yet. In 2010 it unveiled its Copper House Distillery, making not only gins, gin liqueurs and vodka but whiskies of various types too including Spirit of Broadside, an eau de vie *de bière* in the Alsatian style. Also try their rye whisky and their Dead Man's Finger collection of rums. Some 20 years after it started its clamber back into the sunlight, there seems to be no end to the new visions it wants to show us.

◀ *The visitor centre*
▲ *A postcard from Southwold*

And that goes for the old Swan Hotel, too. The Swan is the face the brewery shows to the street (the brewery visitor centre is in its old coachyard), and in the mid-19th century its brewhouse was almost literally the acorn from which modern Adnams grew. For generations the Swan served as Adnams's de facto brewery tap, but it was a cut above all other brewery taps. It was very conscious of being a hotel, and a good hotel at that – the sort of place whose patrons knew which knife to use. It is now contemporary, a change that has split opinion. Those who liked it as it was don't like it as it currently is, and those who like it as it is never used it as it was. But the latter comfortably outnumber the former.

THE BEER Traditional bitter Broadside 6.3% ABV, for summer Ghost Ship 4.5% ABV or a really dark ale Tally-Ho 7.2% ABV.
THE GIN Copper House Dry Gin 40% ABV.
THE WHISKY Rye Malt Whisky 47% ABV, giving you a drier and spicier finish, or the single malt 40% ABV.

13 GREENE KING

IT TOOK A BIG APPETITE TO MAKE A GREAT BREWERY.

⌂ Westgate St, Bury St Edmunds IP33 1QT ✆ 01284 763222 ⏴ greeneking.co.uk ⏰ 10.00–18.00 Mon–Sat; must book in advance.

Greene King has long been excoriated for buying and closing smaller rivals to absorb their tied estates. Rayment's, Ruddle's, Ridley's, Hardy's & Hansons, Morland, Wells & Winch – these are just some of the fine old names that lie trampled in the wake of Greene King's long career of aggrandisement. The brewery's eager adoption of modern methods – in particular its former use of hop oils instead of the cone, the whole cone and nothing but the cone – was also apt to draw a sharp intake of breath from the true CAMRA real ale warrior.

"YOUR TOUR WILL TAKE YOU UP TO THE BREWHOUSE ROOF FOR A STUNNING VIEW OF THE TOWN"

But there's a lot more to Greene King than that. It's a huge and rambling company full of nooks and niches and unexpected twists in ill-lit corridors: at times more like Gormenghast than a modern corporation, and the visitor will come across some surprising treasure from the past.

The company gives 1799 as its foundation date; 'there or thereabouts' might be more accurate. Benjamin Greene was the son in a family of well-to-do drapers who went into brewing thanks

to a connection with Samuel Whitbread, a fellow member of the Bunyan Independent chapel in Bedford. After pupillage at Whitbread, Benjamin was able to buy the Westgate Brewery in Bury St Edmunds. It ticked over, but there were few opportunities for growth, and in 1836 Benjamin handed it over to his son Edward and became a slave-owning planter in the West Indies.

The growth-spurt started in 1887 when the company merged with a neighbour, Frederick King, and started expanding into the countryside.

Christmas's (really!) of Haverhill, Simpson's of Baldock and many other country brewers succumbed to its advances so that by 1920 it owned nearly 500 pubs. All these takeovers meant that the Westgate Brewery couldn't cope with demand, and in the midst of the hungry 1930s, Greene King built itself a whole new brewhouse whose splendidly towering, boldly geometric Art Deco façade was revealed to the world in 1938 and resembles no other brewery in the country, or at least none that survive. If anything it's more like that imperious parade of 1930s factories that line the A40 heading west out of London – Hoover, Firestone and Gillette – that tell you that the 30s weren't hungry everywhere. (Your tour will take you up to the brewhouse roof for a stunning view of the town and surrounding country.)

As an efficient and modern producer, Greene King suffered less than its neighbours from wartime shortages, although the attempt to ferment potatoes failed because the slurry fouled the brewery pipework and the beer caused epic flatulence. But efficiency and modernity aren't the whole story. Greene King has its traditions, and if you take the tour you will find three enormous oak vats in a dark corner, their lids weighed down with piles of soil. They contain maturing stocks of 5X, a 12% ABV old ale never sold under its own name but aged for two or even three years and blended with the 5% APV BPA (Best or Burton Pale Ale, also never sold in its own right) to make Strong Suffolk. Slightly sour old ales and strong stock ales for blending used to be big in the east, but it's only here at Greene King that they are still actually made.

So don't write Greene King off as just a giant faceless corporation like any other: turn up at its old maltings (now the visitor centre and tap) and demand a pint of 5X.

◀ Greene King's bold Art Deco brewhouse
▲ On tour at Greene King

THE BEER Abbot 5% ABV full-bodied, smooth and mature taste with fruitcake and toffee flavours, Old Speckled Hen 5% ABV and Ruddles Best 3.7% ABV.

ROOTS OF REVIVAL

FROM ECCENTRIC HOBBY TO BOOMING BUSINESS – TODAY ENGLISH WINES CHALLENGE THE WORLD.

As everyone probably knows, in the last 60 years or so there has been an astonishing resurgence in English and Welsh winemaking, more astonishing even than the subsequent resurgences in artisan brewing and distilling in that its practitioners have had to grow their own ingredients in a less-than-ideal climate. Since 1951 the number of working vineyards rooted in our unforgiving soil has grown from virtually none to more than 500. But it was seldom 'none', almost always 'virtually none'.

> **"THERE IS NOW INCONTROVERTIBLE ARCHAEOLOGICAL EVIDENCE OF VITICULTURE ON SEVERAL SITES IN ROMAN BRITAIN"**

Viticulture has a long history in Great Britain, especially south and east of the Severn and Trent. There is now incontrovertible archaeological evidence of viticulture on several sites in Roman Britain, and DNA testing has even established that a strain grown at Fishbourne in Sussex, the Wrotham Pinot, is directly descended from Roman-era vines. As Christianity spread in the 4th century more and more sacramental wine was required: when St Augustine landed in Kent in 597, one of King Æthelberht's first gifts to him and his followers was supposedly a vineyard, and Anglo-Saxon charters contain many references to vineyards, often as gifts to monasteries. *The Domesday Book* lists 42, a dozen of them attached to monasteries and the rest on aristocratic desmenes.

This promising start proved a dead end when Henry II, the first Plantagenet, succeeded Stephen, the last Norman, in 1154. Henry brought with him possession of a sizeable chunk of France – the whole of the southwest of the country in fact, where the vineyards were located. Grape growing continued on a limited scale in England, but it seemed a bit like keeping a dog and barking yourself; and by the time Henry VIII succeeded in 1509 there were only 139 vineyards in the country. The Dissolution of the Monasteries in the late 1530s reduced the number sharply, and with odd exceptions – mostly in the form of experimental plantings by aristocratic enthusiasts – viticulture gradually died out. Table grapes were grown in the greenhouses of the rich and as ornamental garden-plants, but apart from the produce of the Marquis of Bute's vineyard of more than 60,000 vines, which he grew at Castell Coch near Cardiff between 1875 and 1911, no wine was made for sale.

The first stirrings of the resurgence came immediately after World War II, when three key pioneers – Ray Barrington Brock, George Ordish and Edward Hyams – emerged simultaneously but independently of each other. Of the three, Brock is generally dubbed the Father of English

winemaking. A research chemist by trade, he set up a research station at Oxted Surrey in 1946 to discover which varieties were best suited to English growing conditions. Of the 600 types he planted in the 25 years of his time in Oxted, Seyval Blanc and Müller-Thurgau proved the most successful. Ordish was a pest-control specialist who returned home from working in the Champagne region just before the war, and noticing a similarity in its soil, he planted a few vines in his Maidstone garden. He specialised more in the practicalities of technique and terroir, publishing the seminal *Wine Growing in England* in 1953.

The third of the trio, writer and broadcaster Edward Hyams, was also from Kent: the popularity of *The Grape Vine in England* (1949) and *Vineyards in England* (1953) proved there was an eager following for all matters viticultural. This must have come as something of a surprise since England's table wine consumption was tiny and confined almost exclusively to the upper class. Most wine drunk in Britain was fortified and sweet, and much of it was made here from imported grape concentrate – so-called British wine. Perhaps the interest had been sparked by the recent adventures of hundreds of thousands of men in Italy and France.

The first vintage of commercial English wine since 1911 was produced at a 2½-acre vineyard at Hambledon, Hampshire, by a soldier called Major-General Sir Guy Salisbury-Jones in 1955. Two more vineyards were planted in the mid-1950s at the Beaulieu Estate in Hampshire and the Merrydown Wine Company in Sussex, better known for its country wines and later for its cider. The English wine revival had started.

CHAPTER EIGHT
NORTH

NORTHUMBERLAND

TYNE & WEAR

COUNTY DURHAM

CUMBRIA

LANCASHIRE

THE YORKSHIRES

MERSEYSIDE

CHESHIRE

GREATER MANCHESTER

COUNTY DURHAM

1 CAMERONS

LOOK OUT – THERE'S AN ESCAPED LION ON THE LOOSE.

✉ Lion Brewery, Waldon St, Hartlepool TS24 7QS ✆ 01429 868686 ⌁ cameronsbrewery.com
☺ visitor centre 12.00–16.00 Wed, 11.00–23.00 Thu–Fri, 12.00–23.00 Sat; tours must be booked.

Camerons may not have such a high profile as Fuller's (page 76) or Marston's (page 128), yet it's one of Britain's biggest breweries in terms of potential output, with a capacity of more than a million barrels a year. When you actually see it for yourself you'll be impressed by its sheer size. It's an enormous red-brick barracks of a place, entirely functional and more than a little daunting, but with a charming little Victorian villa tacked on to the front that is the office where the directors and clerks of old passed their working days in slightly cosier surroundings.

"AT ITS PEAK, CAMERONS OWNED 750 PUBS AND COMPLETELY DOMINATED THE REGION"

The company gives its date of foundation as 1865, but there may have been brewing on the site for centuries before that, and the original Lion Brewery was built by one William Waldon in 1852. He died only two years later, leaving the enterprise to his son William Jr. In 1865, 24-year-old John William Cameron was appointed manager and, seven years later, William Jnr also died. Young Cameron took a 21-year lease on the brewery and its 16 pubs, expanding the estate to 119 tied pubs and buying the business outright in 1892. Thenceforward the company's destiny was nothing short of the conquest of the North East.

The first move was to build an efficient new brewhouse with the capacity to increase production as it absorbed rival after rival. The first was Camerons' Hartlepool neighbour, Nixey Coleclough & Baxter with its 80 pubs, bought in 1895 and soon closed. John William himself died the following year, but the company was now set on its course of expansion. Next was Chapman's of Sunderland with 83 pubs in 1897, then in 1910 Heslop's of Stockton with 28 pubs. The war intervened, and the brewery was damaged during the German bombardment of December 1914. But things were soon back on track: in 1920 Newton's of Newcastle fell with 35 pubs, as did Plews of Darlington with 100; 1953: Hunt's of York, Scarborough and Whitby, 221; 1956: Fryer's of Brompton; 1959, West Auckland; 1961: Russell and Wringham of Malton… At its peak, Camerons

owned 750 pubs and completely dominated the entire region, but things were about to change.

Then in 1974 Camerons was bought by Ellerman Lines, a shipping conglomerate owned by a long-standing family connection, and from that moment forth it was a shuttlecock in the game of corporate badminton, passing through the ownership of the Barclay Brothers, Brent Walker and finally Wolverhampton & Dudley, and along the way it was stripped of almost all of its pubs, which ended up with Punch Taverns. Having invested in upgrading the brewhouse, Wolves sold Camerons on in 2002, this time to father-and-son entrepreneurs David and Chris Soley, who have revived its fortunes by bidding for big third-party production contracts, slowly rebuilding a tied

estate and bringing out appealing new brands such as Motörhead Röad Crew, a USA pale ale.

In 2004 an adjoining pub was converted into a brewery tap and visitor centre with exhibition area and interactive displays. Tours must be booked but are worth it to see the marble-lined brewhouse and the 12 open square fermenters built of slate – a now-rare system not entirely unlike the Burton Union (page 128) in principle and once extremely common locally.

THE BEER Craft beer Anchor and Tooth & Claw and an artist collaboration – all the rage these days – with Motörhead complement traditional brands such as its ruby-coloured best bitter Strongarm 4% ABV, a well rounded ruby red ale giving a creamy head.

▲ *The brewery tap and visitor centre in the Anchor*

CUMBRIA

BREWERIES

2 JENNINGS

✉ Brewery Ln, Cockermouth CA13 9NE
📞 01900 820362 🔗 jenningsbrewery.co.uk
🕐 10.00–16.00 Mon–Sat. With no bar or café, Jennings is not one of the most entertaining breweries to visit. However, there's a well-stocked gift shop selling a wide variety of goods and produce as well as the brewery's own beers. Of these, the best-known are probably Snecklifter and Cocker Hoop and for some reason its own-label port. But tours are free (always ring ahead for times and availability) and it has to be admitted: this is one of the prettiest and best-located breweries in Britain. Founded in the nearby village of Lorton in 1828 by a maltster named John Jennings, it moved in 1874 to the wooded dell squeezed between the castle ruins and the little River Cocker, where it still stands today. And very charming it is too.

3 HAWKSHEAD BREWERY

See page 168.

WHISKY DISTILLERY

4 THE LAKES DISTILLERY

See page 170.

▶ *Jennings Brewery at Cockermouth*

3 HAWKSHEAD BREWERY

AFTER ALL THOSE WARS, A FEW BEERS…

✉ Mill Yard, Back Ln, Staveley LA8 9LR ✆ 01539 825260 🖊 hawksheadbrewery.co.uk ⏱ 12.00–19.00 Mon–Thu, 12.00–23.00 Fri–Sat, 12.00–20.00 Sun (bar & shop).

At 50, top broadcaster and globetrotting foreign correspondent Alex Brodie began to think it was time to stop wandering the war zones of the world on behalf of the BBC, or getting up before most people's bedtime to host the *Today* programme on Radio 4 for nine consecutive years. He yearned for a more normal life – like, for instance, running a microbrewery in rural Cumbria. Well, it might not seem normal to most of us, but then Alex had had a thing about beer since childhood, when he used to get dragged along on his dad's pub-hunting expeditions. He joined the Campaign for Real Ale in 1972, the year after its foundation, and made a point of seeking out good beer – well, beer – wherever fate found him, from pints of Morrell's while at Oxford to Heineken out of a teapot in Iraq.

And so it was that in 2002 Hawkshead was set up on a secondhand seven-barrel plant in a barn in a yard in the eponymous village. The beers soon gained a following for their aromatic hoppiness, thanks perhaps to the influence of Kiwi head brewer Matt Clarke, and before long the brewery had reached its capacity. The move to its current home and a brand-new 20-barrel plant came only four years after the first gyle had been mashed in, but that still wasn't enough. Another four years

down the road and today's familiar glass-fronted brewery tap and visitor centre, the Beer Hall, had to be built to make space for additional capacity in the brewhouse.

"THE BEERS SOON GAINED A FOLLOWING FOR THEIR AROMATIC HOPPINESS"

The Lake District has proved fertile ground for many microbreweries, especially those that throw open their doors to tourists. By the same token, competition is fierce and quality is paramount. Hawkshead's Beer Hall with its dining room – the Beer Kitchen – has ensured its place on the tourist trail by pitching itself as a family-friendly pub with a brewery attached rather than the other way round. So, dogs welcome, baby-changing facilities available, high chairs, children's menu and a pubbish main menu concentrating on solid food at sensible prices, but also top-notch beers – and a big assortment of them – fine wines and a nice selection of artisan gins. It's a formula that ensures plenty of repeat custom from annual visitors and a brisk local trade as well. There are brewery tours with tastings at

▶ *Visitor centre, terrace and new brewery*

13.00 every day, but if you can't get on one you can still see the brewhouse in action because the Beer Hall looks down on it. There's also a gift shop, an international beer shop – and plenty of free parking, so fill your boot! – a function room and conference facilities.

Hawkshead has been going through some changes of late, but nothing that affects the visitor. In 2017 Alex decided it was time to relax and actually enjoy his beer, so he sold the business to Liverpool-based Halewood International and retired. However, Matt Clarke's hand is still on the lever, so even though things are changing they

aren't being altered. And Hawkshead has opened a new brewery. Once again it's grown out of itself but rather than close down a good thing; the Beer Hall and Beer Kitchen will go on, with the extra supplies coming from a big new plant at Flookburgh a few miles away.

THE BEER Windermere Pale 3.5% ABV, Bitter 3.7% ABV has a slight elderflower aroma from Slovenian hops. Red 4.2% ABV, and Lakeland Gold 4.4% ABV – this is a refreshing, well-hopped golden ale with complex fruit flavours.

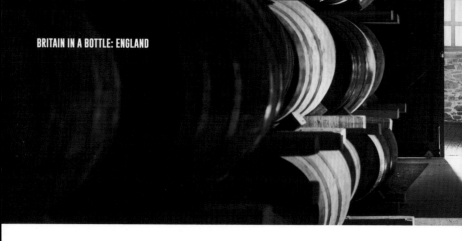

4 THE LAKES DISTILLERY

DON'T VISIT THE LAKES WITHOUT VISITING THE LAKES.

✉ Setmurthy, Bassenthwaite CA13 9SJ ✎ 01768 788850 ✆ lakesdistillery.com ⏲ 10.00–22.00 daily.

Soon after its official opening in December 2014 The Lakes Distillery became one of Cumbria's leading tourist attractions, with more than 100,000 visitors a year. Perhaps people were just surprised to find a whisky distillery in Cumbria – surely it should be a few miles further north? – but if that was the case the novelty has worn off now, and they come because it's lovely.

It's set in the Derwent Valley where the River Derwent leaves Bassenthwaite Lake and heads for the sea, in low-lying country surrounded by frowning fells that demand to be seen dusted with snow. The distillery itself is like a little castle, snug and safe against the outside world and all its dangers, its stout stone buildings ranged around a spacious courtyard. It was originally a model dairy farm, designed and built in the 1850s as a

practical test-bed for theories and experiments in agricultural efficiency, but it had lain empty for 20 years when Paul Currie found it in 2011, bought it and restored it with whisky in mind.

Paul has a track record here. His father Harold, having retired as a very senior executive in the Scotch whisky industry, opened the Isle of Arran Distillery (page 228) in 1995 with Paul and brother Andrew as his right and left hands. When Currie Snr retired, this time for good, Isle of Arran Distillery was sold to a group of independent investors in 1999. Paul stayed on for a while but eventually left to pursue his own dream... and he found it here.

The key to success in a venture such as this – as at Isle of Arran, which in some ways it resembles – is to be the best at everything you do. That's

not just marketing hyperbole: when you've invested £6 million for starters with another £4 million later on you need to be able to count on a premium that people are willing to pay. So the three-year restoration of the farm was painstaking and original, with no short cuts – even the ironwork gates to the courtyard were designed and made by blacksmith-cum-artist Alan Dawson of Workington, and absolutely astonishing they are too.

"THE THREE-YEAR RESTORATION OF THE FARM WAS PAINSTAKING AND ORIGINAL"

Whisky distilling was always the objective here, but like all start-up whisky distilleries, The Lakes started out with gin and vodka while the whisky matured. The gins, Lakes and Lakes Explorer, have been particular hits owing to their locally sourced botanicals, including heather, mint and hawthorn. Even the junipers are gathered on the fells nearby. While waiting for its own whisky to come of age, The Lakes has also come out with two blends of whiskies from all over Britain, The One and Steel

Bonnets. Its own malt, Genesis, was released in 2018 and there's now quite a range.

For the visitor there's an upmarket shop and an elegant 130-cover bistro occupying the original milking parlour: it's bright and airy and has its own terrace and, unusually for a visitor centre eatery, it is open every evening as well as during the day. It describes itself as 'informal' but it's a good deal posher than your average pub and the menu, although pub-inspired, is a bit pricier too. You could just settle for coffee and cake or afternoon tea, though, perhaps followed by a riverside walk when you can also say hello to the alpacas. Guided tours are frequent, but you should book, and the enhanced tours definitely have to be booked in advance to avoid disappointment.

THE WHISKY The Lakes Single Malt Whiskymaker's Reserve at cask strength 60.9% ABV is rich and complex with dry fruits and treacle plus a touch of vanilla.
THE GIN The Lakes Gin 46% ABV with juniper, coriander and angelica notes.

171

CIDERMAKING

TOUGH NUT, YOUR APPLE. IT TAKES SOPHISTICATED MECHANICAL ENGINEERING TO GET AT ITS JUICE.

People often claim cider to be the oldest and most natural alcoholic drink in the world. Here's why they're wrong. Get some apples. Put one on a (moppable) floor and stand on it. There — you've squashed it. Now put half a dozen on the floor and stand on them. They will bear your weight easily, even scornfully. Apples have compressive strength, and getting the juice out of them in worthwhile quantities is a gloriously messy and sticky two-stage mechanical operation in which great numbers of wasps seem keen to participate.

Two-stage, because before you can press the fruit you have to mince it. The traditional cider mill is a circular trough with a millstone in it that is turned by a horse with a low boredom threshold. This is a very primitive mechanism, identical to the olive presses of the ancient world; a donkey-powered version is still in use in the more rustic parts of Greece and Italy. The more modern scratter mill — well, 17th century — comprises a hopper mounted above a hand-turned crankshaft with little blades on it. It worked alongside the horse-powered trough mill for many centuries and is still used by enthusiasts today, sometimes with an electric motor fitted.

Milling is the easy bit. It's the pressing that's really hi-tech. Pliny the Elder in the 1st century AD records several types of what he called 'artificial wine' being made from various fruits, including

apples and pears, presumably crushed in the vast and cumbersome beam presses described in earlier texts. The beam press is basically a giant seesaw, with a huge boulder at one end and some slaves at the other, used mainly for smashing ore but also for various purposes on huge agricultural estates.

> **"APPLES HAVE COMPRESSIVE STRENGTH, AND GETTING THE JUICE OUT OF THEM IN WORTHWHILE QUANTITIES IS GLORIOUSLY MESSY"**

The whole business of industrial-scale crushing, though, was made immeasurably easier and cheaper by Pliny's contemporary Hero of Alexandria, who first described the screw-press in his *Mechanica*. Its only drawback was that it was very difficult to make because the corresponding male and female threads had to be hand-carved to fit properly and it was judged purely by eye. Not surprisingly they spread only slowly, and don't appear to have reached Britain until 1184 when cider is first mentioned in official records. This was 30 years after the Angevin dynasty succeeded the Normans, bringing with them from their native southwest France the winemaking technology that included the screw-press.

Once you have worked out how to cut corresponding threads, the rest of the screw-press

▲ *A cider press*

could hardly be simpler or more efficient. It's just a flatbed with a raised flange around it and a spout in one corner, on to which you load alternate layers of straw (or sacking) and apple pulp to build a 'cheese'. The screw controls a flat board that you lower just to the top of the cheese.

The sweet first running that flows without pressure can be fermented separately; the trick then is to increase the pressure gently bit by bit until the cheese is dry. The juice is fermented quickly and furiously in common-or-garden tanks, then transferred to overwinter in oak barrels (some of them being enormous ex-porter tuns) for a long, slow, secondary fermentation, during which it will ferment out to complete dryness.

That makes proper traditional cider a boon to diabetics, but a bit mouth-puckering for the uninitiated. You can't just chuck in some sugar because if there's even a tiny vestige of live yeast in there it will all start up again, so you have to either pasteurise the cider or treat it with sulphites first. The natural alternative is to dose the freshly pressed juice with lime to precipitate all the nitrogen and inhibit the growth of the yeast, leaving a sweet, rich, luscious but low-alcohol delicacy. Of course, no modern industrial cider is made like this. But then no tourist would dream of strolling around a modern industrial cider plant. There is absolutely nothing to see, not even apples – modern industrial cider is nearly all made from concentrate.

173

GREATER MANCHESTER

5 ROBINSONS

DIG THAT CRAZY HOPNIK, DADDY-O.

✉ Apsley St, Stockport SK1 1JJ ✆ 0161 612 4100 ✎ robinsonsbrewery.com 🕐 09.00–17.00 Mon–Thu, 09.00–18.00 Fri, 10.30–18.00 Sat, 10.30–16.00 Sun.

Stockport's old town with its near-derelict warehouses and factories is in line for a multi-million-pound regeneration, with upmarket leisure and retail facilities and improved transport links at its heart. And the square, massive and brooding bulk of Robinsons' 100-year-old brewhouse is, believe it or not, one of the attractions.

The Frederic Robinson story began in 1838 when William Robinson bought the early Georgian Unicorn Inn. In 1849 his son George installed a brewery; things went well and ten years later George's younger brother – the man who put the Frederic into Frederic Robinson – bought the warehouse and yard behind the Unicorn to build a bigger brewery. He also started acquiring a tied estate, which stood at 12 by the time of his death in 1890. But that was just the beginning.

Work was started on a new growth spurt at the Unicorn Brewery in 1908 with the installation of a big bottling plant. Filtered and pasteurised bottled beers were becoming more and more popular for their shelf life and consistency, but until the invention of the crown cork by William Painter in 1892 they were prohibitively expensive (the automatic filling line wasn't invented until 1923). But with its economies of scale, Robinsons could bottle not only its own ales (particularly the 8.5% ABV Old Tom, first brewed in 1899 and still a stormer today) but also those of smaller breweries that couldn't afford the gear – a service that continues to this day and without which many microbrewers would never have been able to bring their beers to market.

"WHEN YOU TAKE THE BREWERY TOUR YOU WILL SEE THE WORLD'S BIGGEST HOPNIK"

The outbreak of World War I made it impossible for many of these smaller breweries to continue, and conditions didn't get much better after the conflict ended. In 1915 Robinsons bought Heginbotham of Stalybridge; in 1926 Schofield of Ashton-under-Lyne; and in 1929 Kay's Atlas Brewery of Ardwick. All these breweries came with their complement of tied houses so in the 1920s Robinsons had to build and equip the current brewhouse to supply them; the last piece of kit from that refit was only retired in 2012.

174

▲ *The 100-year-old brewery located in Stockport old town*

The strange sculptural object that forms the centrepiece of the visitor centre used to be the copper in which the wort was boiled with hops before fermentation: it's been displayed in a sort of eviscerated presentation with its innards – its heating elements – gruesomely on show. When you take the brewery tour you will see its successor: the world's biggest hopnik. Not beatnik, no. Not Sputnik, either. The hopnik (of which there are only a few in the UK) passes the boiling wort through a bed of hops rather than casting the hops into the furiously boiling wort, as is traditional. The process extracts more of the aromatics from the hops and creates fewer off-flavours, so the beer is truer to the real character of its hop grist.

The visitor centre was developed in 2015 at a cost of £2 million and marks a complete reversal of the older disposition that regarded visitors as a nuisance. It's all part of a new approach that has seen Robinsons branch out into craft brewing with beers such as the Trooper range, designed in partnership with Iron Maiden singer Bruce Dickinson and including Sun & Steel, a pilsner brewed with Japanese sake. The Unicorn bar and restaurant is part of a complex that includes meeting and function rooms, a big heritage display featuring the above-mentioned copper, a timeline walk and a dray (and yes, there are shire horses you can nuzzle up to, but not in the bar). And with its central location, it's all part of the process of making Stockport buzz again.

THE BEER Old Tom 8.5% ABV, rich, malty and warming, with a distinctive deep port wine finish. Ginger Tom 6% ABV, specially brewed using an infusion of Chinese bruised ginger root and botanical extracts.

GIN DISTILLERY

6 THREE RIVERS DISTILLERY

✉ 21 Red Bank Parade, Manchester M4 4HF
✆ 0161 839 2667 ⌖ manchesterthreerivers.
com ⏰ tours start 19.30 Thu–Fri, 13.00 & 19.30
Sat, 13.00 Sun; must book in advance. Based in a
railway arch in Manchester's 'green quarter', Three
Rivers (named after the Irk, the Irwell and the
Medlock, at whose confluence the city stands)
aims to offer a rather more hardcore course than
many of the gin schools now springing up. For
starters, students get a lecture on the history,
technology and art of making and tasting
gin; then they get to meet Angela, the 450l
custom-made Holstein gin still; then they get a
tutored tasting not just of Three Rivers gin but
of other genres as well, including Genever and
Old Tom. Finally people get to try their hand at
formulating their own botanical grists from a
range of 50, using an array of miniature stills.
It's all very intense, and a long way from sipping
a complimentary G&T after a cursory look at a
rectifying column!

LANCASHIRE

BREWERY

7 LANCASTER BREWERY

✉ Lancaster Leisure Park, Wyresdale Rd, LA1 3LA
✆ 01524 848537 ⌖ lancasterbrewery.co.uk
⏰ 10.00–16.00 Mon–Wed, 10.00–17.00
Thu–Sun. Well, here's a novel idea: a retail estate
with a bar worth drinking in! And not only that,
but a brewery as one of the main attractions!
Lancaster Leisure Park occupies the site of the
Horndean Pottery, which closed in 1988, and is
home to the Countrystyle Meats farm shop and
kitchen, The Original Factory Shop, Giggles Play
& Adventure, Cam Portrait Photography, Turning
Point Theatre Arts Studio and the GB Antiques
Centre, the largest antique and furniture centre
in the country. After browsing that lot you'll want
a beer, so it's just as well that Lancaster Brewery
moved here in 2011.

MERSEYSIDE

GIN DISTILLERY

8 LIVERPOOL GIN DISTILLERY

✉ 52–54 Castle St, L2 7LQ ✆ 0151 481 5555
⌖ liverpoolgindistillery.com ⏰ 12.00–22.00
Sun–Wed, 12.00–midnight Thu–Sat. The
commercial potential of combining an artisanal
distillery and a stylish bar-brasserie, especially if
it's in an up-and-coming inner-city wining-and-
dining quarter, is huge, and the Liverpool Gin
Distillery is the proof of the pudding. By 2016 its
Liverpool Original, Valencian Orange, Rose Petal
and Lemongrass & Ginger gins were selling so
well that the company was bought by one of the
biggest independents in UK wines and spirits,
Halewood International.Its new home is in a
Grade II-listed former Bang & Olufsen showroom
and comprises a dark spirits bar with a limited
menu in the basement, a gin bar and the main

attraction – the 600l copper pot still itself – on the ground floor. On the first floor there is also a gin lab with 32 miniature pot stills where you can mix your own botanicals. Tours, tutored tastings and lab sessions can all be booked. This is reinventing the factory as an attraction in its own right and it's going to be big.

NORTHUMBERLAND

BREWERY

9 HIGH HOUSE FARM BREWERY
See page 178.

▲ *Castle Street – Liverpool, home of the Liverpool Gin Distillery.*

9 HIGH HOUSE FARM BREWERY

IT WAS A VERY CHILL WIND INDEED, BUT IT HAD A SILVER LINING…

⌂ Matfen NE20 0RG ✎ 01661 886192 ⊘ highhousefarmbrewery.co.uk ◷ 10.30–17.00 (closed Wed); tours 11.00 & 15.00 Sun, must book in advance.

It was the foot-and-mouth outbreak of 2001 that persuaded Steve and Sally Urwin that their 200-acre farm on Hadrian's Wall, where they grew wheat and barley and ran a small beef herd and a flock of 150 sheep, needed future-proofing.

At the time the Hadrian's Wall Walk had just been completed and public access to it crossed the farm, so the Urwins were quite used to visitors hiking through their yard. And a lovely yard it is to hike through, with its early Victorian stone buildings, all Grade II listed, and its glorious setting in the rolling Northumbrian hills. Given a large, handsome and disused granary building and the proximity of so much barley, brewing suggested itself as an obvious second string. In fact all the farm's natural advantages convinced the Urwins not just to install a brewery and join the scramble for pub trade distribution but to share everything they had with the thousands of visitors who flock to the region.

The brewery opened in 2003 with the support of English Heritage, which co-operated with their plans to reroof and repoint the sturdy farm buildings sympathetically to make room for a purpose-built ten-barrel brewery and backed their application for listed building consent. Creating a visitor centre was always part of the plan, and

what a centre the Urwins have created! As well as brewery tours, there's an exhibition of the brewing process and the farm's history in the old malt loft (incidentally, High House beers are all brewed from the farm's own barley). Then there's the bar; a well-patronised café that sells everything from coffee and cake to main meals; a brewery shop that also sells beer mustard, beer chutney, beer pickles, beer chocolate and even beer ice cream – all locally made; a three-mile farm walk; a children's playground; and a function room.

"WHILE THE URWINS HAD RECKONED ON 3,500 VISITORS IN THEIR FIRST YEAR, THEY ACTUALLY SAW MORE THAN 9,000"

Within minutes of opening in September 2006, High House had been named Rural Retailer of the Year in the Countryside Alliance's Diversification Awards and had won bronze in the North East England Tourism awards. And while the Urwins had reckoned on 3,500 visitors in their first year, they actually saw more than 9,000.

In 2009 the Urwins decided they were ready to go back to full-time farming and sold the brewery to Heather and Garry Scott, who run it with the help of their two sons and a nephew, and

▲ *Farm buildings, bar and restaurant at High House*

haven't really changed a great deal. However, and perfectly understandably, High House has become an incredibly popular wedding venue. As such, if planning a visit it might be prudent to ring ahead, just to be on the safe side.

THE BEER Auld Hemp 8% ABV, the very first beer brewed. Matfen Magic 4.8% ABV has a beautiful aroma of blackberries and autumn fruits with malty and chocolate overtones.

THE YORKSHIRES

BREWERIES

10 BLACK SHEEP
See page 182.

11 KELHAM ISLAND BREWERY
✉ 23 Alma St, Sheffield, South Yorkshire S3 8SA
✆ 0114 249 4804 🖉 kelhambrewery.co.uk
🕘 12.00–23.00 Sun–Thu, 12.00–midnight Fri–Sat (Fat Cat pub). The Fat Cat, previously the Alma, in Sheffield's historic Kelham Island industrial quarter, was bought at auction by the late Dave Wickett, a university lecturer, in 1981 with the intention of bringing real ales from small brewers to a city dominated by Whitbread and Bass. It was restored as a very traditional urban pub with real fires, real ales, real pie and peas and other such delicacies, and no TV, jukebox or fruit machines, and in 1990 a ten-barrel brewery was built on part of the garden. It was so successful that a new, much bigger brewery had to be built in 1999; and the new brewery itself had to be doubled in capacity after Kelham Island's strong pale ale, Pale Rider, was voted Champion Beer of Britain in 2004. Meanwhile the original brewhouse was converted into a visitor centre. Group tours on Fridays and Saturdays must be booked in advance and include drinks and a pie and pea lunch; private tours are available by arrangement.

12 THEAKSTONS
See page 184.

CIDER MILL

13 AMPLEFORTH ABBEY
✉ Ampleforth, North Yorkshire YO62 4ER
✆ 01439 766000 🖉 ampleforth.org.uk 🕘 call ahead. Making cider isn't Ampleforth Abbey's core business: educating the 600 boys and girls in its college is. Well, prayer is really – but be that as it may – Ampleforth's estate (donated on its foundation in 1802) includes more than ten acres of orchards originally intended to provide table and kitchen fruit for the monks. Although there are no cider varieties among the 50-odd represented there, a little cider has always been made for the refectory table. Commercial production of sparkling cider was only started as a fundraiser in 2001. Since then sales have burgeoned, with still cider added to the range and some of the liquor being sent to Somerset to be distilled. The abbey is immensely welcoming, with a visitor centre, tea room and shop (which also sells an abbey-style beer brewed by Little Valley at Hebden Bridge); visitors are even encouraged to attend services in the Abbey Church. There are also woodland walks and orchard tours (check website for dates). A text you will see and hear often on your visit is John 1:39, 'Come and see', repeated in the avowed hope that by seeing the monks' world you might get a glimpse of your own heaven.

WHISKY DISTILLERY

14 SPIRIT OF YORKSHIRE
✉ Hunmanby Industrial Estate, Filey, North Yorkshire YO14 0PH ✆ 01723 891758

spiritofyorkshire.com 09.30–17.00 Mon–Sat, 10.00–15.00 Sun. Yorkshire's first whisky distillery owes its existence to the fact that the malting barley grown on the Wolds is so fine that it would be a crime not to distil at least some of it. So Jim and Gill Mellor, proprietors of Hunmanby Grange Farm and Wold Top Brewery at Driffield in the East Riding of Yorkshire, decided to correct the omission, bought two big Forsyth pot stills, installed them in a unit on a rather forbidding industrial estate and in May 2016 flicked the 'on' switch. And although there'll be no whisky bottled for a while yet, there have been releases of new make and the distillery is very much live. The Pot Still Café has become something of an attraction in its own right in a tourist area with plenty of competition, and the tours (11.00, 13.00, 15.00 Mon–Sat, 13.00 Sun) are often booked out well in advance. The evening live music and other events are a big draw with locals and tourists alike.

▲ *Black Sheep's collection of legendary ales*

10 BLACK SHEEP

A TALE OF TWO THEAKSTONS PART I.

✉ Wellgarth, Masham, North Yorkshire HG4 4EN ✆ 01765 680101 🖉 blacksheepbrewery.com
🕐 10.00–17.00 Sun–Tue, 10.00–22.00 Wed, 10.00–23.00 Thu–Sat.

With its fine Georgian façades, its opulent parish church and its huge market place, Masham is one of the most charming towns in the Dales. If the building stone hereabouts were yellow instead of grey it could almost be in the Cotswolds – although a Yorkshireman would undoubtedly retort that if Chipping Norton's stone were grey instead of yellow it could almost be in the Dales. There is a unifying factor: Masham, like Chipping Norton, built its medieval wealth on wool. The Cistercians of the various neighbouring abbeys ran their estates pretty much as sheep ranches, and Masham was the entrepôt where live beasts and fleeces were traded in huge numbers.

The ovine connection proved a good hook to hang the branding on when in 1992 Paul Theakston chose to set up a new brewery in the town where his family had lived and brewed for five generations. T&R Theakston, founded in 1827, hit a rough patch in the 1970s and in 1984 was sold to Lancashire brewer Matthew Brown. Paul, who had become managing director at the tender age of 23, at first accepted the inevitable, but when Matthew Brown in turn was bought by Scottish & Newcastle in 1988 it was a takeover too far. Most of the family stayed on, but Paul made himself the black sheep by departing. He

made himself a bit more of a black sheep, perhaps, by siting his enterprise in the old maltings of another brewery, Lightfoot's, that Theakstons had bought and closed in 1919 and which is right next door to a Theakstons' pub, the White Bear. He even thought of using the Lightfoot name, but Theakstons still owned it and in fact has started using it again.

"EYE-CATCHING PROMOTIONS SUCH AS TEAMING UP WITH MONTY PYTHON TO PRODUCE HOLY GRAIL ALE"

With no pubs of its own but with hungry and thirsty tourists streaming past the brewery door, it made sense to open a bar, dining room and shop, which Black Sheep duly did in 1996. Opening up to the public so completely was quite a pioneering step at that time, and the menu of hearty pub-style fare was built on the Yorkshire heritage and location. The beers, too, were and are of sound Yorkshire character: Best at 3.8% ABV and Special at 4.4% emphasise the traditional British hop's bitterness rather than the floral and tropical fruit aromas that overpower some modern beers. Meanwhile the malt character tends towards the sweet, just how they like it in Yorkshire. Riggwelter

at 5.9% ABV, meanwhile, is not a million miles away from the Old Peculier produced just down the road.

Without a tied estate or national advertising, the brewery's open-door policy – which includes tours at 11.00, 12.30, 14.00 and 15.30 every single day (but do book) – has proved an excellent way of spreading the word about its beers. Eye-catching promotions such as teaming up with Monty Python to produce Holy Grail Ale towards the end of 1999, one of the first of the artist collaborations that are now so popular, have also raised its public profile. More recently still it has broadened its corporate base by taking over the struggling York Brewery and its four pubs. Which is all well and good, but a blow-out at the brewery itself is still an essential part of any trip to the Dales.

THE BEER Black Sheep Ale 4.4% ABV, a premium bitter, 54° North 4.5% ABV, a Helles lager using German pilsner malt. To celebrate 30 years of Monty Python they have brought out Monty Python's Holy Grail Ale 4.7% ABV, a golden ale packed with hops.

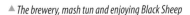
▲ *The brewery, mash tun and enjoying Black Sheep*

183

12 THEAKSTONS

A TALE OF TWO THEAKSTONS PART II.

⌂ The Brewery, Masham, North Yorkshire HG4 4YD ✆ 01765 680000 ✎ theakstons.co.uk
🕑 09.00–17.00 Mon–Fri, 10.30–17.00 Sat–Sun.

▲ *The cooperage at Theakstons*

Like Camerons (page 164), Theakstons is living proof that there can be life after takeover; and in the case of Theakstons, not only was it eventually delivered from the shackles of corporate servitude, but it was liberated by the very family that founded it!

The company was established by Robert Theakston in 1827 at the Black Bull in Silver Street

(today a wine merchant, Corks & Casks, which owns a gin distillery, Spirit of Masham). In the 1870s it moved to its present site in Paradise Fields where there was space to build the handsome but somewhat stumpy tower brewery you see before you. There, nothing much happened for several generations apart from the takeover and closure immediately after World War I of the town's other brewery, Lightfoot's, and its ten pubs. Then in 1974, with beer volumes growing, the youthful MD Paul Theakston made a fateful decision to increase production and acquire a tied estate by buying the Carlisle State Brewery, which had been government-owned since World War I and for which the government had no further use. But it was too big a financial stretch, and after ten years of struggle the family accepted a white knight offer from Lancashire brewer Matthew Brown.

"AT A TIME WHEN REAL ALE WAS BEGINNING ITS RESURGENCE, XB WAS UP THERE IN THE ESTIMATION OF DRINKERS"

Matthew Brown proved to be no rock. For some time Theakstons had been stalked by Scottish & Newcastle, whose 1987 takeover bid narrowly failed. The 1988 bid succeeded, and a large part of the prize was the value of the Theakston name, made legendary by the 5.6% ABV Old Peculier but underpinned by the solid performance of the 3.8% ABV Best and the 4.5% AVB XB. At a time when real ale was beginning its resurgence, XB was up there with contenders like London Pride and Pedigree in the estimation of drinkers and (just as important) of publicans, who wanted brands that were popular yet credible. Theakston Best was one of them: it proved such a success with Scottish & Newcastle publicans that production had to be moved from Masham to the Tyne Brewery.

By 2003, though, Scottish & Newcastle was losing interest and was more interested in investing in its new Russian venture. The Theakston brothers, Simon, Edward, Tim and Nick

— cousins of Paul's — offered to return their mess of pottage and reclaim their inheritance, and to everyone's delight Scottish & Newcastle accepted.

The intervening years have been good to Theakstons. It was able, fairly early on, to expand the brewery and reclaim production of XB; in 2010 it launched an innovative 4.1% blonde beer, Lightfoot, a hybrid of ale malt and lager hops; and Old Peculier, first brewed in the 1890s, was as legendary as ever. (The name recalls Masham's medieval status as a 'peculier' of the Archbishop of York's: the parish was administered directly on his behalf and the landowner had no say in the appointment of clergy or claim on the tithe. The beer is thought to date back to the days before refrigeration, when summer-brewed beers often went off and a reserve of strong winter-brewed stock ale was kept as an emergency back-up.)

The brewery visitor centre, the Black Bull in Paradise, used to be the stables where the dray horses lived with digs in the loft for the draymen who started work very, very early. It includes a tap, a shop and a collection of Theakstons memorabilia and is the base for brewery tours (ring for further information). Take the tour and you'll see England's last full-time brewery cooper, Jonathan Manby, hard at work repairing old barrels and maybe even making a few new ones too.

THE BEER Pale Ale 3.5% ABV, Barista Stout 4.2% ABV, giving you coffee blended with malted barley, and Best Bitter 3.8% ABV, a well-balanced golden-coloured ale. Try Smooth Dark 3.5% ABV with toffee finish.

VINEYARDS

15 HOLMFIRTH VINEYARD

✉ Woodhouse Lane, Holmbridge, Holmfirth, West Yorkshire HD9 2QR ✆ 01484 691861 ✎ holmfirthvineyard.com ⏱ tours run year-round at 10.30 & 15.00, restaurant open from 09.00 daily. Holmfirth's character has been so firmly fixed in the public mind by the dreamlike, quasi-nostalgic second-childhood antics of the *Last of the Summer Wine* posse that the style and character of Holmfirth's vineyard is as much of a shock as the fact that it's there at all.

Back in 2006 Ian and Becky Sheveling gave up lucrative careers – he as a designer, she as a Formula 1 engineer – to buy a run-down sheep farm overlooking the Holm Valley and turn it into one of Britain's most northerly and highest vineyards. They knew they could overcome the climatic challenges by planting the adapted Rhine hybrids – Seyval Blanc, Solaris and Rondo – so beloved of English winemakers, so what was going to be really special about their vineyard was not so much its altitude and latitude as its buildings. At the top of the slope, sheltered from the north wind by the bulk of the winery building, they built a futuristic semi-circular restaurant, all picture windows to make the most of the views and with a sunny terrace. Further downhill they took advantage of a worked-out quarry to hide The Retreat, a block of seven self-catering apartments with spa, all cunningly designed so that although the occupants can enjoy the panorama from their balconies, nobody can really see them. The progress of the building and planting was followed by the TV reality series *Build a New Life in the Country*, and the build went so well that the Shevelings were able to plant in 2007 and produce vintages of white and rosé for sale in 2010, a year earlier than planned.

16 RYEDALE VINEYARDS

✉ Earfield Farm, Westow, North Yorkshire YO60 7LS ✆ 01653 658035 ✎ ryedalevineyards.co.uk ⏱ 09.00–17.00 Mon–Fri, 09.00–12.00 Sat; tours & tastings are held at 15.00 every Sat from Easter to end Oct (check availability & book in advance); alternatively, groups of ten or more can book private tours ending up in the tasting room – a recently converted stable – for brunch, tea or tapas. The farmhouse is also a B&B. You hear a lot about the north–south divide, but to a winegrower it's the east–west split that really matters. For Ryedale, whose 10,000 Chardonnay, Pinot Noir and Pinot Meunier vines were mostly planted in 2006, really is Britain's northernmost vineyard and yet always gets decent-sized crops of good quality. The latitude may mean short growing seasons, but it also means long days; the altitude means that on frosty nights the cold air rolls down into the valley and forces the warmer air back up; and the longitude means less rain, which is mostly dumped on Manchester before the cumulonimbus can cross the Pennines. That's the theory: it's borne out by a full trophy cabinet. The business is family-run and they have planted more vines at nearby Howsham.

▶ *Holmfirth Vineyard, overlooking the Holm Valley*

17 WHIRLOW HALL FARM TRUST

⌂ Whirlow Ln, Sheffield, South Yorkshire S11 9QF ✆ 0114 236 0096 ✎ whirlowhallfarm. org ⊙ 10.00–17.00 Wed–Sun. Sheffield ends with a bang. One moment you're in the city, the next you're out in the Peak District, but still within the city limits. And one of those dignified stone farmhouses you will see perched on a hillside is Whirlow Hall, a 140-acre working farm and, since 1979, an educational trust treating underprivileged kids to a day out in the open air shovelling manure and manhandling wheelbarrows. And it really is a working farm: the produce the trust sells in the Cruck Barn Café and the farm shop (where they sell meat, fruit and vegetables as well as craft beer) is a vital source of income. The produce now includes red, white, rosé and sparkling wines from 2½ acres of Phoenix, Rondo and Solaris planted in 2010, and since 2018 yielding enough to be worth vinifying. Wine may not be the trust's main focus, but a day spent at Whirlow Hall is exhilarating, even inspiring, and contributes to a very good cause; plus you get to come away with a bottle of bubbles!

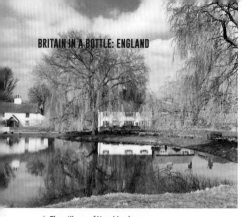

▲ *The village of Nun Monkton*

18 YORKSHIRE HEART VINEYARD & BREWERY

✉ Pool Ln, Nun Monkton, North Yorkshire YO26 8EL ☏ 01423 330716 ⌖ yorkshireheart.com ⏱ 09.00–16.30 Mon–Sat (shop & visitor centre), 11.30–17.30 Wed & Sat (café). The history of microbrewing is widely populated by hobbyists who got a bit good and decided to venture beyond the kitchen table. Not so the history of English winemaking – with the exception of Chris and Gillian Spakouskas, who started off making country wines out of garden and hedgerow fruits, and then found room in their garden for 35 vines. That was in 2000 and, once they had honed their skills, they branched out planting 12,500 vines on a carefully chosen seven-acre site on their 35-acre holding between 2006 and 2011. In fact more recently Chris, Gillian and their family have extended the vineyard yet further: it now covers ten acres and runs to 17,000 vines, mostly Rhine hybrids such as Solaris, Ortega, Rondo and Bacchus but now including Chardonnay and Pinot Noir as well: Yorkshire Heart's white and rosé sparklers come very highly regarded.

But a fully equipped winery isn't enough for the Spakouskas family, and since 2011 they've been running a microbrewery on the farm as well. The brainchild of son Tim, it's a five-barrel plant with its own bottling line and produces a wide range of beers from the 3.3% ABV Lightheart to the 7% ABV Molly's Chocolate Stout. And as if that wasn't enough, in 2013 they planted an orchard. There will be cider. All this bounty has to be shared, and in 2017 Yorkshire Heart opened its shop and café, The Winehouse.

TYNE & WEAR

GIN DISTILLERIES

19 NEWCASTLE GIN COMPANY

✉ Bealim House, 17–25 Gallowgate, Newcastle-upon-Tyne NE1 4SG ☏ 0191 221 1880 ⌖ newcastlegin.co.uk ⏱ 11.30–23.00 Mon–Thu (food served until 21.00), 11.30–midnight Fri, 11.00–24.00 Sat, 12.00–22.30 Sun. Opened in 2015, Newcastle Gin Company is one of the latest additions to the chain of bars across the North East that make up Vaulkhard Leisure – one of whose directors, motor racing champion Harry Vaulkhard, numbers home distilling among his hobbies. As a former printworks, Bealim House is decorated in appropriately industrial style, with the 400l Portuguese copper still as the central feature of the ground-floor bar. The gin is made by vapour infusion, the botanicals first being macerated in warm spirit and then hung in a basket in the neck of the still. Upstairs an open-plan kitchen dispenses colourful small-plate tapas. Tutored tastings lasting 45 or 90 minutes can be booked in advance.

20 POETIC LICENSE

✉ Roker Hotel, Roker Terrace, Sunderland SR6 9ND ✆ 0191 510 3564 ✎ poeticlicensedistillery. co.uk ⏱ 11.00–23.00 Mon–Thu, 11.00–01.00 Fri–Sat, 12.00–21.00 Sun. Boutique distillery bars are such a good idea it's a wonder there aren't far more of them. In this case, the venue is a grand old seafront hotel that was bought and totally revamped in 2014 by pub and restaurant chain Tavistock Leisure, which already owned the Sonnet 43 Brewery (named after Elizabeth Barret Browning's *How Do I Love Thee?*). The hotel tea room became Let There Be Crumbs, the dining room became the Italian Farmhouse and the bar became Poetic License, with one end glassed off to install Gracie, the 500l hybrid gin still. A huge range of limited-edition gins along with regulars Northern Dry and Old Tom are made in the pot, while a vodka is made in the six-plate column. All are beautifully packaged in distinctive, eye-catching designs. A boutique bar may not strictly be a visitor attraction, but it suits the purpose: visitors can sample the products while 'touring' the facility without stirring from their chairs; Poetic License has its own rather funkified pub-style menu; and the host venue sees a lot more trade. There will be more joints like this to come. Many more.

▶ *Roker Lighthouse, Sunderland*

THE IDEAL VINEYARD

FOR THE BEST VINEYARD EXPERIENCE FORGET THE FERRY, TURN BACK FROM THE TUNNEL AND HEAD FOR HOME.

If you're about to embark on a vineyard tour, prepare yourself for a treat. The big vineyards of regions such as Champagne, Bordeaux and the Rhine can frankly be a bit monotonous with row upon row of ruthlessly managed vines receding to the horizon and precious little interstitial planting to vary the view.

English vineyards tend to be very much smaller than their continental counterparts, which from an aesthetic point of view creates variety and context and from an arthritic point of view puts less strain on the visitor's hips and knees. In many cases they command fine views because their favourite position is halfway up a modest slope – halfway so that cold air rolls downhill to create a frost pocket out of harm's way in the valley below; modest because while vines don't like wet feet and need to be efficiently drained (bonus point: leave your wellies at home!) they also have to be worked – pruned, grafted, picked, that sort of thing – which is not easy on a near-vertical mountainside. Elevated sites can be exposed to the wind, though, so most vineyards are well protected by shelter-belts composed of attractive trees and shrubs that not only guard the vines but also delight the eye.

And it gets better. The best-located vineyards will have been chosen for their microclimate and will face broadly south to get as much sun as possible during the growing season. Growers prefer an aspect facing slightly east of south to get the morning sun, so the ground can start heating up as early in the day as possible, so by the time you arrive for your tour all will be as sunny and warm as it can be.

> ## "GROWERS PREFER AN ASPECT FACING SLIGHTLY EAST OF SOUTH TO GET THE MORNING SUN, SO THE GROUND CAN START HEATING UP AS EARLY AS POSSIBLE"

So what will you see on your tour of this garden of visual and meteorological delights? Well, that depends on the time of year. Visit between November and March when the vines are dormant and you won't see much. That's when the pruning is done, but you probably won't even see that because the place is almost bound to be closed. But come April and May when the sap rises, the buds burst and the shoots, little fresh leaves, tendrils and inflorescences begin to emerge. Now's the time when a late frost can wipe out the entire crop, and the vineyard begins to fill up with workers attending to the wiring, rubbing out ectopic buds, spreading manure, hoeing to break the surface of the soil and planting new vines.

In June, the toilers' industry is rewarded by the appearance of the flowers that, once fertilised,

▲ *Rathfinny Vineyard, East Sussex (page 108)*

will metamorphose into tiny bunches of fledgling fruit that must be nurtured and pampered: the leafy canopy must be shaped to an even height so that all the fruit gets an equal share of sun, and plucked through with channels for air and rain. Swelling bunches must be thinned out and unwanted shoots removed.

Finally in August the grapes start to change colour as they ripen. It's an anxious time when you will see the grower taking ceaseless samples of fruit to measure its sweetness and acidity; only when they are judged to be as close to perfect ripeness as possible will the army of pickers be summoned and their secateurs unleashed. These are scenes you may rarely get to witness as a wine tourist in France or Italy or Spain or Germany where the vendange – or vendemmia, or vendimia, or Trauben Ernte – is so often mechanised. So if you want to see pre-Machine Age peasants hard at it out there in the fields earning their bread by the sweat of their brow, Sussex is a better bet than Sicily.

191

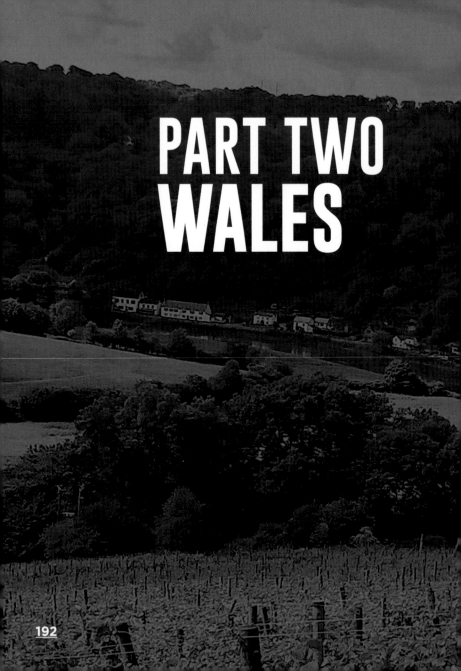

PART TWO
WALES

09 WALES   194

CHAPTER NINE
WALES

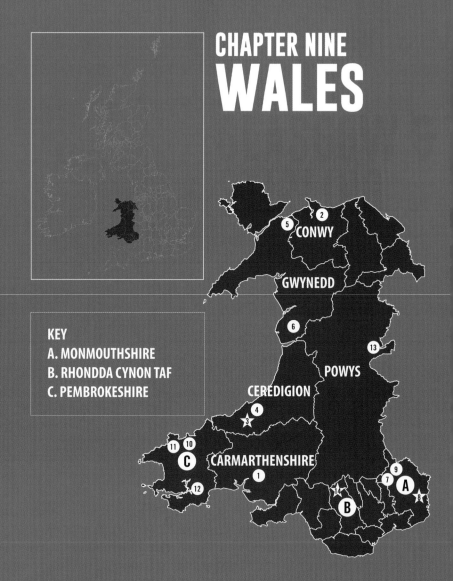

KEY
A. MONMOUTHSHIRE
B. RHONDDA CYNON TAF
C. PEMBROKESHIRE

CONWY

GWYNEDD

POWYS

CEREDIGION

CARMARTHENSHIRE

CARMARTHENSHIRE

GIN DISTILLERY

1 COLES DISTILLERY & BREWERY

⌂ White Hart, Llanddarog SA32 8NT
✆ 01267 275395 ☍ coles.wales ⏲ 12.00–
15.30, 18.00–23.00 Mon–Tue & Thu–Sat, 12.00–
15.30, 19.00–22.30 Sun, closed Wed. If you love
kitsch you're going to die of joy when you open
the door of this thatched late-medieval drovers'
inn. If floor-to-ceiling knick-knacks, technicolour
soft furnishings and wildly over-carved benches
and tables aren't your thing, however, concentrate
on the beer and gin. Brothers Cain and Marcus
Coles and their families bought the pub in 1993
and in 1999 added a five-barrel microbrewery in
which they now produce upwards of 15 beers. In
2011 they started making cider too, and in 2017
installed a still designed and fabricated by Cain
from which comes a range of gins and liqueurs and
Wales's first and so far only white rum. A whisky
may have been released by the time you read this.
Ring to book distillery tours. The pub kitchen is
famed for the generosity of its portions.

CONWY

BREWERY

2 BRAGDY CONWY

⌂ Ty Mawr Enterprise Park, Tan y Graig Rd, Lysfaen
LL29 8UE ✆ 01492 514305

☍ conwybrewery.co.uk ⏲ see website for
opening times. Founded in 2003 by former
electrical engineer Gwynne Tomas and his
wife Adele, Bragdy Conwy is one of a clutch of
microbreweries here that rapidly became successful
after the opening of the North Wales Expressway
in 2001 that revived the region's tourist trade.
It's not the prettiest brewery in the world, being
no more than a unit on an industrial estate, but
its newly opened micropub, Mash (formerly the
sample room; dog-friendly), has a terrace with a
wonderful sea view. Conwy is one of a consortium
of local micros along with Nant and Purple Moose
that owns the Albion Alehouse (also dog-friendly)
in Conwy itself. It brews two ranges of beers: the
core variety of traditional choices such as bitter, a
dark ale and a golden ale; and the West Coast craft
range that is more experimental in inspiration.

CEREDIGION

GIN DISTILLERY

3 DÀ MHÌLE ORGANIC DISTILLERY
See page 198.

MEADERY

4 NEW QUAY HONEY FARM

⌂ Cross Inn, New Quay SA44 6NN ✆ 01545
560822 ☍ thehoneyfarm.co.uk ⏲ Easter–end
Oct 12.00–17.00 Tue–Sat. When Sam Cooper

▶ *New Quay beach*

was only nine, a neighbour got him interested in beekeeping. As often happens with apiculture it was an interest that grew and grew until in 1995 his parents decided to give up on dairy at their 40-acre farm and switch to herding bees instead. The operation now has 500 hives on its own land and at other locations around Ceredigion to take full advantage of different food plants, while the farm buildings have been transformed into a shop and

visitor centre selling all kinds of honey and related products – including a range of meads made (not brewed – making mead does not involve extracting flavours using hot or boiling water!) in Sam's purpose-built meadery. There's also a tea room that sells cakes made on the farm and an exhibition of beekeeping through the ages that includes a number of living hives buzzing away safely behind a glass partition.

3 DÀ MHÌLE ORGANIC DISTILLERY

FROM A WELSH DISTILLERY WITH A SCOTTISH NAME…

✉ Glynhynod Farm, Llandysul, Ceredigion SA44 5JY ✆ 01239 851998 ⬦ damhile.co.uk
🕐 10.00–17.00 Mon–Fri.

Glynhynod organic farm made news back in 1992 when owner John Savage-Onstwedder decided he wanted an organic whisky to see in the millennium with, but couldn't find one. So John, who is also co-owner of Teifi Farmhouse Cheese, gathered up 11 tonnes of organic barley and delivered it to the legendary Springbank (page 298) malt distillery in Campbeltown, which in 1999 returned it to him in the form of 15 hogsheads of delectable whisky: Dà Mhìle, pronounced 'da vila', which is Gaelic for 2000. The Welsh would have been Dwy Fil, but John stuck with the Gaelic; and it was such a success that he decided to repeat the experiment, this time commissioning Loch Lomond Distillery to produce both a malt and a grain whisky.

By now the bug had bit, and in 2008 John started planning a small-batch distillery all of his very own. The drawback was that small-batch distilling was still very new, and Customs was still trying to enforce the old anti-moonshining ban on portable stills of less than 1,800l capacity. But it was only a convention, not an actual regulation; rectifying stills of far less than 1,800l were allowed; and specialised distillers making mashes of fruit, who obviously couldn't simply buy commercially made base spirit, were being grudgingly licensed to operate smaller spirit stills. After all, it wasn't as if they were going to heave the still on to the cart the moment the gaugers hove into view and escape into a glen with it!

John was one of a generation of putative distillers with a vision of a new way of doing things, who found that Customs was becoming rather less sclerotic in its attitude; and in 2012 he duly commissioned his 350l still. Despite its size

it's a proper spirit still: Dà Mhìle has its mash tun and fermenter, and although it can and sometimes does buy in its base spirit it can also ferment and distil from scratch just about anything John wants. The creative potential unleashed by possession of such a small still is limited only by the scope of the distiller's imagination. If you're Rembrandt and you're working on a canvas 14' x 12' you take your time, you concentrate and you produce *The Night Watch*. If you're Picasso and you've got a pile of napkins and a stub of pencil, you can afford to be far more prolific. And that's one of the reasons why Dà Mhìle is so fascinating: literally anything is fair game. There's a gin flavoured with seaweed gathered from the beach at New Quay just up the road.

"JOHN WAS ONE OF A GENERATION OF PUTATIVE DISTILLERS WITH A VISION OF A NEW WAY OF DOING THINGS"

There's an apple brandy distilled from a cider made of the crabs and wildings that stud the farm's hedgerows. White clover and camomile, also foraged on the farm, go into the Farmhouse Botanical Gin. The pink gin is reddened not with Angostura bitters but with local strawberries. Wonderful things are all around you if you're not afraid to try them.

The distillery itself, at the end of its rather hair-raising lane, has another echo of Scotland. Like some Islay distilleries it's a long low building of white painted stone, with its name emblazoned across it in an almost aggressively bold sans-serif font. The foreground isn't sullen sea, though, but West Wales's rolling green hills; and once inside any trace of sullenness is instantly dissipated. A new viewing gallery has been built as a mezzanine, constructed entirely by hand, with never a crane called in, using only fallen trees from the farm and full of sun from the many skylights. Here you can watch the distillery team at work; here you can buy both Dà Mhìle's products and the Teifi cheeses made in a dairy in the same yard; and here you can enjoy and learn from the after-tour tasting.

THE GIN A choice of Oak Aged 42% ABV, Botanical 42% ABV, Seaweed 42% ABV, or try their Sloe Gin 25% ABV, fruity body, nutmeg, cinnamon and cloves.

▲ *The River Dyfi*

GWYNEDD

GIN DISTILLERIES

5 ABER FALLS DISTILLERY

✉ Station Rd, Abergwyngregyn LL33 0LB
☎ 01248 209224 🌐 aberfallsdistillery.com
🕐 12.00–17.00 Mon–Fri, 11.00–17.00 Sat–Sun;
tours are frequent during school holidays – check
the website for availability & booking. This is
the distillery that no visitor to North Wales can
miss, mainly because it's no more than a few
hundred yards off the A55 Expressway. It also has
a wonderful view over the Menai Strait towards
Anglesey and stands at the very foot of the
120ft Aber Falls and will, after the appropriate
maturation period, produce whisky. And given that
both wash and spirit still are unusually tall and
ought to produce a fair bit of reflux, the whisky is
destined to be very smooth. The distillery was set
up in 2017 by Liverpool-based drinks distributor
Halewood International as part of a venture into
artisan distilling (although whether one can be a
multinational company and an artisan at the same
time is open to debate) and is located in a sternly
handsome 19th-century slateworks. There is a
newly opened visitor centre where you can sample
(and buy) Aber Falls' range of Welsh-accented gins.
To get hold of their whisky (due in 2021), become
a member of their Clwb Llechi.

6 DYFI DISTILLERY

✉ Corris Craft Centre, Machynlleth SY20 9RF
☎ 01654 761551 🌐 dyfidistillery.com
🕐 Apr–Oct 10.00–17.00. The Dyfi Valley that
snakes from Creiglyn Dyfi down to the Irish Sea
is Wales at its wildest. Not the wild Wales of crag
and scar and bald sheep-studded mountain, but
the wild Wales of dripping trees, mossy boulders
and spongy sphagnum underfoot. The wild Wales
where Merlin likes to come for a picnic. And for a

gin, too, for in a clearing in the woods is the Corris Craft Centre, in one of whose nine studios is Dyfi Distillery. Established in 2016 by the brothers Cameron – hill farmer, forager, beekeeper and biologist Pete and wine consultant Danny – Dyfi is within Wales's only UNESCO World Biodiversity Reserve and is less than three miles from the Centre for Alternative Technology. Dyfi's gins are spiked with wild local flora, gathered by moonlight with a golden sickle and rectified in pots so small they're more like retorts than stills. Visit any time, don't book: from every point in the shop you can see all the equipment bubbling away; there are placards to tell you what everything is; and if you fancy a cuppa, the Corris Craft Centre has a rather good café and a number of craft shops.

MONMOUTHSHIRE

BREWERY

7 RHYMNEY

⌂ Gilchrist Thomas Estate, Blaenavon NP4 9RL ✆ 01685 722253 ✐ rhymneybreweryltd.com ◷ 11.30–17.30. Founded in Merthyr Tydfil in 2005 by father-and-son team Steve and Marc Evans, the enterprise was named to commemorate one of the great independent breweries of South Wales. Rhymney Brewery was originally established in 1839, taken over with more than 300 pubs by Whitbread in 1966 and unceremoniously closed in 1978. The reborn brewery relocated from its first home in 2011 to a much bigger facility in the Blaenavon World Heritage Industrial Landscape, between the Big Pit mining museum and the Iron Works. The brewery has a Victorian look but is in fact purpose-built and has a visitor centre with a shop, an exhibition space devoted to the history of the original Rhymney Brewery and a bar decorated in the style of a 1970s working men's club.

VINEYARDS

8 PARVA FARM
See page 202.

....

9 SUGARLOAF VINEYARD

⌂ Dummar Farm, Pentre Ln, Abergavenny NP7 7LA ✆ 01873 853066 ✐ sugarloafvineyard. co.uk ◷ 10.00–17.30 Tue–Fri, 10.00–18.00 Sat, 11.00–17.00 Sun. Set on a south-facing slope of Sugarloaf Mountain and with long views over the broad Usk Valley, Dummar Farm with its five acres of vines has to be visually one of the loveliest of British vineyards. Owners Simon Bloor and Louise Ryan are fully conscious of the views as one of Sugarloaf's key assets: the pair of stone-built self-catering holiday lets share a patio with a panorama, while the recently built shop, licensed café and function room also have large, well-placed terrace so you can sit snugly in the café and watch Wales being Wales. The vines are generally of the Rhine/Alsace family, with the two still whites and the Hiraeth vintage white sparkler all being single-varietal – Reichensteiner, Madeleine Angevine and Seyval Blanc respectively. Self-guided vineyard trails don't need booking; guided and group tours do.

8 PARVA FARM

A VINEYARD WHERE ROMANCE – OR AT LEAST, AN OLD ROMANTIC – IS NOT DEAD.

✉ Tintern, Chepstow NP16 6SQ ✆ 01291 689636 ✎ parvafarm.com ◷ Nov–Mar 11.30–16.00, Apr–Oct 13.00–17.30; closed Tue–Wed.

The magical Wye Valley and the hill country surrounding it – if not this actual patch of ground, at least somewhere very near it – is the subject of one of the loveliest of Wordsworth's nature poems, *Lines Written a Few Miles above Tintern Abbey*. Perhaps when you visit Parva Farm you might carry a copy with you to read as you stroll among the vines, for the sloping vineyard powerfully evokes the scenery that enraptured the poet and might similarly enrapture you.

There's also a strong possibility that this same vineyard enraptured the monks of Tintern themselves, all those centuries ago: there are few sites in the vicinity of the abbey as suited to viticulture as this, so it may well be the spot where they raised the grapes for their communion wine. Today's vines, though, date back mostly to 1979 when the four-acre vineyard was established by Martin and Gay Rogers, who planted Bacchus, Seyval Blanc, Müller-Thurgau and Pinot Noir to become the first commercial vineyard in Wales.

In 1996, ownership passed to the present incumbents, Colin and Judith Dudley, who found they weren't getting a satisfactory red from the Pinot Noir and added 750 Regent plants, which means they can now make a Pinot rosé as well as well as a better red. Including a demonstration yard, Parva Farm now has 4,500 vines of 17 varieties, from which the Dudleys, having completely re-equipped the winery, now make an intriguing range. Their first harvest yielded just 56 bottles of medium-dry white, but in 1999 they made a sparkling wine, Dathliad, for the millennium (*dathliad* means celebration; there's now a rosé Dathliad as well). In 2001 they experimented a little further and based a mead on their Seyval Blanc. Seyval Blanc is also the basis for a dessert wine flavoured with summer fruits, and more recently they've turned to cidermaking, using apples from the farm itself and also from the organic orchard next door. It is barrel-fermented in an old wine cask and is light, dry and reputedly very drinkable.

> **"THERE'S ALSO A STRONG POSSIBILITY THAT THIS SAME VINEYARD ENRAPTURED THE MONKS OF TINTERN THEMSELVES, ALL THOSE CENTURIES AGO"**

Parva doesn't have a visitor centre as such, but its shop doubles as a sampling room where proper tutored tastings are given after guided

▲ *The farm and vineyard*

tours (which must be booked). The shop carries all the farm and winery products, other local produce of all sorts, gifts, merchandise and plants. There isn't a café either, but then the Wye Valley Hotel is immediately across the road and visitors can either drop in for a pint and a sandwich or book a post-tour table for something more substantial. Alternatively you can bring a picnic to enjoy on your self-guided tour while you:

> 'repose ... and view
> These plots of cottage-ground,
> these orchard-tufts,
> Which at this season, with their unripe fruits,
> Are clad in one green hue, and lose themselves
> 'Mid groves and copses. Once again I see
> These hedgerows, hardly hedgerows, little lines
> Of sportive wood run wild: these pastoral farms,
> Green to the very door; and wreaths of smoke
> Sent up in silence from among the trees.'

Wordsworth, *Lines Written a Few Miles above Tintern Abbey*

THE WINE Tintern Parva Bacchus 11% ABV, Tintern Parva Dathliad sparkling 12% ABV. They also now produce their own cider, Tintern Parva Siedr 7.5% ABV, giving you a light dry finish.

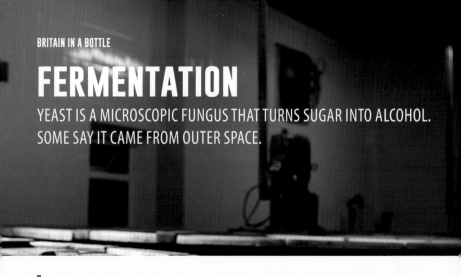

FERMENTATION

YEAST IS A MICROSCOPIC FUNGUS THAT TURNS SUGAR INTO ALCOHOL.
SOME SAY IT CAME FROM OUTER SPACE.

If you're in luck, then on the day of your brewery tour there'll be a gyle in the fermenting vessel and you'll be treated to a ringside view of the action. Or to put it more intelligibly, there'll be a batch heaving and burping away in the fermenting vessel that you can watch, er... heaving and burping. (Strange that in an industry so larded with archaic jargon there isn't a late medieval Dutch word for 'fermenting vessel'. Small prize for the likeliest sounding attempt.)

Fermentation is the most important part of the action, not just in the brewery but in the winery and the cider mill as well. It's a three-stage operation: when the warm yeast slurry is first pitched into whatever syrupy substance awaits, its first priority is to reproduce. For this it needs air. Traditionally most fermentation vessels were open to the elements, the yeast shamelessly and rapidly throwing a thick rocky crust of dense coffee-coloured foam as it frantically reproduced in what was effectively an orgy of pulsating lust, millions upon millions of writhing single-cell fungi

splitting, then splitting again and again and again relentlessly until... well, until they got hungry.

"FERMENTATION IS THE MOST IMPORTANT PART OF THE ACTION, NOT JUST IN THE BREWERY BUT IN THE WINERY AND THE CIDER MILL AS WELL"

From lust the yeast cells turn to gluttony. Understandably, too: after anything up to a week of such frenzied activity the little dears need to build their strength back up. This part of the process is anaerobic. Indeed the yeast's ability to live and feed without oxygen has led to speculation that it might even predate oxygen. After all, the planet is about five billion years old and free oxygen has only been around for a billion of them. It seems likely it was produced when aquatic blue-green algae began to photosynthesise, using solar energy to split molecules of water and carbon dioxide and reform them as organic compounds and free oxygen. And if aquatic blue-green algae could do their thing

without oxygen, maybe yeast cells were out there partying anaerobically too? And if, as some of the wackier scientists have posited, these organisms actually arrived from outer space, wafted on some ineffable cosmic current, then maybe yeast and booze really are gifts from God?

Back down here on Earth you'll see tiny bubbles forming on the loose, foaming cap that has succeeded the original craggier version. This is CO_2, protecting the protean liquid from invading bacteria and other spoilage organisms as it undergoes its transformation. Do not breathe it in! CO_2 is both painful (it burns) and lethal. It's killed plenty of brewery workers over the years – its toxicity is one of the reasons why more and more fermenters today are closed in. (The other reasons are that enclosed fermenters give better control of temperature and protection against infection.)

The third stage of fermentation is maturation, the slow respiration of the few surviving yeast cells

helping the beer or cider or wine to remain almost in suspended animation as it reaches its apogee of condition. Generally the exhaust gas of this last stage gently dissipates, but if you put the liquid into a sealed pressure-bottle along with a nugget of sugar, the CO_2 continues to build up and up and up until releasing the cork becomes a nervous affair – yes: you've got Champagne! For the record, the modern technique of bottling Champagne using *pupîtres* and *dégorgement* and so forth was not an English invention. Bottle-glass strong enough to take the pressure was, though; and in the mid-17th century cidermakers started using pressure-bottles to preserve the delicious gentle fret of the last stage of fermentation. Champagne in those days used to arrive by barrel in the spring, still sparkling from its long, slow winter ferment. The English preferred it like that, and bottled it in their new pressure-bottles with their corks tied down with string. But it was the French who developed and refined the process, making it all controllable and utterly delectable.

▲ *Taking samples of wort from the washback.*

PEMBROKESHIRE

BREWERIES

10 BLUESTONE BREWING COMPANY

✉ Tyriet, Cilgwyn, Newport SA42 0QW
☏ 01239 820833 ⊗ bluestonebrewing.co.uk
🕓 10.00–17.00 Mon–Fri, 12.00–18.00 Sat.

Established in 2013 in the dairy and former stables of a working farm, the brewery takes its name from the Preseli Mountains' most famous export: the 40-odd three-tonne slabs of dolerite quarried here some 5,000 years ago and dragged on sledges (probably) 180 miles to Wiltshire to form the first ring of Stonehenge. Tyriet and its buildings are of the same material, so it's fitting that founder Simon Turner, who runs the brewery with his family, should have named the range of British and continental-inspired beers Rock Solid Ales, which include Fossil Fuel stout, Preseli Pils, Bedrock Blonde, Pierre Bleu and Rockhopper. The springwater used in the brewing is filtered through layers of bluestone and can be used untreated; brewery by-products are used on the farm; and the whole shooting match is solar powered. In order to cut down their carbon footprint they have now installed their own bottling plant and they feed all the by-products to the farm animals. The brewery doesn't currently do formal tours, although in the brewery tap (dog- and child-friendly) you can see a video of Simon doing his stuff. The tap's furniture and fittings are mostly made of old beer barrels, and that includes the urinals. The yard and tap often host live music in the evening.

11 GWAUN VALLEY

✉ Killifreth Farm, Pontfaen, Fishguard SA65 9TP
☏ 01348 881304 ⊗ gwaunvalleybrewery.co.uk
🕓 10.00–18.00 Mon–Sat, also 19.00–22.00 Sat.

A farm brewery similar to Bluestone complete with campsite, holiday cottage and spectacular views, Gwaun is set at the head of one of those delightful hidden valleys in which Wales abounds. The little River Gwaun rises near the brewery and falls steeply to the sea through ten miles of woods and pastures, forming pools and waterfalls along the way. Its course includes a five-mile guided wildlife trail. The brewery itself was started in 2009 by homebrewing enthusiast Len Davis and his wife, accomplished singer-songwriter Sarah. She's responsible for the beers' eye-catching pump clips and bottle labels, and the paintings that adorn the brewery and its tasting room/function room. The ten beers, all in the 4–4.5% ABV range, are adaptations of Len's homebrew recipes.

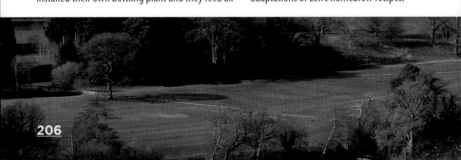

VINEYARD

12 CWM DERI

✉ Martletwy, Narberth SA67 8AP ✆ 01834 891274 ⌾ cwm-deri.co.uk 🕑 10.00–17.00; restaurant open daily for lunch & Fri–Sat for dinner. Cwm Deri was first planted in 1990, making it one of West Wales's older vineyards. The vines are of the cold-resistant Rhine hybrid school of thought – Madeleine Angevine, Seyval Blanc, Phoenix, Orion, Golden Riesling, Leon Millot and Triomphe D'Alsace – and Cwm Deri has also branched out into country wines, fortified fruit liqueurs, mead and preserves using the produce of its own estate, all available along with other local produce at the on-site shop and a branch in Tenby, some 14 miles away. The setting, overlooking rolling hills towards Cardigan Bay, is the epitome of rural tranquillity and visitors are welcome to roam the estate's vineyards and woodlands. One of the owners is a chef by trade, and the restaurant is highly regarded but mercifully well priced. The estate is a working farm with a camping and caravanning site, and a glamping experience is available in shepherds' huts for additional accommodation.

▼ *The Usk Valley*

POWYS

BREWERY

13 MONTY'S BREWERY

✉ Cottage Inn, Pool Rd, Montgomery SY15 6QT ✆ 01686 668933 ⌾ montysbrewery.co.uk 🕑 12.00–18.00 Tue–Thu, 12.00–19.00 Fri–Sat. Founded in 2009 by Pam and Russ Honeyman – unusually but not uniquely she makes the stuff, he sells it – Monty's Brewery is on a completely different site from its visitor centre. The actual brewing is carried out in a unit on an unlovely industrial estate just up the road at Hendomen. Then in 2015, by which time Monty's beers were serial award-winners, the old Cottage Inn on the edge of the tiny town become available. The Honeymans snapped it up, and what a showcase it makes for their beers! Not only is there a comfortable and even elegant bar, there's also a 250l nanobrewery that Pam uses for formulating new brews and trying out different hop varieties. There may not be any tours of the main brewery, but watching the little pilot plant at work is just as good. The beer range includes three gluten-free ales, Magnitude barley wine and CAMRA national champion golden ale, Monty's Pale Ale.

RHONDDA CYNON TAF

14 PENDERYN DISTILLERY

IN A UNESCO GEOPARK, ONE MAN'S DREAM BECAME ANOTHER'S REALITY.

⌂ Penderyn, Rhondda Cynon Taf CF44 0SX ✎ 01685 813300 ◷ penderyn.wales ☉ 09.30–17.00 (Jul & Aug 18.00) daily.

Wales's first whisky distillery since the closure of a short-lived venture in Bala in 1903, Penderyn was not only Wales's but Britain's first new distillery, beating Somerset Royal and King Offa by a decade.

It was actually the brainchild of the late Daffydd Gittins, owner of the Brecon Brewery and something of a dreamer, who sold Swn y Mor (Sound of the Sea) – a blended Scotch liquored down with Welsh water and filtered through a bed of Welsh herbs – as Welsh whisky for 18 years before the Scotch Whisky Association sued him and put him out of business. He was no rogue, though: in the meantime he had been helping to finance Dr David Faraday of the University of Surrey in the development of the ingenious Faraday still. Put simply, it's an ordinary pot but with a condensing and rectifying column instead of a neck and lyne arm. It looks like a gin still; but what's really clever is the internal system of pumps that allows the vapour to be moved between plates, giving the distiller absolute control over which fractions to retain and discard. It is also supremely efficient, producing 92% pure spirit in a single pass with no need for separate wash and spirit stills, which saves a great deal of energy and creates a whisky that is not only drinkable but excellent at only four years old – quite a rarity for a whisky this young.

> **"THE VILLAGE LIES BETWEEN THE RHONDDA AND THE BRECON BEACONS ON THE VERY EDGE OF ONE OF THE MOST GLORIOUS LANDSCAPES IN BRITAIN"**

The first Faraday still was built by McMillan of Prestonpans and installed at Brecon but hadn't had the chance to produce when the company ceased trading. Shortly afterwards it was bought by the Welsh Whisky Company and moved to Penderyn, where in 2000 Dr Faraday finally got to commission his invention. The early years were admittedly a struggle: distribution was hard to get; a pioneering cask club failed to find acceptance; white spirits didn't generate the hoped-for cash flow; and only when substantial new investment was found did Penderyn finally take off. A second Faraday still was installed along with two conventional pot stills that together

would more than double capacity and also create a richer, rounder product: a downside of the Faraday stills is that the spirit they make is very pure and can err on the light side. Finishing the whisky in Madeira casks has also added some fat to its bones, and the use of other casks, together with the still's versatility, has made it possible to turn out a wide variety of expressions.

The investment programme included the opening of a visitor centre in 2008. The village lies between the Rhondda and the Brecon Beacons on the very edge of one of the most glorious landscapes in Britain, the twisted glacial wonderland of the UNESCO Fforest Fawr Geopark. The area was therefore already well visited by tourists of the well-waterproofed and heavily

▲ *Penderyn's visitor centre*

booted kith, among whom a warming whisky is always welcome. The rather austere building itself is clad in dark-stained weatherboarding in keeping with its wooded and, to be frank, often overcast surroundings. Inside, though, it's all light and air, with partitions of stacked casks creating a suitable ambience. There's an exhibition space that will tell you all you want to know, although no café. As the centre is the start and finish point for distillery tours and tastings that were taken by 45,000 people in 2019, though, the lack of a coffee and a cake doesn't seem to be of much account.

THE WHISKY Penderyn Madeira 46% ABV, if you want some smoke Penderyn Peated 46% ABV, or Penderyn Legend 41% ABV, aromas of fresh apples and citrus fruits intermingled with cream fudge and sultana raisins.

WINEMAKING

OUR VINEYARDS MAY BE RUSTIC BUT OUR WINERIES ARE HI-TECH, SO WHEN VISITING AN ENGLISH WINERY KEEP YOUR TROUSERS ON.

Of the 500-plus vineyards in England and Wales, only 150-odd (forgive the arithmetic vagueness: the numbers seem to increase every time you look) are equipped with wineries to vinify their own and other growers' grapes. So if it's winemaking that you want to see, do check in advance that your destination is more than just a pretty place.

"GONE ARE THE DAYS WHEN EVERYONE SIMPLY TOOK THEIR TROUSERS AND SOCKS OFF AND JUMPED UP AND DOWN IN A VAT FULL OF GRAPES"

Adding a winery to the vineyard has generally been a step too far for most English growers because it means a complete shift in the financial balance of the business. The capital investment, maintenance budget, mechanical and winemaking skills, running costs and burden of compliance all seem to be slewed towards the winery rather than the vineyard – many of the first vineyards were simply too small either to afford the investment or to justify the effort. In those circumstances it makes perfect sense to offload the whole sticky business on to someone trained and equipped for the task.

When you embark on your tour you will see the logic behind this. Gone are the days when everyone simply took their trousers and socks off and jumped up and down in a vat full of grapes. All around you will be an apparently random tangle of vats, pipes, pumps and valves of (hopefully) gleaming stainless steel. This is what (in most cases – every winery is custom-built and no two are entirely the same) you are likely to see:

Destemmer
Used especially for red grapes that ripen only in full sun and might therefore be a little less than ripe when harvested, essentially the destemmer is a worm mounted in a perforated horizontal pipe fed by a hopper. The worm rips the grapes off the stems, which are likely to be green and might therefore taint the wine, and breaks their skins before they fall through the perforations into a crusher. They are then fermented, complete with skins and pulp, to extract the pigment.

Press
Grapes for white wine (some of which will be red) are pressed and strained before fermentation; and just as you are unlikely to see grapes being trodden so you are unlikely to encounter a screw-press in a modern winery. Presses today are usually either hydraulic or pneumatic and exert gentle and even pressure. Not so picturesque, granted, but they make better wine. And the annular bladder, should you be fortunate enough to encounter one, is bound to amuse.

▲ *Inside the winery at Hush Heath Vineyard (page 100)*

Fermenter

Precise control of fermentation temperature is perhaps more critical in winemaking than it is in brewing or cidermaking, and cooling equipment will account for a great deal of the energy consumed by a winery. And fermentation in general is a great deal more complicated in wineries than elsewhere since every type of wine seems to need a different regime and hence a different type of vessel. Red wine fermentation is particularly devilish since the floating cap of grape skins has to be prevented from drying out.

Riddling and disgorging room

There are two ways of carbonating an alcoholic drink: mechanically pumping it full of carbon dioxide under pressure or skilfully refermenting it in bottle so that it produces its own bubbles. This is an involved business – and a highlight of the tour – that starts with a spell in the *pupître*. This construction looks just like an A-board with holes in each just big enough to accommodate the neck of a Champagne bottle. The bottles of unfiltered or half-filtered wine are fed with a little priming sugar and possibly some yeast nutrient, crown-corked and stacked upside-down in the holes. There they remain, sometimes for years, gently fermenting away and being turned a little every so often, all in semi-darkness so the wine isn't damaged by ultraviolet light. When the exhausted yeast and other bits and pieces have all settled into the neck, the tops of the bottles are dipped in glycol at -28° to create a frozen plug, which shoots out as the crown cork is removed. The bottles are then topped up and properly corked and wired and that, ladies and gentlemen, is why bottle-fermented sparkling wine is so blooming expensive.

And finally, the tasting room...

PART THREE
SCOTLAND

CHAPTER TEN
SOUTHERN SCOTLAND

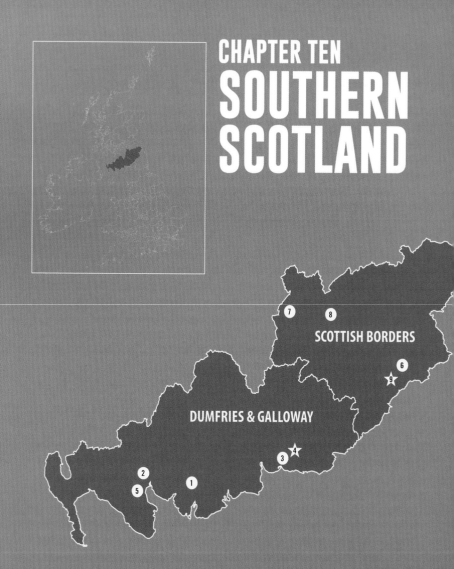

SCOTTISH BORDERS

DUMFRIES & GALLOWAY

DUMFRIES & GALLOWAY

BREWERY

1 SULWATH BREWERS

✉ 209 King St, Castle Douglas DG7 1DT ✆ 01556 504525 ⌖ sulwathbrewers.co.uk ⌚ 10.00–18.00 Mon–Sat; tours 13.00 Mon, Fri – check for availability. Founded in a courtyard off King Street in 1995, Sulwath is one of 50 food- and drink-related businesses whose quality and variety have led to Castle Douglas being designated Dumfries & Galloway's food town. Sulwath – the name is an obsolete form of Solway – produces eight regular brews, all named after local personalities and landmarks. The cosy brewery tap has become a cask beer landmark in the district.

GIN DISTILLERIES

2 CRAFTY DISTILLERY

✉ Wigtown Rd, Newton Stewart DG8 6AS ✆ 01671 404040 ⌖ craftydistillery.com ⌚ 10.00–18.00 Mon–Sat; tours 12.00 & 15.00 daily, call ahead for availability. Purpose-built in 2014, the home of Hills & Harbour gin commands panoramic views over the surrounding hills and forests and was always planned as a destination. Unusually, Crafty brews its own wash and makes its own base spirit and, as is becoming standard practice in Scottish gin distilleries, it sources its own botanicals too, using local flora such as noble fir needles and bladder wrack. It also runs the Galloway Gin Escape where you can forage

for them. The Galloway Picnic invites you to help yourself to local cheeses, charcuterie and fresh bread in the glass-walled Tree Bar.

3 ORO GIN

✉ Dalton, Nr Lockerbie DG11 1DU ✆ 01387 840381 ⌖ orogin.co.uk ⌚ 13.00–20.00 Wed, 13.00–22.00 Thu, 13.00–midnight Fri–Sat, 13.00–20.00 Sun. Originally founded in 2015 as the Quintessential Distillery by the Clynick family from Rugby in Warwickshire, ORO Gin made its first Oro and Oro V ('oro' being the Spanish for gold) gins in 2017 by the traditional one-shot method, macerating the botanicals – which are also very traditional – in neutral spirit for 24 hours before redistillation. The tasting room and restaurant is Spanish-themed, offering tapas and boccadillos. There's also a Finnish-style grill hut or *kota* and a Bavarian-style Bierkeller on site too.

WHISKY DISTILLERIES

4 ANNANDALE

See page 218.

5 BLADNOCH

✉ Bladnoch DG8 9AB ✆ 01988 402605 ⌖ bladnoch.com ⌚ 10.00–17.30 Tue–Sat; tours must be booked in advance. Nestling on the banks of the little river by the same name and

▶ *Bladnoch Distillery*

surrounded by low grassy hills, Bladnoch goes all the way back to 1817 and had a somewhat chequered history until 2015, when it was bought out of receivership by Australian businessman David Pryor and completely restored. The shop is a whisky-lover's dream of bliss, Café Melba serves lunch and tea, and tours have recently been restarted.

217

4 ANNANDALE

ROBBIE BURNS WOZ 'ERE. NO, REALLY.

⌂ Northfield, Annan DG12 5LL ✐ 01461 207817 ⬠ annandaledistillery.com ☺ coffee shop 09.00–17.00 Mon–Sat, 10.00–17.00 Sun; tours must be booked online.

The nearest distillery to England is also, in a sense, one of Scotland's newest. Annandale is a mere seven miles up the A75 from Gretna: turn right on to the B722 just north of Annan, and about half a mile up on your left is a lane leading to a group of imposing stone buildings whose purpose is quickly revealed by a tall chimney and pagoda-style roof. But if this is such a new distillery, you ask, how come it's so obviously old?

Actually, Annandale was one of the rush of distilleries opened after the 1823 Excise Act: the original buildings date to 1830. Over the years it was extended and expanded – hence the pagoda maltings – but like so many others it was mothballed after World War I. A few years later it became a farm and the maltings were used as a grain-dryer.

By 2006 the grand old buildings were disused and near-derelict. That's when international industrial research gurus David Thompson and Theresa Church stumbled across the place, and since they had always contemplated running a distillery that was also a visitor attraction, they bought it and spent over £10 million on a long and painstaking restoration. The distillery had commissioned the late Dr Jim Swan to assist them in producing a great whisky and his demise truly

affected all those who worked at the distillery. The first spirit ran in November 2014 and at the same time a moderately Burns-themed (he was, after all, an excise officer in Dumfries for most of his adult life) café was opened.

In December 2017 they involved Doddie Weir and Gary Armstrong (two very well-known Scottish rugby players) to come along and hand fill their very first peated whisky into specially commissioned Man O'Sword branded bottles and these were sold to help raise money for Doddie's Motor Neurone Disease charity.

"DAVID THOMPSON AND THERESA CHURCH STUMBLED ACROSS THE PLACE; THEY HAD ALWAYS CONTEMPLATED RUNNING A DISTILLERY THAT WAS ALSO A VISITOR ATTRACTION"

Many distilleries are now tying in their whiskies with films and TV and, to coincide with the release of *Outlaw King* – a Netflix film all about Robert the Bruce – the distillery released a blended whisky based on their Man O'Sword but also containing other malt and grain whiskies.

Annandale's three tours include the Restoration Tour focusing on the rebirth of the distillery, the

The water source at the distillery

Technical Tour delving more deeply into the whisky and the distilling process, and the Owners' Tour where David will personally escort you, giving his personal perspective on how the distillery was brought back to life.

David and Theresa have now renovated the Globe in nearby Dumfries, a 17th-century inn that has very close ties to Robert Burns. As well as Michelin-experienced staff, the inn has a range of 200-plus whiskies.

THE WHISKY The first two single malts were released in June 2018, both matured in ex-Bourbon casks. One, Man O' Words, is unpeated, and the other, Man O' Sword, is peated at 18ppm; both are bottled at cask strength 61.1% ABV.

FORMATS

REAL ALE GOOD; KEG BEER BAD. SIMPLE! TELL THAT TO A CRAFT BREWER...

For the last half-century, Britain's beer world has been embroiled in controversy with ferocious zealotry, fanatical passion and superheated debates sparked off by how beer should be transferred from barrel to glass. The old-fashioned way of doing it was to hold the glass under the nozzle of a hand-operated vacuum pump with a barrel of beer at the other end of the pipe and pull the handle. Then in the 1930s keg beer was introduced to prolong shelf-life by processing draught beer in the same way as bottled. Filtered, pasteurised and carbonated – it was virtually imperishable. Air that might have oxidised it was excluded and microbes were gassed to death. The aim was to allow big breweries to supply far-flung tied estates with beers that would survive the journey to the remotest pub intact. As a bonus, every pint in the keg was saleable – unlike old-school draught whose dregs had to be poured away.

"REAL ALE IS FAR MORE SENSITIVE, WITH A SHELF LIFE OF ONLY THREE OR FOUR DAYS AND PRONE TO SPOILAGE"

The stability and shelf life of keg allowed British brewers to take a step further. They found that CO_2 rendered the natural preservatives – the alcohol, the dutiable and therefore expensive fraction of the liquid, and the acid-rich and also very expensive hops – almost redundant. So they started making weaker and fizzier beer, served cold to mask the lack of hop flavour. It didn't go unnoticed: founded in 1972, the Campaign for Real Ale was so successful because it struck a chord with almost every adult male in Britain. Beer has been classed as much by format as by style ever since.

Yet the very expression 'real ale' is nonsense. Everyone claims to understand what it means, but it means nothing. All ale is real: it is all made by mashing malted barley in hot water, boiling the resulting syrup with hops and then fermenting it. Keg beer is not synthetic, it is merely processed, and real ale started life not as a classification but as a slogan. However made-up the terminology may be, though, the liquids thus described are genuinely different. Keg beer is almost inert and will keep almost forever. Real ale is far more sensitive, with a shelf life of only three or four days and prone to spoilage. Those in the know prefer the terms 'cask-conditioned' (ie: the ale continues to ferment gently in the cask and only comes into perfect condition in the pub cellar) and 'brewery-conditioned' (ie: it leaves the brewery as good as it's ever going to get).

Things used to be so simple. Cask equalled good, keg equalled bad. Then came the upsetter: craft. Craft, like 'real', is a term that in the context of beer has no inherent meaning. It emerged when a new generation of microbrewers, inspired by the example of small brewers in the USA, began

producing top-quality keg beers that, they argued, would always reach the drinker in the condition they intended. The word 'craft' was taken up as a polite way of sidestepping the awkward truth that their beers were in fact straightforward keg. But upsetting the 'cask equals good' equation wasn't enough for them. They had to go and make cans respectable. Once cans were taboo in pubs, but not any more. Because we're not talking about the mainstream cut-price multipacks depressingly but accurately known to supermarket beer-buyers as 'slabs' here, we're talking about high-class beers from craft brewers. Having decided that the liquid was more important than the packaging format, those cheeky imps of the brewing world started putting their beers in cans. And people actually started buying them...

Real ale and craft beer may make all the headlines, but they don't make all the sales. Far from it. Most of the beer served in Britain is still filtered, pasteurised, carbonated and chilled and is not even ale. Big-brand lager makes up the bulk of UK sales, both draught and packaged, and it is therefore true to say that more than half of Britain's beer drinkers choose full-on fizzed-up ice-cold stone-dead beer because that's the way they like it.

SCOTTISH BORDERS

BREWERIES

6 BORN IN THE BORDERS BREWERY & LILLIARD GINNERY

✉ Lanton Mill Farm, Jedburgh TD8 6ST ✆ 01835 830495 🖉 bornintheborders.com🕙10.00–17.00 daily. Lanton Mill Farm is quite a find for any tourist interested in drink – it's got a brewery and a distillery! Converted into a highly visitable business centre in 2014, the farm's ten units include Born in the Borders Brewery, which – like more and more craft breweries and distilleries – is an environmentally friendly 'plough to pint' operation using locally grown barley; and a small-batch gin distillery named after a local heroine – Lilliard – allegedly killed by the English in the Battle of Ancrum Moor in 1545. The complex has a café and restaurant where keen birders can watch the pair of ospreys who nest nearby via CCTV. The brewery offers free self-guided tours throughout the day – just turn up – but access to the distillery is limited. Phone ahead and they'll fit you in if they can.

....

7 BROUGHTON BREWERY

✉ Main St, Broughton, Biggar ML12 6HQ ✆ 01899 830345 🖉 broughtonales.co.uk 🕙 shop 08.00–17.00 Mon–Fri; tours by arrangement. Although the brewhouse at Traquair Castle reopened as part of a restoration project in 1965, Broughton claims to be Scotland's original small independent commercial brewer having turned 40 in 2019. Its ambition was to restore some traditional flavour to a Scottish beer market drowning in lager and dull, uninspiring keg ales. By introducing characterful offerings such as Greenmantle, Old Jock, Merlin's Ale and Scottish Oatmeal Stout it succeeded not only in carving its own niche but also in re-energising Scottish ale brewing. Old Jock at 6.7% ABV will give a good flavour of malt with a slight hoppy bitterness. Housed in a cluster of modern-ish agricultural buildings on the edge of Broughton village, it's not the most appealing brewery to look at.

▲ *Peebles in the Scottish Borders*

8 TEMPEST BREW CO

✉ Block 11, Units 1 & 2, Tweedbank Ind Estate, Tweedbank TD1 3RS ✆ 01896 759500 🖰 tempestbrewco.com ☺ 10.00–17.00 Mon–Fri, 10.00–14.00 Sat; tours/tastings 12.30 Sat, must book in advance. Scottish-born chef Gavin Meiklejohn and his New Zealander wife Annika met while working in a gastropub-cum-microbrewery in Canada and started a journey together that took them to New Zealand, where they set up a 50l pilot brewery in their garage, via a brewing course in Sydney, to Scotland where in 2007 they bought the Cobblers pub/restaurant in Kelso. Gavin was itching to brew, though, and in 2010 they cobbled up Tempest in an old dairy using secondhand kit. Here Gavin brewed the kind of beers chefs brew when they brew: packed with flavours, meticulously made and as fresh as humanly possible. Tempest's take on modern IPAs is legendary. In 2015 the brewery moved to a much bigger all-new plant with its own lab to ensure consistency; a centrifuge to clear the beer, making it finings-free and vegan-friendly; and a bottling line enabling it to bottle its beers fresh from the tank without pasteurisation.

WHISKY DISTILLERY

9 BORDERS DISTILLERY
See page 224.

9 BORDERS DISTILLERY

WHAT IS TWEED WITHOUT WHISKY? WELL, UNTIL RECENTLY IT WAS HAWICK.

⌂ Commercial Rd, Hawick TD9 7AQ ✆ 01450 374330 ✎ thebordersdistillery.com ⊙ 10.00–17.00 Mon–Sat; tours must be booked in advance.

Opened in 2018 by a partnership of ex-William Grant directors, Borders Distillery is the first for nearly two centuries in a region better-known for its wool industry. Hawick has been a mill town since the 18th century, producing tweeds for sale around the world and, more recently, luxurious cashmere knitwear. In the 1960s it earned more export dollars per head than any town in Britain and even today its largest employer, Johnstone's of Elgin (founded 1797), has 1,000 workers and is expanding. But it seems the industrious and God-fearing textile workers had less of a thirst for the water of life than their compatriots further north: perhaps the strict regimen of shift-work and long hours dulled their appetite, and a solitary attempt in the wake of the 1823 Excise Act to open a distillery proved abortive: the Kelso Distillery opened in 1825 and closed only 12 years later.

All that changed when the partners saw Hawick's advantages as a hometown. It came with a skilled and disciplined workforce, and good water as the River Teviot runs just behind the distillery. There's also a growing tourist trade, but the real distinguishing feature was that it was the only whisky distillery in the Borders rather than just another face in the crowd on Speyside. So after five years in the planning and an investment of £10 million, the painstaking restoration of an 1880s factory in the town centre was completed and two pairs of enormous whisky stills, with a fifth for gin and vodka, were installed. (You can watch them being winched in through the roof in a video on the company website – improbable though it seems, they all arrived wrapped in plastic!)

> **"THE DISTINGUISHING FEATURE OF BEING THE ONLY WHISKY DISTILLERY IN THE BORDERS RATHER THAN JUST ANOTHER FACE IN THE CROWD ON SPEYSIDE"**

The factory is not especially distinguished architecturally but it does possess a glass roof and a row of big leaded first-floor windows that flood it with natural light and give the passer-by a good view of the stillheads. At the moment, of course, those stills are hard at work but have produced no whisky – not until 2021, anyway. In the meantime the partners have drawn on their skill and experience to create two blends, Clan Fraser and Clan Fraser Reserve, and a vatted (or, as we are supposed to say nowadays, a blended) malt.

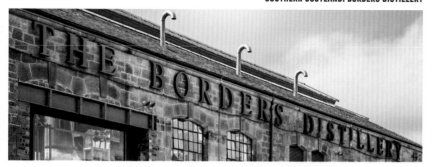

The future plans involve installing an anaerobic digester, where waste products from the distillery will be used to create a biogas and from this you can create steam, which in turn will then help power the distillery.

▲ *The still house containing two pairs of stills*

THE WHISKY Clan Fraser Reserve 40% ABV gives delicate sweet peat smoke, honey and buttery with hints of cinnamon and vanilla. On the palate fragrant blossom honey, raisins and figs, sweet butterscotch and more peat smoke.

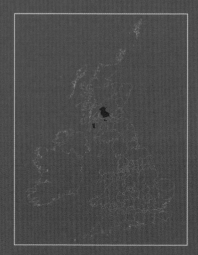

CHAPTER ELEVEN
ARRAN, GLASGOW & STIRLING

STIRLING

GLASGOW

ARRAN

ARRAN

BREWERY

1 ARRAN BREWERY

Cladach, Brodick KA27 8DE 01770 302353
 arranbrewery.com Apr–Sep 10.00–17.00
Mon–Fri, 12.30–16.30 Sun, Oct–Mar 10.30–16.30
Mon–Sat. Founded in 2000 by Richard and
Elisabeth Roberts, Arran Brewery enjoys a
dramatic location between the island's largest
mountain – Goatfell at 874m (2,866ft) – and the
imposing Brodick Castle. The 20-barrel brewing
plant came from the defunct Tipsy Toad brewery
and its 11 ales are serial award-winners, with the
5% ABV Arran Blonde perhaps being the most
popular. After a change of ownership in 2008, the
brewery added a purpose-built visitor centre that
includes a viewing gallery allowing the curious to
observe the Arran crew at work. All tours include a
complimentary tasting.

WHISKY DISTILLERIES

2 ISLE OF ARRAN DISTILLERS

Lochranza KA27 8HJ 01770 830264
 arranwhisky.com Mar–Oct 10.00–17.15
daily, for winter hours call ahead; tours should
be booked in advance. Distilleries both legal and
(mostly) illegal once flourished on Arran, simply
because lookouts could so easily see the excise
men coming. When the 1823 Excise Act relaxed
restrictions on distilling, the island's isolation
became more of a handicap than an advantage,
and the illegal trade died out. More than 150
years later industry executive Harold Currie chose
the island for the site of his new whisky distillery,
which opened in 1995 and was one of the true
pioneers of new-wave artisan distilling in Britain
and indeed the world. The official ribbon-cutting
was marked by an impromptu fly-past by a pair
of golden eagles from the crag above, and the
venture was consequently a huge success. Arran
has recently added the CASKS café to its roster of
attractions, where you can sample many different
types of local produce including cheeses, speciality
breads and meat. A sister second distillery,
Lagg, has been opened at the south end of
the island.

3 LAGG

Kilmory KA27 8PG0 01770 870565
 laggwhisky.com Apr–Sep 10.00–17.30
daily, Oct–Mar 10.00–16.00 Tue–Sat. With the
success of the Isle of Arran Distillery, the owners
decided that another distillery on Arran had
potential and chose the south of the island. Work
started in 2017 and the first spirit was produced in
early 2019. The distillery was opened to the public
only recently and the architecture is stunning, with
the roof covered with a sedum blanket that contains
a mixture of plants that change colour with the
seasons. Visit the Sheiling Bar and Bistro, both of
which offer panoramic views of the mainland.

►*Lochranza, home of Isle of Arran Distillers*

GLASGOW

BREWERIES

4 DRYGATE BREWERY

✉ 85 Drygate, G4 0UT ✆ 0141 212 8815
🖊 drygate.com 🕐 tours 17.00 & 19.00 Sat,
13.00, 15.00 & 17.00 Sun. Drygate was founded
in 2014 in a 50-year-old factory. The building had
had many uses in the past, including box factory
and screen-printing works, and much of the original structure and evidence of its past lives have been conserved and are on display. It includes a German-style beer hall and separate brasserie on different floors, stocking a vast range of beers from both Drygate and other international and domestic brewers. Not only can you arrange a tour, but you can also brew your own on Wednesdays and Saturdays, when the pilot plant can accommodate up to three people brewing 50l or six people brewing 100l. Why not spend five hours under expert tutelage creating your beer?

5 WEST BREWERY

See page 232.

WHISKY DISTILLERIES

6 AUCHENTOSHAN

✉ Dalmuir, Clydebank, G81 4SJ ✆ 01389
878561 🖊 auchentoshan.com 🕐 year-round
10.00–17.00 daily. Thought to have been founded
in about 1800, Auchentoshan is not only the
oldest-attested malt distillery in this part of the
world but was, for a while, the last survivor in the Lowland region. Its claim to fame is that it is the only distillery in Scotland that triple-distills all its whisky, putting it more in line with Irish and American whiskeys than Scotch. With its proximity to Glasgow it has become an extremely popular location and the whisky is fast becoming popular with young adult drinkers.

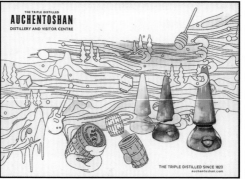

7 THE CLYDESIDE

✉ The Old Pumphouse, Queen's Dock, 100
Stobcross Rd, G3 8QQ ✆ 0141 212 1401
🖊 theclydeside.com 🕐 year-round 10.00–17.00

▲ *Auchentoshan uses three stills for their distillation*
▶ *The Clydeside*

daily. A relatively recent addition to Glasgow's roster of distilleries, Clydeside was opened in 2017 by brothers Tim and Brian Morrison, descendants of the great independent bottler and distiller Stanley P Morrison. Determined to bring malt distilling back to Glasgow, they were able to buy the building that once controlled entry into Glasgow Queen's Dock and provide the hydraulic power to operate the swing bridge. The distillery is close to other attractions, including The Riverside Museum of Transport and the Glasgow Science Centre. It hosts an excellent range of tours, with the top of the range being the two-hour excursion conducted by the distillery manager. There's also a bottle-shop and a bar-café where the speciality is whisky and food pairings.

8 GLENGOYNE

See page 236.

5 WEST BREWERY

GERMAN BEER ON GLASGOW'S GREEN.

✉ Templeton Bldg, Glasgow Green, G40 1AW ✆ 0141 550 0135 ✎ westbeer.com ☾ year-round 18.00 Fri, 12.00 & 15.00 Sat, 15.00 Sun; book online.

When Bavarian-born Petra M Wetzel's father came to visit her in Glasgow and wasn't all that impressed with the beer, she decided to put matters right by starting a brewery of her own. And to make sure that the old boy would like the beer she stuck to the Bavarian *reinheitsgebot* or purity law of 1516, which forbids the use of any ingredients except malted barley, hops, yeast and water – a law that was extended to cover the whole of Germany in the 1860s.

Petra has also sought to make her artisan lagers and wheat beers using ingredients that are as close to the German original as she could find. Her malt is mostly made from British barley, but she does import strains from Germany to help recreate the authentic flavour. The hops are mainly Hallertau, one of the 'noble' varieties used by German and Czech brewers. Finally the house yeast is an imported bottom-fermenting strain that is skimmed after each brew and propagated for consistency. St Mungo, WEST's first brew and now the flagship brand, is named after Glasgow's patron saint and supposed founder.

WEST Brewery incorporates a bar and restaurant, WEST on the Green, all very attractively sited in the Templeton Building, an 1890s carpet factory designed to look like – or something

like – the Doge's Palace in Venice and overlooking Glasgow Green. Also on the Green is the People's Palace, which is home to a collection of artefacts, photographs, prints and film giving a unique view of how Glaswegians used to live. Hardly surprising that WEST on the Green has become a popular

"ST MUNGO, WEST'S FIRST BREW AND NOW THE FLAGSHIP BRAND, IS NAMED AFTER GLASGOW'S PATRON SAINT"

wedding venue. Its seating capacity was increased in 2016 by the addition of the WEST courtyard, while a £5 million expansion of the brewery resulted in two plants operating on the site. There are a number of different tours – the original tour and tasting session; the WEST experience, which ends with a three-course meal accompanied by a pint of St Mungo; and private tours can be arranged but advance booking is essential.

THE BEER St Mungo 4.9% ABV, malty, crisp and golden. Heidi-Weisse 4.9% ABV, fruity, cloudy and with a hint of banana. Munich Red 4.9% ABV, a sweet biscuit flavour. Black 4.6% ABV, a smooth stout with a fudge finish.

▲ The Templeton Building

HOPS

IN THE 15TH CENTURY, HOPS TURNED ALE INTO BEER AND TURNED HOMEBREW INTO THE BASIS OF A MIGHTY INDUSTRY.

The hop was – is – one of those wonderplants for which our thrifty medieval ancestors found a long list of uses. Its flowers produced not only a muddy red-brown dye but also a tannin-based mordant (dye fixative), especially effective on wool. They also made an aromatic, astringent and mildly antibacterial tisane – a medicinal herbal tea – considered particularly good for treating catarrh and other respiratory ills. Picked young, the shoots could be eaten raw or cooked (and still are in Belgium). The bines could be plaited for coarse twine or soaked and beaten for their fibre (although the bines are less easy to work than hemp, flax and nettles, so hop textile was not a common product). The litter left over after stripping the bines was used to pad pillows and quilts. Oh, and from at least the 6th century (earlier than once thought, thanks to a recent archaeological find in Baden-Württemberg) people were using them as a preservative and flavouring in beer.

As far as we can tell, the use of hops in brewing started in southern Germany and spread gradually throughout the Teutonic world. The first mention of hopped beer being imported into Britain comes from the 1360s when Dutch merchants started shipping limited quantities into Great Yarmouth, presumably for their own consumption. The first record of brewing with hops in Britain comes from Colchester, Essex, in 1412; but all the hops used in Britain were imported until 1520 or thereabouts, when the bines were first cultivated in Kent. Previously the English had drunk ale, from the Danish øl, a malt mash infused with a bewildering variety of gathered or garden herbs and, despite the hop's huge advantages, ale lingered on for many generations, probably because unlike beer it didn't require boiling for at least 90 minutes.

"TODAY THERE ARE SOME 300 VARIETIES OF HOP CULTIVATION AROUND THE WORLD"

Finally, the hop won out. As a climber it was easier to grow and pick on a commercial scale compared with ground-hugging herbs, while its acids and oils added early in the boil were highly effective preservatives and conferred delightful aromas and flavours. Commercially, its use altered the economics of brewing and started driving out the small and, in particular, female operators: well-capitalised brewers who could afford the extra vessels and fuel required for beer brewing could produce greater quantities using less malt (because the preservative hop acids enabled brewers to get away with producing less alcoholic beer), pricing the smaller operators out of the market.

Armies on campaign were among the first bulk customers for longer-lasting hopped beers,

and as soon as large-scale beer-brewing became profitable the female brewsters of yore found themselves being frozen out of the market.

Hop-growing quickly spread out all over the country as farmers set aside small parcels of land to supply their local brewers; but equally quickly it contracted to today's two main regions – Kent/Sussex and Herefordshire/Worcestershire, as growers discovered that economies of scale and shared services were necessary to make the business viable. Hop dryers – kilns in the west, oasthouses in the east – were expensive to build, as were the hop-poles and wiring (strung by trained and experienced 'stiltmen') on which the bines grew. Seasonal influxes of extra pickers were necessary too, since the hop harvest coincides with both the apple and grain harvests. Travellers were a welcome sight in autumn in Hereford and Worcester then, while the whole East End decamped to Kent and Sussex for a paid holiday.

Today there are some 300 varieties of hop in cultivation around the world from dear old English favourites such as Fuggles and Goldings to new strains such as Australia's Krakanup and the Czech Kazbek, developed from plants found growing wild in the Caucasus Mountains. Among craft brewers, playing with blends of all these strains amounts almost to mania, and long may it last.

8 GLENGOYNE

YOU TAKE THE HIGH ROAD AND I'LL TAKE THE LOW ROAD.

✉ Dumgoyne by Killearn, G63 9LB ✆ 01360 550254 ✐ glengoyne.com ⏱ 10.00–17.00 daily.

Is Glengoyne a Lowland or a Highland distillery? It's a moot point and one to argue about over a friendly dram. For the distillery actually straddles the imaginary Greenock–Dundee dividing line, and while the whisky here is distilled in the Highland region, it's aged in the Lowland.

> **"ALL THE ELECTRICITY COMES FROM RENEWABLE SOURCES AND IT HAS CREATED ITS OWN WETLANDS TO TREAT SPENT LEES FROM THE STILL HOUSE"**

The best place to have this friendly argument is Glengoyne itself. Only 14 miles from Glasgow on the A81 Aberfeldy Road, its setting makes an interesting backdrop to the debate. For the dividing line here is as much geographical as imaginary, with the Earl's Seat on the Campsie Fells rising to over 1,900ft and a 15m (50ft) waterfall crashing down the sheer basalt slopes of Dumgoyne providing the distillery's mashing liquor. It helps that Glengoyne is frequently rated as one of the prettiest distilleries in Scotland.

Given its setting and its proximity to Glasgow, it's no surprise that the 180-year-old distillery – founded by a local landowning family to displace the 'small stills' that flourished in the hills hereabouts – is one of the most visited in Scotland. It's only half-an-hour's drive from Glasgow, but if you don't have a car the No 10 from Buchanan Street Bus Station stops right at the distillery gate and takes about an hour.

The distillery is extremely conscientious about the environment. All the electricity comes from renewable sources and it has created its own wetlands to treat spent lees from the still house through a series of reed beds. This process takes out anything harmful and eventually the treated water re-enters the local burn that in turn feeds into nearby Loch Lomond. The wetlands also

provide excellent biodiversity with a large range of plants that attract birds, insects and other wildlife. It has also taken on two beehives.

What makes Glengoyne unusual is that it takes an inordinate amount of time to make its whisky. Having an unusual set-up in the still house – one spirit still to two wash stills – the new make runs through the stills at about a third of the usual rate. This lethargy is compounded by some of the slowest fermentation time in Scotland: fermentation can last up to 110 hours. It all results in a bold fruit and sweetness to the whisky.

▲ *Nosing and tasting in the warehouse and the different types of oak used in maturation*
◄ *Making your own whisky in a Masterclass*

A wide range of tours including the basic Wee Tastings lasting about an hour, the Malt Master at nearly two hours and the top-of-the-range Masterclass where over five hours you will taste five of their whiskies and at the conclusion create your very own Glengoyne Single Malt. This all takes place in the engaging sample room.

THE WHISKY The core range of 10, 12, 18, 21 and 25 Years Old. Classic fruit with some vanilla and ginger notes. For something different try The Legacy Series 2019 at 48% ABV, non-chill filtered that creates an amber colour with rich sticky toffee pudding, dates and warm pear.

237

STIRLING

BREWERY

9 ALLANWATER BREWHOUSE

⌂ The Brewhouse, Queens Ln, Bridge of Allan FK9 4NY ✆ 01786 834555 ✐ allanwaterbrewhouse.co.uk ⏲ 12.00–23.00 Mon–Fri, 12.00–midnight Fri–Sat, 12.00–22.00 Sun. Now approaching its silver anniversary, the Allanwater Brewhouse & Bar has a range of 30 cask and keg beers and, unusually, produces its own craft ciders as well. There are three levels of tour available, of which the silver and gold variants offer not just the head brewer's talk, the tour and the samplings but a delightful meal of soup or stew as well.

GIN DISTILLERIES

10 MCQUEEN GIN

⌂ Trossachs Distillery, The Barn, Upper Drumbane, Callander FK17 8LR ✆ 01877 339929 ✐ mcqueengin.co.uk ⏲ 10.00–17.00 Mon–Fri; book tours online. Tucked away up a single-track road not far from the small town of Callander you'll find the Trossach Distillery, a converted stone barn that is home to McQueen Gin. Since it first fired up the still in 2016, McQueen has made a name for itself with some adventurous flavour combinations such as spiced chocolate orange and fruits of the forest, which reputedly changes colour. All are available from

the on-site shop; one-hour tours are held every weekday and must be booked.

....

11 STIRLING GIN

The Old Smiddy, 9 Lower Castlehill, FK8 1EN 01786 596496 stirlinggin.co.uk various tours available throughout the week 10.00–18.00, book in advance online. Under the frowning walls of Stirling Castle you'll find a single-storey stone building with an interesting past: built in 1888 on the site of a medieval forge, the Old Smiddy was originally a temperance hall but in 2018 started a new life as a gin distillery. Owners June and Cameron McCann have carefully restored the building before installing state-of-the-art stills, a visitor centre and a shop; they are now working on renovating the garden. You can either attend the gin school where over two hours you will learn

the history of Scottish gin and make some of your own, or you can take one of the three other tours on offer. Try their Stirling Gin 43% ABV, sealed with a hand-dipped wax seal, and decorated with unique illustrations by Ritchie Collins, an artist influenced by the Scottish wild coast and countryside. Their signature gin has six botanicals carefully chosen to reflect the unique flavour of Stirlingshire's countryside. Basil and citrus peel combine with bold juniper notes to give you a complex spirit. By using local nettles they are working to provide a sustainably sourced spirit with links to their Stirling heritage. Try serving with ice, or with Fever Tree Mediterranean tonic with basil leaf garnish.

WHISKY DISTILLERY

12 DEANSTON

Nr Doune FK16 6AG 01786 843010 deanstonmalt.com 10.00–17.00 daily. Strictly speaking a southern Highlands distillery, Deanston is so handy for Glasgow that it might as well be classed as Lowland itinerary. The distillery buildings were originally a cotton mill built in 1785 by the Father of the Industrial Revolution himself, Richard Arkwright, and powered by the waters of the busy little River Teith on whose banks it stands. Apart from the standard tour, look out for the Whisky and Chocolate tour which is a quadruple taster matching four Deanston whiskies with four great chocolates created by chocolatier Iain Burnett.

◀ *Deanston distillery on the River Teith*

YEAST

GOD IS GOOD AND TO PROVE IT HE GAVE US YEAST. IT'S THE MIRACLE MICROBE THAT TURNS WATER (PLUS SUGAR) INTO WINE.

The yeast cell is an amazing little beastie. A fungus and a distant relative of the mushroom, it's the Jim Royle of microbiology: all it does is eat sugar, fart, defecate and reproduce. And unseemly though it may sound, it's the flatulence and defecation that are of interest, for the former produces the CO_2 that makes dough rise and Champagne sparkle, while the latter produces the alcohol that makes life a little happier. (Bread dough can be 2% alcohol until you bake it.)

For an organism so small and so limited in its horizons, it's really quite versatile. Some are more or less interchangeable: you can brew with baker's yeast and bake with brewer's yeast. At Antwerp's De Koninck brewery it was traditional to hand out free scoops of barm from the top of the fermenting beer for people to take home to use in their baking; today in the brewery tap they give you a free shot to down with your beer and it's deliciously creamy, a bit like coffee and very good for keeping you regular. The internet is alive with home brewers, winemakers and cidermakers who claim to have baked bread with the yeasts peculiar to their hobbies, with wine and natural cider yeasts giving better results than wild beer yeasts.

Other strains are much more specialised: Belgian lambic brewers and the most traditional English, Norman and Galician cidermakers allow their worts and juices to be infected with wild ambient yeasts and bacilli that create some… ahem… most unusual flavours that to most of us are more to be prized for their authenticity than their taste. In fact British brewers prize their own strains so highly that they keep clean samples in a freezer at the University of East Anglia in Norwich as standbys should their working strains become infected.

Then there are the highly tolerant strains used by winemakers: yeast cells eventually die because the CO_2 and alcohol they excrete are actually extremely poisonous, and while even the most valiant ale yeasts by and large are overwhelmed at 10–11% ABV, wine yeasts are quite happy at 13–14% and some will be fine at even higher than this.

"THE EYEBROW-RAISER ABOUT ALL THIS IS THAT UNTIL 1858 NOBODY KNEW WHAT YEAST WAS OR DID"

In the 18th century people had already started asking questions about what yeast was and did and, although at first they came up with some pretty weird answers, their curiosity couldn't be quenched. Humans have been deliberately fermenting sugary liquids, pastes and pulps for around 9,000 years and, although for all that time they knew how to get wine from grapes or mead from honey or arak from palm sap, nobody had a clue what made the magic work. That's even after

▲ Fermentation taking place in the washbacks – after the addition of yeast

humankind realised that yeast was the stuff that did the trick and could be harvested and even stored from batch to boozy batch. 'God is good' was one of yeast's medieval names, and if there was one thing everyone in Christendom understood it was that God moved in mysterious ways and if His son could turn water into wine then perhaps the best thing to do was just to accept it without asking too many questions.

The theory at the time was that processes such as putrefaction arose from the nature of the substance in question – it was called 'spontaneous generation'. The theory when the young chemist Louis Pasteur first identified the real culprit was that fermentation was a process akin to putrefaction. As the son of a tanner, Pasteur knew that it took an external agent to stabilise change, so perhaps it took an external agent to start it? In fact that was pretty much what Pasteur was researching as Director of Scientific Studies at the École Normale Supérieure in Paris when he made one of the first of many major breakthroughs in his long and distinguished career. The discovery of yeast in 1858 was truly earth-shattering and led to many, many more equally important advances – including pasteurisation – that made Pasteur as great in his field as his contemporary Charles Darwin was in his.

CHAPTER TWELVE
EAST LOTHIAN, EDINBURGH & MIDLOTHIAN

EDINBURGH

EAST LOTHIAN

MIDLOTHIAN

EAST LOTHIAN

BREWERIES

1 BELHAVEN

✉ Brewery Ln, Dunbar EH4 1PE ✆ 01368 869200 ⊘ belhaven.co.uk ⏰ 09.00–17.00 Mon–Fri; tours must be booked in advance. Scotland's oldest brewery, founded in 1719, is also one of its most beautiful, and the seaward views take in sandy beaches, the volcanic bulk of the Bass Rock and the mysterious Bridge to Nowhere. The entire complex is Grade A listed, even though the machinery inside is very up to date. Belhaven's visitor facilities, including its tours, shop and bar, underwent a prolonged and expensive upgrade in preparation for its tercentenary celebrations, but everything is up and running again now. Call or check the website for details.

2 KNOPS BEER COMPANY

✉ Archerfield Brewery, Archerfield Walled Garden, Dirleton EH39 5HQ ✆ 01620 388588 ⊘ knopsbeer.co.uk ⏰ 09.30–17.00 daily; tours by arrangement. Heriot-Watt-trained brewer Robert Knops set up on his own in 2010 after stints at Castle Eden and Stewart Brewing. At first his range of modernised traditional styles was brewed under contract, but in 2013 he moved into a unit at the walled garden on the Archerfield Estate, alongside a restaurant and a farm shop. As well as touring the state-of-the-art brewhouse you can spend time exploring the gardens themselves, which include a willow walk and a fairy trail.

GIN DISTILLERY

3 NB DISTILLERY

✉ Halfland Barns, North Berwick EH39 5PW ✆ 07733 321759 ⊘ nbdistillery.com ⏰ 10.00–16.00 Mon–Fri; taster tours 11.30, 13.30, 15.30 Wed–Thu, 11.30 Fri; Connoisseur Tour 17.00 Fri, 14.00 Sat. After teaching themselves how to distil using a pressure-cooker and some radiator pipes, Steve and Viv Muir moved into their purpose-built eco-friendly (and rather luxurious) base in 2018 to make classic gins and a citrus vodka. They then added a double-retort still and are now making dark rums as well.

WHISKY DISTILLERY

4 GLENKINCHIE

✉ Pencaitland, Tranent EH34 5ET ✆ 01875 342012 ⊘ malts.com ⏰ Mar–Oct 10.00–17.00 daily, Nov–Feb 10.00–16.00 daily. Just 20 miles from Edinburgh city centre, Glenkinchie is set in an attractive glen in the hamlet of Peastonbank two miles south of Pencaitland, from which it is signposted. It's not actually too hard to find, and is well worth the effort. A shuttle bus runs direct from Edinburgh city centre to the distillery three times a day. The distillery was first licensed in 1837 by local farmers John and George Rate, although it's suspected that they had been operating for some time before that. They ran it until 1859 before converting it into a sawmill. But in 1890, with phylloxera ravaging the vineyards of

▶ *Glenkinchie distillery*

France and severely curtailing the world's supply of Cognac, a consortium of Edinburgh businessmen stepped in and reopened it, installing the two largest stills in Scotland. Apart from a brief closure during World War I when barley was short, it's been thriving ever since. The old maltings were closed in 1968 and have been converted into an award-winning visitor centre and museum, the centrepiece of which is a scale model of a distillery made for the Empire Exhibition in 1925.

EDINBURGH & MIDLOTHIAN

BREWERIES

5 CROSS BORDERS BREWING COMPANY

✉ Hardengreen Industrial Estate, Dalkeith EH22 3NX ✆ 0131 629 3990 ◇ crossborders.beer ◷ tap room 16.00–22.30 Fri, 14.00–22.30 Sat; tours at 14.00, 15.00, 16.00 Sat. Many Scottish gin distilleries make a feature of using botanicals largely foraged in the wild, surrounding the distillery. Well, here's a brewery that does the same sort of thing. Cross Borders was set up in 2016 by Gary Munckton and Jonny Wilson, friends since childhood, after Jonny had graduated from the Heriot-Watt Institute of Brewing & Distilling. A collaboration between the brewery and wild food expert Amy Rankine of Hipsters & Hobos has resulted in a range of beers that all incorporate locally foraged ingredients. These include Summer that contains honeysuckle, Autumn with bramble and rowan, and Winter with spruce tips.

6 EDINBURGH BEER FACTORY

✉ Unit 15, Bankhead Industrial Estate, Edinburgh EH11 4EQ ✆ 0131 442 4562 ◇ edinburghbeerfactory.co.uk ◷ tap room 12.00–18.00 Mon–Thu, 12.00–21.00 Fri, 11.00–17.00 Sat; tours Fri & Sat, book online in advance. Opened by the Dunsmore family in 2015, the Edinburgh Beer Factory is as much a shrine to the Edinburgh-born father of pop art Eduardo Paolozzi as it is to beer. Paolozzi took everyday objects and transformed them into works of art;

Edinburgh Beer Factory takes beer styles from Britain and the continent and transforms them with unconventional hops and other twists into something new and strange. The beers' names come from Paolozzi works; the prints in the tap room walls are Paolozzis; the brewery exterior is pure Paolozzi – a perfectly ordinary industrial building absolutely metamorphosed. Oh, and a portion of the profit goes to the Paolozzi Foundation. Someone here is a fan!

7 FERRY BREWERY

✉ Bankhead Farm Steading, Bankhead Rd, South Queensferry, Edinburgh EH30 9TF ✆ 0131 331 1851 ◇ ferrybrewery.co.uk ◷ tap & shop 10.00–17.00 Tue–Thu, 10.00–19.00 Fri–Sat, 12.00–17.00 Sun; tours/experience, tours/half-day golf tour Sat–Sun, must be booked in advance. The first brewery in 'The Ferry' since 1851 stands virtually in the shadows of the Forth Railway Bridge, the Forth Road Bridge and the Queensferry Crossings. Founded in a converted cowshed by Mark Moran in 2016, the brewery produces a wide range of traditional beer styles including a red ale, a porter, an 80/- and a stout. There is a selection of tours including half a day of beer and golf, where you can combine a brewery tour with a round at the nearby Dundas golf club. The Tap has become a popular social centre hosting regular live music.

▶ *The Forth Railway Bridge*

8 STEWART BREWING

26a Dryden Rd, Bilston Glen Ind Estate, Loanhead EH20 9LZ 0131 440 2442 stewartbrewing.co.uk shop, tap 10.00–18.00 Sun–Thu, 10.00–22.00 Fri–Sat; tours Fri evening & Sat afternoon must be booked in advance. Since starting in 2004, Jo and Steve Stewart have gone from strength to strength. The brewery they originally ran all by themselves now has 30 employees and their cobbled-up ten-barrel plant was succeeded in 2010 by a gleaming Bavarian-built kit, 30 times as big, to which they commissioned a striking black, purpose-built brewhouse. Inside it's almost a beer-lover's theme park where you can craft your own in the Craft Beer Kitchen, try flights fresh from the tank, fill up your growler at an 18-tap filling station or just chill in the Tap Room.

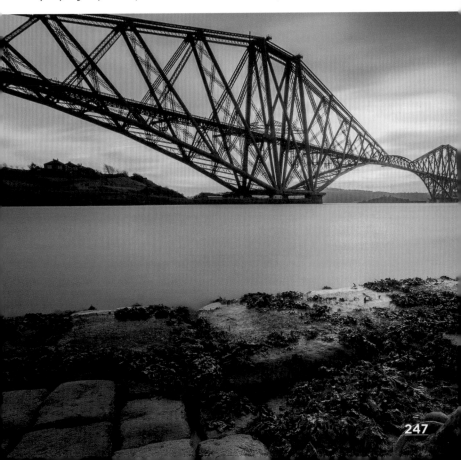

GIN DISTILLERIES

9 EDINBURGH GIN

✉ 1A Rutland Pl, Edinburgh EH1 2AD ✆ 0131 656 2810 🖱 edinburghgin.com 🕑 09.45–16.45 daily; tours must be booked in advance. Edinburgh Gin was an offshoot of Spencerfield Spirits, an independent blender and bottler that was having its Edinburgh Original Gin contract-made until 2014. They then installed two small stills, Flora and Caledonia, in the Heads & Tales bar in the basement of Edinburgh's Rutland Hotel. Given the size of the place, Spencerfield has opened a more sensible production unit in an old biscuit factory in Leith, but Flora and Caledonia are still at work producing small-batch specials during the day. After 17.00 they return to their slumber behind glass screens and the Heads & Tales cocktail bar takes up the reins once more.

10 PICKERING'S GIN

✉ Summerhall, Edinburgh EH9 1PL ✆ 0131 290 2901 🖱 pickeringsgin.com 🕑 shop 10.00–17.00 Mon–Fri, 12.00–19.00 Sat–Sun; tours Thu–Sun, must be booked in advance. Built in 1925, Summerhall was until 2011 the home of the Royal Veterinary School and was universally known as 'Old Dick's' after founder William Dick. More recently it became the Summerhall Arts Complex, where engineer Matthew Gammell and mixologist Marcus Pickering spotted the derelict dog kennels in the small animals' infirmary, which they thought would make an ideal site for a distillery. Working to a botanical recipe supposedly found in a coat pocket and dating from 1947, they started to produce a classic Bombay gin based on a particularly pure neutral grain spirit sourced from France and gently simmered in a rectifying still called Gert. This is neither direct-fired nor steam-heated but goes back to a method common in the 18th century: a *bain-marie*, which distributes the heat absolutely evenly. Next to the distillery is the complex's pub, the Royal Dick, into which Pickering's Gin is actually piped. Also on draught are ales from Barney's Brewery, which occupies the oldest part of the Summerhall site where in the 18th century there stood… a brewery!

WHISKY DISTILLERY

11 HOLYROOD

✉ 19 St Leonard's Ln, Edinburgh EH8 9SH ✆ 0131 285 8977 🖱 holyrooddistillery.co.uk 🕑 year-round 10.45–18.30 Sun–Thu, 10.45–20.00 Fri–Sat. Very centrally located, close to the Royal Mile, this distillery is located in a converted Victorian railway building dating back to 1835. It is the first single malt distillery to open in the city for nearly 100 years. Their first whisky will not be available until early 2022, but in the meantime they have selected a range of whiskies from Scotland with four base flavours: smoky, spicy, sweet and fruity. They have started to produce their own range of gins. These include Holyrood Pink, Spiced and Dry.

VISITOR ATTRACTION

12 SCOTCH WHISKY EXPERIENCE
See page 252.

▲ *Edinburgh Gin Distillery*

MALT 1

OUR FIRST RELIABLE SOURCE OF SUGAR TRANSFORMED MANKIND'S FORTUNES. IT MAKES YOU THINK.

When you consider that humans have been brewing beer, or something very like it, for around 14,000 years, it makes you realise what a clever species we are. Because the very first thing you have to do when making beer is produce sugar from a plant that doesn't actually contain any. And how clever is that?

It's not only clever, it's important. Modern society wallows in sugar, but 23,000 years ago when hunter-gatherers in what is now Israel are thought (according to the latest research) to have made their first tentative stabs at cereal cultivation, it was hard to come by. And people need sugar to help them think straight: at cellular level, the brain is the busiest and most crowded organ in the body and devours half of the sugar we take in. For hunter-gatherers the only readily available sources of sugar were honey, seasonal fruits and tree saps. The surely accidental discovery that the starch in the various grains they were beginning to cultivate could be turned into a reliable, plentiful and year-round supply of sugar was an epoch-making game-changer.

One of the many advantages of grain over more ancient foodstuffs was that it could be stored. However, in granaries that might be rat-proof but weren't necessarily watertight it wouldn't take much rain or even dew seeping in to persuade the grain that it must be spring, and therefore time to start germinating. To the humans, the only outward sign of this was the appearance of a tiny rootlet on each grain; but inside there was plenty going on as the diastatic enzymes woke up and started creating the food the seed needed for its growth spurt by breaking down proteins and turning starch into accessible sugar. Horrified humans set about salvaging the soggy and apparently spoiled grain by drying it over a slow fire or a bed of embers; and when the work was done they made a delicious discovery. Far from being spoiled, their precious harvest had been transformed.

"ONE OF THE MANY ADVANTAGES OF GRAIN OVER MORE ANCIENT FOODSTUFFS WAS THAT IT COULD BE STORED"

Once they had worked out how to manage the processes involved, people found a multiplicity of uses for their grain. They could bake sweet flatbreads or biscuits with it, boil it up for sweet porridge, or simply steep it and pour off the sweet water. At any of these stages, wild yeasts and other microorganisms attacked, as eager for digestible sugar as the humans were themselves, and this effected a second biochemical transformation every bit as magical as the first. Leavened, their flatbreads rose to become soft and fragrant loaves; fermented, their gruel became

▲ *A traditional floor malting with an operator turning the barley by hand*

beer. This was pretty exciting stuff in itself, but there was more.

The year-round availability of a good source of brain-food can only have helped our ancestors to exploit and eventually gain control of the world around them. And learning the arts of making and using malt also taught our ancestors a skill that was an absolutely essential precursor to the next stage in human development: judging and controlling temperature. It was easy enough to tell if you were kilning your sodden barley at too high a temperature: it dried out completely and turned black. But it can only have been by trial and error that the humans found that if you dried it at too low a temperature – ie: below 35°C – the enzymes weren't activated and the magical transformation didn't happen. When it came to mashing malt for brewing they had to be even more accurate: those enzymes needed to reach a temperature range of 60–70°C and be held there for up to two hours to complete the job of turning all the starch into sugar. Any lower and they'd never get going; any higher and they'd be scalded to death. Once people had solved these challenges – a process that, without thermometers or any aid more scientific than trial and error, took about 9,000 years – they were able to start smelting and working copper.

So: no malt, no metal. And no lots of other stuff, too.

12 SCOTCH WHISKY EXPERIENCE

NOT SO MUCH A MUSEUM, MORE A PALACE.

✉ The Royal Mile, 354 Castle Hill, Edinburgh EH1 2NE ☎ 0131 220 0441 ⏱ 10.00–18.00 daily, check website for tour availability.

Not a distillery, but somewhere the dedicated whisky tourist won't want to miss. It was opened in 1988 in an imposing Victorian school building after 19 Scotch whisky companies got together to create a showcase for the industry to visitors from all over the world. The centrepiece is a barrel-ride similar to the one at the Jorvik Viking Centre in York, which glides around a replica distillery explaining the finer points of making and maturing malt whisky en route. But the centrepiece has to be one of the most extensive collections of whiskies in the world. The Diageo Claive Vidiz collection has been the focal point ever since it went on display in 2009 and totals 3,384 bottles, with the oldest dating back to 1897.

> **"THE DIAGEO CLAIVE VIDIZ COLLECTION HAS BEEN THE FOCAL POINT EVER SINCE IT WENT ON DISPLAY AND TOTALS 3,384 BOTTLES"**

On top of its heritage and entertainment functions, the Scotch Whisky Experience runs some pretty heavyweight educational events such as the

Morning Masterclass and the Sense of Scotland tasting tutorials. These are all great fun and highly informative, but they are more than that: the certificate issued at the end is recognised by the Scotch Whisky Association and the courses are attended by trade and industry students as well as tourists.

For those who really want to develop their own whisky there is an opportunity for 'Blending your own', which is an informative interactive session that not only unlocks the mysteries of Scotch whisky, but allows the group to put their knowledge into action, as well as take home their very own whisky. Following a whisky tasting under the guidance of a whisky expert, each guest creates their own unique blend in a 100ml bottle to take home, along with their 'blending certificate'. If you are into whisky pairing with food then try their Taste of Scotland.

▲ The Diageo Claive Vidiz collection
▲ A Masterclass underway
▲ The Amber Restaurant
▲ The large range of whiskies on sale

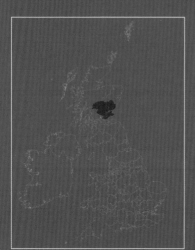

CHAPTER THIRTEEN
EASTERN
SCOTLAND

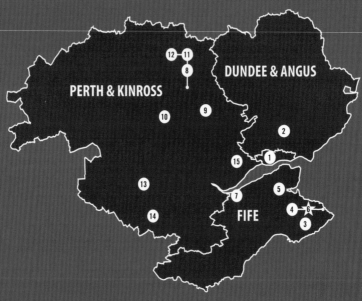

DUNDEE & ANGUS

BREWERY

1 71 BREWING

✉ 36–40 Bellfield St, Dundee DD1 5HZ ✆ 01382 203133 🖉 71brewing.com 🕑 check website for tap room & bottle shop opening hours; book tours online. How does any business start? Sometimes it just takes an event to give you that idea – which is exactly what happened when founder Duncan Alexander, on a whim, visited a brewery when on holiday in Australia. He had always been interested in beer and, on his return to Scotland, ended up back in his hometown of Dundee. There he has created a good range of beers including Poko Yoko, a raspberry and vanilla sour as well as Cloud Fall, an American pale ale. Why not try something different – Breakfast Toast, a coffee stout.

GIN DISTILLERY

2 GIN BOTHY

✉ Kirk Wynd, Glamis DD8 1RT ✆ 01307 840979 🖉 ginbothy.co.uk 🕑 12.00–14.00 & 15.00–17.00 Thu–Sun. Gin Bothy has the historic and somewhat spooky Glamis Castle right on its doorstep, but aims to provide you, alongside a gin experience, an opportunity to discover the history behind the bothy. These were originally small refuges for shepherds out on the hills but are also traditional homes for farm workers in eastern Scotland. And, of course, it was also a euphemism for an illegal

distillery. The distillery produces a traditional gin but also raspberry liqueur and Gunshot, which is a gin infused with cinnamon, cloves and mixed spices.

FIFE

BREWERY

3 OVENSTONE 109

✉ Ovenstone, Anstruther KY10 2RR ✆ 01333 311394 ⬦ ovenstone109.com ⏱ 10.00–17.00 Mon–Fri; call ahead to arrange a tour. The brewery takes its name from the bond angle between the hydroxyl group and the alkyl group in a molecule of ethanol – but then you knew that. You can probably guess that the enterprise was created by a scientist and an engineer who wanted to produce beer using renewable and sustainable technology and eschewing fossil fuels of any kind. The brewery produces a Golden Ale and a Blonde at present, and there are plans to produce a fruit beer due to the abundance of delicious produce growing locally.

GIN DISTILLERY

4 DARNLEY'S GIN

✉ East Newhall Farm, Kingsbarns KY16 8QE ✆ 01333 451300 ⬦ darnleysgin.com ⏱ see website for tour details & opening hours. Tucked behind Kingsbarns Distillery (page 258) is a cottage that lay derelict until the Wemyss family identified the opportunity to bring their

◀ *Glamis Castle*

gin production to Fife, where they have lived and worked for centuries. In 2017 they opened Darnley's Distillery & Gin School and it is here that their distiller produces award-winning gins covering the entire flavour wheel, from fresh and floral to warm and spicy, with a new smoky gin just released. They are passionate about making great tasting spirit using time-honoured skills and all natural ingredients; some are sourced from their cottage garden and some from further afield. For those who really want to get to the heart of making gin, sign up for their Distil Your Own Gin Experience where you learn all about the botanicals, take part in the distillation process and finally label and bottle your own gin.

WHISKY DISTILLERIES

5 EDEN MILL

✉ Main St, Guardbridge, St Andrews KY16 0US ✆ 01334 834038 ⬦ edenmill.com ⏱ call ahead. Eden Mill's near-epic story started in 2012 when former Molson Coors sales director Paul Miller decided to start his own brewery on a historic site that had once been home to the Seggie Brewery and before that to a distillery owned by the legendary Haig brothers. Perhaps the ghosts of the previous owners possessed him, since before long he also opened a distillery on the site producing first gin and now whisky. At the time of writing, further expansion is being carried out, so tastings are being held at The Gatehouse in Guardbridge.

6 KINGSBARNS

See page 258.

6 KINGSBARNS

AT THE HEART OF THE LOWLANDS REVIVAL.

✉ East Newhall Farm, Kingsbarns KY16 8QE ✆ 01333 451300 ⊘ kingsbarnsdistillery.com ⌚ see website for opening hours and tour details.

▲ *The distillery*

Officially opened on 30 November 2015, Kingsbarns was a welcome addition to the Lowland region of Scotland, once rich in distilleries but not so very long ago down to just one. With the craft distilling boom came a revival in the region, which covers the area south of a line between the Firth of Clyde in the west and the Firth of Tay in the east, and which at the time of writing boasts 14 artisan distilleries.

This is one of Scotland's most popular golfing districts and in fact the distillery was started back in January 2009 by professional caddy Doug Clement, its first single malt being released in the summer of 2018. It's now owned by the Wemyss

▲ The distillery shop

Family Spirits portfolio consisting of blended malts, independent bottlings and Darnley's Gin (page 257).

Kingsbarns Distillery only ever uses barley grown in the sun-soaked fields of Fife from a handful of local farmers. The mineral-rich water used in the distillation process is sourced from an aquifer 100m directly below the distillery.

"GREAT LENGTHS HAVE BEEN TAKEN TO SOURCE QUALITY OAK CASKS SUPPLIED FROM AROUND THE WORLD TO MATURE THEIR NEW MAKE"

Membership of their Founders' Club earns you a welcome pack containing a 200ml bottle of new make spirit and a cask strength, single malt 70cl bottle. Kingsbarns Distillery's unhurried fermentation, using both traditional distillers' and French yeast strains, produces an intensely fruity character that, when slowly distilled in their Scottish copper pot stills, creates a remarkably clean, complex spirit. Great lengths have been taken to source quality oak casks supplied from around the world to mature their new make spirit and impart distinct flavours. The Kingsbarns spirit, securely matured in Fife bonded warehouses, is imparted with intricate oak character and subtle wood spices.

There are three types of distillery tours suitable for all levels of whisky interest. You can book online or by phone for a visit – taking in the distillery's exhibition, a guided tour of the distillery and a tutored tasting. If you don't have time for a tour, try a flight of whiskies in the café.

Visitors can also tour Darnley's Gin Distillery that operates in the neighbouring cottage, where they learn about the Darnley's story, meet 'Dorothy' the 350l copper still and hear all about the history of gin and the botanicals they select to make this award-winning spirit.

THE WHISKY Kingsbarns Dream to Dram 46% ABV is light, intensely fruity and floral. Kingsbarns Single is bottled at cask, strength 62% ABV, and uses a selection of different woods for maturation.

MALT 2

IT'S NOT WHAT YOU'VE GOT, IT'S THE WAY THAT YOU KILN IT.

Malt is one of the two most important substances on the planet to anyone with a more than passing interest in alcoholic beverages. The other is grape pulp and, of course, what they have in common is fermentable sugar. Other sources are used in making drinks, even whey, but few if any of them have the versatility of the Big Two. Perhaps the closest third would be orchard fruit – apples and pears – but even they produce a far narrower range of expressions than either malt or grapes. Red perry, anyone?

> **"ANY GRAIN CAN BE MALTED AND USED IN BREWING, AND EACH GRAIN HAS ITS SIGNATURE – OATS, FOR INSTANCE, PRODUCE A VERY SMOOTH BEER"**

Wine buffs, especially the snobbier ones who write off beer as 'just beer', are always surprised by the rich variety of flavours that malt can produce, but when you stop to consider the breadth of the range of grains available, there's nothing to be surprised about. Any grain can be malted and used in brewing, and each grain has its signature – oats, for instance, attract solid particles and produce a very smooth, polished beer; rye has a sharp, astringent, some would say smoky flavour; wheat creates a mix of very distinct tastes and aromas including bubble gum, banana and clove. Barley is the brewer's favourite partly because it's

the grower's favourite – it's tough and rugged and thrives on shallow, dry soils in temperate regions – and partly because it's so overloaded with the enzymes that turn starch into sugar that it can be mashed with unmalted grain. And in the days when malt was taxed, the less malt you had to use in the mash the bigger your profit margin.

Unlike grape varieties, which all produce very different flavours and aromas, malting barley varieties differ mainly in their performance in the field and the mash tun. It's in the kilning of the malt when its astonishing gamut of expressions becomes clear. The three basic malts – lager malt, pale ale malt and distiller's malt – are all light-coloured at 2–3° on the Lovibond scale, with a high proportion of fermentable sugars at 80–80.5%. They're bred for efficiency rather than character, and they're all very good mixers. Distiller's malt is high in nitrogen for fast, thorough fermentation and has the diastatic power to convert or 'saccharify' a wash of 80% unmalted grain. It is also sensational when kilned over peat to produce that iodine smokiness that characterises most Islay whiskies. Lager malt is a natural fit with wheat and rye, and pale ale malt is a precursor to any number of darker, sweeter, richer, juicier variants – amber, biscuit, brown, crystal, chocolate, coffee, mild, stout, roasted…

These variations come at the end of a process that used to take several days. In the system known as floor malting, which has almost but

▲ *One of the floor maltings at Highland Park Distillery with the operator 'turning' the barley (page 340)*

not quite died out in making brewing malt but is still common in the whisky industry, clean grain (dried down to 12–13% moisture for safe storage) is steeped in a tank of water through which air is periodically bubbled. When its moisture content rises to 40–45% it's drained and the malt is allowed to stand for a while. This is repeated two or three times. The grain is then spread evenly on a concrete floor to germinate at an even temperature of 10–16°C, and is turned using a special fork or rake to ensure evenness. Finally it goes into the dryer or kiln to free-dry at ambient temperature for a while, then to be force-dried by a warm air jet down to 5% moisture, and finally to be cured at 80°C or more to create all the different types of malt.

And there you have it: tiny nuggets of malty goodness just waiting to be milled and mashed, packed with flavours of biscuit, caramel, bubble gum, toffee, coffee, toast, green fruit, marmalade or burnt wood. And all of these flavours and aromas are achieved naturally by the manipulation of moisture, temperature and time.

7 LINDORES ABBEY

✉ Abbey Rd, Newburgh KY14 6HH ✆ 01337 842547 ⌖ lindoresabbeydistillery.com
🕐 10.00–16.00 daily. This, they say, is where it all started – the abbey whose infirmarer Brother John Cor distilled the first recorded *uisge beatha* (water of life) from malt rather than wine back in 1494 (although the spirit he produced, unaged and infused with medicinal herbs, was closer to gin than whisky). The abbey had been in ruins since 1559 but when ownership passed to the Mackenzie Smith family they decided to bring the old place back to life by building a distillery and visitor centre overlooking the abbey ruins, with the River Tay in the distance. The location has the most stunning views and you can enjoy a dram and something to eat in The Legacy Bar. The distillery welcomes dog owners.

▶ *Blair Athol Distillery*
▼ *Lindores Abbey Distillery*

PERTH & KINROSS

BREWERY

8 MOULIN BREWERY

✉ The Moulin Hotel, Pitlochry PH16 5EW
✆ 01796 472196 ⌖ moulinhotel.co.uk
🕐 10.00–16.00 Mon–Fri; call ahead. One of Scotland's oldest microbreweries, Moulin was opened in the former coach house and stables of the 17th-century Moulin Hotel in 1995. The brewery's first beer, Ale of Atholl, was quite sweet and dark, in keeping with traditional Scottish tastes; it was followed by a lighter, drier beer that was named after the movie that Mel Gibson was shooting in the area at the time. (Yes, *Braveheart*.) Old Remedial is a strong winter warmer often called on to counteract the weather in these parts. The beers are also served at the Moulin's sister pub, the Bothy Bar in Blair Atholl.

GIN DISTILLERY

9 PERSIE DISTILLERY

✉ Bridge of Cally, Blairgowrie PH10 7LQ
📞 01250 886798 🖊 persiedistillery.com
🕐 12.00–18.00 Sun–Thu; reserved for group bookings on Fri, closed Jan. The distillery is the brainchild of Simon Fairclough who came up with the idea of a touring gin club. Laden down with over 150 gins he travelled up and down the length of Scotland trying to find out which gin style came out on top with both wholesale suppliers and consumers. He noticed three very popular styles: fruity, savoury and sweeter. He then knew which ones to produce at his new distillery and has gone on to achieve awards from both the Scottish Gin Awards and Perthshire Chamber of Commerce.

WHISKY DISTILLERIES

10 ABERFELDY

✉ Aberfeldy PH15 2EB 📞 01887 822010
🖊 dewarsaberfeldydistillery.com 🕐 Apr–Oct 10.00–18.00 Mon–Fri, Apr–Oct 12.00–16.00 Sun. Set among the wooded slopes of the Tay Valley, Aberfeldy is a grand, formal building that could be the barracks of a distinguished Highland regiment if it weren't for the telltale pagoda topping the old maltings. The distillery was built in 1898 by John Alexander and Tommy Dewar, sons of Perth wine and spirit merchant John Dewar. You can discover the complete history by visiting the award-winning interactive heritage exhibition.

11 BLAIR ATHOL

✉ Pitlochry PH16 5LY 📞 01796 482003
🖊 malts.com 🕐 Jan–Sep 10.00–18.30; Oct–Dec 10.00–17.00 Mon–Fri. A picture-postcard group of attractive stone buildings set round a pleasant courtyard, Blair Athol is one of Diageo's flagship distilleries and is also a very popular visitor attraction. First founded in 1798 by two local entrepreneurs named Robertson and Stewart, it coasted along, going through many changes of ownership until after World War II. Blair Athol was selected for heavy investment: its capacity was doubled in the 1970s and in the 1980s, when Bell's was becoming Britain's best-selling whisky, it was opened to visitors. The public loved it and soon it was attracting 30,000 tourists a year. Since then it has gone from strength to strength, offering four levels of tour from the standard to the Allt Dour (Blair Athol's original name) Deluxe.

12 EDRADOUR

Pitlochry PH16 5JP 01796 472095
edradour.com Apr–Oct 10.00–17.00
Mon–Sat, Nov–Mar 10.00–16.30 Mon–Fri.
Pitlochry's second malt distillery was Scotland's smallest until the new wave of artisan distilleries got going – and in many respects it's still its most interesting and in the most picturesque setting. It is of the same vintage as its much, much, bigger neighbour, Blair Athol (page 263) and under its present owners, Signatory Vintage, they have built a second distillery on the other side of the river, doubling production. For such a small distillery they produce a very large range of whiskies inlcuding cask strength and heavily peated.

. . . .

13 GLENTURRET

The Hosh, Crieff PH7 4HA 01764 656565
theglenturret.com A variety of tours;
book online. The Hosh is a secluded little glen just outside Crieff which was reputed to be a hotbed of moonshining throughout the 18th century. Until very recently, Glenturret was the home of the Famous Grouse Experience, which has now closed, and the distillery has been bought by luxury goods business Lalique. The restaurant and café are undergoing refurbishment and will be opening in time for the new season. There is a wide selection of tours, from the basic right through to a whole day where you can help hand rouse the barley in the open mash tun. Try the Glenturret 10 Years Old or, for those who like some smoke, Glenturret Peated.

. . . .

14 TULLIBARDINE

Blackford PH4 1QG 01764 661809

www.tullibardine.com A variety of tours; book online. It's got a bit of history, has Tullibardine – which is weird, as it was only established in 1949. But the derelict buildings that the distinguished Welsh-born distillery engineer William Delmé-Evans (also responsible for Jura, page 314, and Glenallachie, page 281) saw and thought ripe for conversion had previously been a brewery, and it's always said that it was from a predecessor on the site that James IV ordered the brews for his coronation at Scone in 1488. The distillery shares a water source with Highland Spring, and some of the whiskies are finished in ex-wine casks from France. Try the Murray Marsala finish or Sovereign with its vanilla notes.

WINERY

15 CAIRN O'MOHR WINES

East Inchmichael, Errol PH2 7SP 01821 642781 cairnomohr.com 10.00–17.00 daily, café 10.00–17.00 (closed Mon), tours Apr–Oct 14.15 Wed & Sun. Founders Ron and Judith Gillies met on a riverboat in the mangrove swamps of the Panamanian jungle and quickly decided, like you do, to open a winery together where they would specialise in making wines including strawberry, raspberry and bramble from the fruit, both wild and cultivated, that grows so profusely here in the Carse of Gowrie. That was way back in 1987, and they have delivered handsomely on their dream, making both still and sparkling wines from local fruits and flowers, and bottled and draught ciders, both pure apple and fruit-flavoured.

▶ *Loch Tummel, Pitlochry*

WHISKY OR GIN?

DRINK IT FRESH, IT'S GIN. LET IT AGE, IT'S WHISKY. WELL... KINDA.

At some point in the 15th century the monastic apothecaries of northern Europe discovered that they could distil the *aqua vitae* they needed for their medical potions a lot more cheaply from native malt liquor than from imported wine. One of vodka's surfeit of charter-myths, dating from about 1430, has a visiting Greek Orthodox monk named Isidore teaching the brothers of the Chudov Monastery in Moscow to make a wash from bread because they were short of wine to distil for their *aqua vitae*. It's credible in every detail including the date, but the first actual record of distilling from grain comes not from Moscow but from Scotland, where in June 1494 King James IV granted Brother John Cor of Lindores Abbey eight bolls or about a ton of malt 'ad faciendum aquavite'.

"THE INTERACTION OF ETHANOL AND OAK IS TRULY TRANSFORMATIVE"

People tend to point to this as the moment of whisky's birth – or at least the signing of its birth certificate – but of course Brother Cor wasn't distilling whisky or anything like it. His neutral(ish) spirit, spiked with healing herbs, wasn't even considered to be a beverage but medicine, prescribed in doses of a few drops taken in a spoonful of wine. In some senses it was closer to gin than whisky. Medicine only became beverage after the Scottish Reformation of the 1550s,

when displaced monastic apothecaries spread out into private practice and when Scottish farmers realised that simply by repurposing their brewing and washing coppers they could benefit from the secularisation of distilling. In good years they would no longer have to accept glut prices for their surplus crop; instead they could malt it, brew it, distil it into imperishable *aqua vitae* and store it in oak casks to await the leaner years.

It was the oak that turned proto-gin into proto-whisky. The interaction of ethanol and oak is truly transformative: the wood's tannin darkens and protects the liquor, its vanillin mellows its taste, age breaks down harsh aldehyde and some of the ethanol – the angel's share – evaporates through the barrel's porous staves. But even when they had discovered the power of the wood it seems that some distillers couldn't shake off the liquor's roots as a compounded medicine. In 1695 James Lightbody, in a treatise entitled *Every Man His Own Gauger*, gives the following recipe for 'Irish Usquebaugh': 'Take of good spirits, 12 gallons. Put therein aniseeds, nutmegs, sugar, carroway-seeds, of each four ounces, distil the whole to proof spirit, put thereto liquorish, raisins of the sun 2 pound, and 4lb. of sugar, let it drain through a flannel bag, and fine it down with the whites of eggs and wheat flour. This is the only way that natives of Ireland make this liquor, which is approved of to exceed all the other new ways of making it, being but

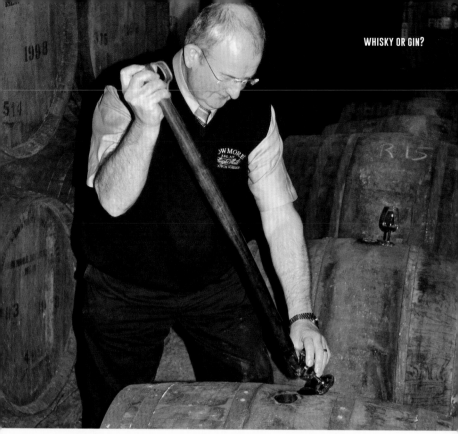

▲ *A warehouseman at Bowmore Distillery (page 302) drawing a sample from a cask using a valinch*

imitations of the original.' George Smith's *Compleat Body of Distilling* (1725) refers to usquebaugh as a compound by rectification of proof spirits. One recipe he gives requires five gallons of rum, six of 'malt brandy' plus mace, cloves, nutmeg, cinnamon, coriander seed, ginger, cubebs, raisins, dates, liquorice, saffron and sugar. It may not sound much like whisky to us, but even as late as 1755 Dr Johnson, in his dictionary, defined usquebaugh as being 'drawn over aromaticks'.

After the conquest of Jamaica in 1655 rum came to the forefront of popularity. But in the afterglow of the Glorious Revolution of 1688 and the ascent of the Dutch Prince of Orange as William III, juniper-flavoured gin swept all before it. Aniseed water disappeared entirely, rum was confined to minority status and whisky — finally bereft of herbs and spices and darkened and smoothed by oak — hardly appeared south of the border for another 150 years.

CHAPTER FOURTEEN
ABERDEENSHIRE
& MORAY

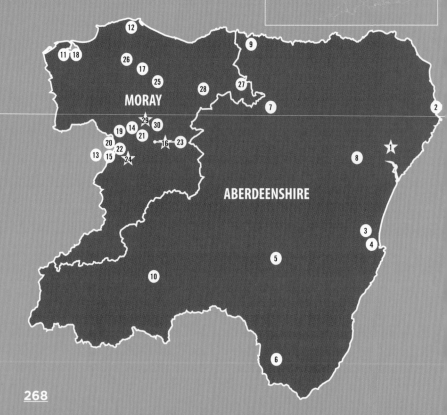

MORAY

ABERDEENSHIRE

ABERDEENSHIRE

1 BREWDOG

SHAKE, RATTLE AND STIR... THE BEER ESTABLISHMENT.

⌂ Balmacassie Industrial Estate, Ellon AB41 8BX ✆ 01358 724933 ⌖ brewdog.com ⊙ 12.00–22.00 Mon–Thu, 12.00–23.00 Fri, 10.00–23.00 Sat, 10.00–22.00 Sun; book tours online.

BrewDog, famously the punk brewery with attitude, started life in 2007. Founders James Watt and Martin Dickie loudly proclaimed that what they wanted was to shake up the brewing industry, and it wasn't long before they were causing waves with the launch of an 18.2% ABV stout. Publicity was and is their speciality, and the less approving it is the better it suits them. They took great delight, for instance, in twisting the tail of the Portman Group – that's the drinks industry's ethics watchdog – with stunts such as launching a seasonal beer called Speedball and naming their low-alcohol beer Nanny State. Never content to rest on their laurels, they decided to create the strongest beer in the world and came up with Tactical Nuclear Penguin (32% ABV), then Sink the Bismarck (41% ABV) and finally The End of History at 55% ABV.

BrewDog underlined its alternative approach when it took to raising capital not by tugging its forelock to the bankers and venture capitalists, but by a spectacularly successful series of crowdfunding campaigns that raised more than £73 million. As a result the company now has breweries in Ellon in Aberdeenshire; Brisbane, Queensland; Berlin and also Columbus, Ohio, which has a hotel attached. But Scotland is where it started.

"PUBLICITY WAS AND IS THEIR SPECIALITY, AND THE LESS APPROVING IT IS THE BETTER IT SUITS THEM"

The Ellon site is a state-of-the-art eco brewery that has expanded over the years to include a second brewhouse called Site3; a fermentation facility called the Overworks that specialises in sour beers; and Lone Wolf Distillery, which produces gin, vodka and a range of whiskies including malt, grain and rye under the Boilermaker series. The DogWalk tour takes in the lot, as well as the canning line for good measure, but if you want to really splash out then go for The Big Dog tour, five hours taking in the DogWalk tour but followed by a meal at the DogTap (their on-site bar which opened in 2014) and finishing off with an after-dinner tutored beer and cocktail tasting.

In the DogTap there are ten taps serving draught beer and the bar sits in the shadow of the giant external fermenters, separated from the brewkit by a single glass door. You will also find the BottleDog (giftshop in layman's terms) where you can buy bottled and canned beers to take away, as well as the latest BrewDog merchandise.

▲ *Lone Wolf Distillery*

THE BEER It all started with Punk IPA at 5.6% ABV, a light, golden classic with bursts of caramel and tropical fruit. Dead Pony Club at 3.8% ABV – dive in to aromas of citrus, lemon-grass and lime zest. If you want to turn it up then try the Amplified range: Hazy Jane 7.2% ABV, with hints of pear and banana and a caramel and biscuit malt finish.

271

BREWERY

2 BREW TOON

🏠 72a St Peter St, Peterhead AB42 1QB 📞 01779 47621 🖱 brewtoon.com ⏱ bar 12.00–23.00; tours can be booked online. Established in 2017 on the site of the old Tanfield Brewery that closed in the 1950s, Brew Toon has become as popular for its lively bar as it is for its beers. The brewery tap serves modern bar food all day and hosts live music every Saturday, a quiz every Sunday, regular stand-up and frequent takeovers. A very distinctive craft beer range includes Raspberry Carronade, M'ango Unchained and Limoncello Soul.

GIN DISTILLERIES

3 PORTER'S GIN

🏠 Orchid, 51 Langstane Pl, Aberdeen AB11 6EN 📞 01224 516126 🖱 portersgin.co.uk ⏱ bar 18.00–02.00 Sun–Thu, 17.00–03.00 Fri, 18.00–03.00 Sat; book distillery visits online. When you open a bar there's always a temptation to start a microdistillery too, and that's exactly what happened here. Orchid was opened in 2009 with plans to install a craft distillery in the basement but, instead of opting for conventional stills, a vacuum still distils botanicals at low temperatures, ensuring a fresh and natural flavour to the gin. Orchid also hosts mixology classes and tutored tastings.

4 THE HOUSE OF BOTANICALS

🏠 Arch 4, Palmerston Rd, Aberdeen AB11 5RE 📞 01224 582992 🖱 doctoradams.co.uk ⏱ call ahead to arrange a visit. This is home to an array of botanical-based drinks, including gins and cocktail bitters and, rather interestingly, it is situated in the railway arches under Aberdeen's main railway line. It was founded by Adam Elan-Elmegirab, who started his career as a bartender and in 2019 made his mark on the cocktail word by reformulating Boker's Bitters 100 years after they disappeared.

5 THE LOST LOCH SPIRITS

🏠 Unit 7, Deeside Activity Park, Aboyne AB34 5BD 📞 01339 883411 🖱 lostlochspirits.com ⏱ book tours & spirit school online. Situated on the edge of the Cairngorms National Park, the distillery produces a variety of spirits including the hybrid Haroosh, a blend of whiskies combined with botanicals including brambleberries (that's blackberries to you and me) and Deeside honey. The distillery is powered by renewable energy generated by a wind turbine, solar panels and a biomass boiler.

WHISKY DISTILLERIES

6 FETTERCAIRN

🏠 Distillery Rd, Fettercairn, Laurencekirk AB30 1YB 📞 340205 01561 🖱 fettercairnwhisky.com ⏱ Apr–Oct only 16.00–10.00 Tue–Sat. Fettercairn is the perfect example of how the landed gentry muscled in on distilling once they saw its potential. The business grew out of an illicit distillery operated by a family named Guthrie in the Drumtochty Forest north of Fettercairn

▶ *GlenDronach Distillery*

village, but almost as soon as the law had been changed in 1823 to make small-scale distilling unviable and large-scale distilling a good bet, Sir Alexander Ramsay of the Fasque Estate took over the operation and moved it down the hill into the village's old grain mill. Today it belongs to Whyte & Mackay, who own another three malt distilleries: Jura (page 314), Dalmore (page 327) and Tamnavulin. The distillery produces a light spirit and the 12 Years Old will give you banana and mango with a really good finish of dried flowers.

7 GLENDRONACH

Forgue, nr Huntly, AB54 6DB 01466 730202 glendronachdistillery.co.uk tours 10.00–16.30 daily. In a district notorious for small-scale unlicensed distilling, a consortium of local landowners came together in 1826 – shortly after the legislation that made large-scale distilling a commercial proposition – to found their own legitimate concern in the grounds of a Georgian manor, Glen House. The group was headed by a colourful character named James Allardes who popularised the whisky in Edinburgh. The distillery changed hands a number of times in the ensuing decades and in 1960 it was bought by William Teacher's. Like Ardmore, it was popular with blenders because its richness meant they only needed to use a little of it to give character to their neutral grain spirits; and this was precisely what Teacher's required. And like Ardmore, its direct-fired stills generated caramel, and the spirit was made even sweeter and richer through ageing in sherry casks. Take the Connoisseur's tour and you can enjoy a tutored tasting of six whiskies after you have looked around the distillery.

8 GLEN GARIOCH

⌂ Oldmeldrum, Inverurie AB51 0ES ✎ 01651 873450 ⬩ glengarioch.com ◯ year-round 10.00–16.00 Mon–Sat, Apr–Oct 12.00–16.00 Sun. Scotland's most easterly distillery on the northern outskirts of Oldmeldrum is also one of its most colourful, with not one but four creation myths and a 20-year dalliance with tomatoes behind it. The tomatoes? Oh yes – Glen Garioch changed hands many times, and in 1971 Stanley P Morrison bought it from DCL. Innovative, environmentally friendly and conscious that energy prices were going through the roof, Morrison made the most of its gas bill by re-using waste heat to warm greenhouses and grow tomatoes. The venture lasted from 1973 to 1993. In the same year that the greenhouses were closed, so was the maltings which has now been converted into the visitor centre.

▶ *The imposing Lochnagar Mountain*
▼ *Glenglassaugh Distillery on the shoreline*

9 GLENGLASSAUGH

⌂ Potsoy, Banff AB45 2SQ ✎ 0131 335 5135 ⬩ glenglassaugh.com ◯ Apri–Oct 10.00–16.00 daily. Founded in 1875, Glenglassaugh is a distillery that has risen from the dead... twice. It was originally established by James Moir, a local businessman, and inherited by his nephews when he died. But in 1892 one of them died too, and the survivor sold up to the newly formed Highland Distilleries. Eventually in 2016 it was sold to the US company Brown-Forman, owner of many well-known brands including Jack Daniel's. Situated on the beach at Sandend Bay there is just one tour available but you can pay an additional £15 to enjoy a selection of their single malts.

10 ROYAL LOCHNAGAR

⌂ Crathie, Ballater AB35 5TB ✎ 01339 742700 ⬩ malts.com ◯ see website for details. In a pretty wooded glen just off the B976 and in the imposing shadow of the 1,160m (3,800ft) Lochnagar Mountain, Royal Lochnagar is only a

stone's throw from Balmoral as the crow flies…
or rather as the Queen and Prince Consort stroll.
For, only a few days after his royal neighbours had
moved in, New Lochnagar Distillery proprietor
John Begg dropped Prince Albert a note enquiring
whether he might perhaps care for a look around
the distillery. Begg was surprised, to put it mildly,
when Albert turned up at the door the very next
day with the Queen and a couple of royal offspring
in tow to take advantage of the offer. Immediately

the word 'new' on the signboard was painted out
and replaced with the word 'royal', and so it has
remained. Today it is the smallest distillery of
the 28 malt distilleries owned by Diageo, but it's
perfect for the visitor as everything is under one
roof. If you've got time, and you are interested
in railways, make sure you visit Ballater railway
station which, although it was destroyed by fire in
2015, has now been completely rebuilt and is fully
open to visitors.

MORAY

BREWERIES

11 SPEYSIDE BREWERY

⌂ 2 Greshop Rd, Forres IV36 2GU
✆ 01309 358082 ⌖ speysidebrewery.com
🕐 10.00–17.00 Mon–Fri; tours by appointment.
Surrounded by whisky distilleries and sharing
their water supply, Speyside Brewery was set up in
2012 because – well, sometimes what you want
is a beer, right? It's a brewery with a local flavour,
naming its brands after the area's icons and
landmarks: Bottle Nose, for example, named after
the pod of bottlenose dolphins that swim in the
nearby Firth, and Randolph's Leap, named after a
Moray beauty spot with a romantic legend. It has
also developed a very distinctive IPA, matured in
whisky casks to give it that extra kick.

12 WINDSWEPT BREWING CO

⌂ Unit B, 13 Coulardbank Industrial Estate,
Lossiemouth IV31 6NG ✆ 01343 814310
⌖ windsweptbrewing.com 🕐 10.00–17.00
Mon–Sat. While so many distillers are trying
to achieve barley-to-bottle control over their
operations, Windswept Brewing is going for
field-to-firkin by sourcing its raw materials locally
and creating a shorter supply chain. Started by
two ex-RAF pilots, Al Read and Nigel Tiddy, both
of whom enjoy outdoor pursuits, the distillery has
encouraged the promotion of both cycling and
running in the local area and finishing off with, of
course, a pint in the tap room.

GIN DISTILLERY

13 CAORUNN AT BALMENACH

⌂ Balmenach Rd, Cromdale, Grantown-on-Spey
PH26 3PF ✆ 01479 874933 ⌖ caorunngin.
com 🕐 tours start 11.00 & 14.00 Mon–Thu,
10.00 Fri. Closely associated with the Balmenach
whisky distillery, they've been making gin here
since way before the current gin trend took off –
although the venture isn't quite as old as some
of its equipment! Neutral grain spirit is pumped
into a unique copper 'berry chamber' where it is
vaporised. This chamber, a cylinder that is laid
on its side rather than upright, dates back to the
1920s and is a form of infusion still originally
used in the perfume industry. It has a copper
framework inside it to increase the precipitation
of sulphites for an exceptionally clean spirit – very
important in perfumery – and trays on which the
botanicals are left to infuse. The 11 botanicals
include six traditional ones along with five locally
foraged. The gin has now become a huge success
in the premium category.

WHISKY DISTILLERIES

14 ABERLOUR

⌂ Aberlour, Speyside AB38 9PJ ✆ 01340 881249
⌖ maltwhiskydistilleries.com 🕐 10.00–16.30
daily; book in advance. Water is a serious matter
around here and has been for centuries. In the
grounds of the distillery at the western end
of Aberlour's high street is St Drostan's Well,

▶ *Ballindalloch Distillery*

supposedly used by the 7th-century missionary to baptise local heathens and probably sacred, therefore, long before Drostan arrived. And before the distilling industry moved out of the shadows, the Spey and its tributaries were lined with watermills, grinding the barley for which this district was renowned. The water that concerns us, though, is the rainwater that filters through the granite slopes of the looming Ben Rinnes range, filling the springs of Aberlour and pure enough to be used untreated. It's not just the water that's taken seriously here: it's the visitor experience as well. The visitor centre, built in 2002, was always intended more for the connoisseur than the general tourist: standard tours take nearly two hours rather than the usual one.

. . . .

15 BALLINDALLOCH

Lagmore, Ballindalloch AB37 9AA ℘ 01807 500331 ⌨ ballindallochdistillery.com ☺ call ahead. The pretty much perfect Scottish baronial Ballindalloch Castle with its surrounding estate has long been one of the few attractions on Speyside that had little or nothing to do with whisky. The 16th-century castle itself, with its turrets and crenellations; the beautiful grounds; the golf; the wildlife; the country sports – this is the Scotland you've dreamed about. And to make it even more charming, Guy McPherson-Grant is the 23rd generation of his family to own it. The first new make ran in September 2014 from the stills he installed in a derelict farmhouse on the estate; and in April 2015 the Duke and Duchess of Rothesay (or, as they're known elsewhere, Prince Charles and Lady Camilla) popped in to cut the ribbon. The distillery takes its water from the nearby Garline Springs and all the barley used is grown on the estate. Unlike many new distilleries, Ballindalloch isn't trifling with gin or vodka or immature spirit: the intention is to give the maturing stocks at least eight years in oak before seeing how it has turned out.

. . . .

16 BALVENIE

See page 278.

16 BALVENIE

DOUBLEWOOD IS THE NAME OF THE GAME.

✉ Dufftown, Keith AB55 4DH ☎ 01340 822210 🖉 thebalvenie.com ⏱ call ahead.

So close to Glenfiddich (page 282) that they're almost a single site, for many years Balvenie played second fiddle to its slightly older sister. William Grant, the founder of both distilleries, was a canny man: he saved money by equipping Glenfiddich with secondhand stills, and when in 1893 he decided to build Balvenie (to cash in on a disastrous fire at Glenlivet (page 284) that led to a serious run on stock for blending), he not only picked up yet more cheap secondhand stills, he also found a cheap secondhand building. Balvenie New House had been designed by the brothers John, Robert and Adam Brothers – Scottish Neoclassical architects – in 1724 but had long been derelict: the distillery malting was fitted into part of it, while dressed stone from more ruinous parts was recycled to build the distillery itself.

During the last half-century while Glenfiddich was being established as Britain's most popular single malt, Balvenie was always regarded as more of a connoisseur's dram – indeed, one noted critic has described its 15 Years Old expression as 'the best whisky in Scotland'. And although Glenfiddich itself is now available in a multitude of expressions (one bottling was over a century old), Balvenie has always seemed the more exclusive and more traditional of the two. The distillery adopts certain rare crafts. It grows its own barley (and malts it

too, but only 15% of its requirements), has one of Scotland's few surviving old-fashioned floor maltings, has its own coppersmiths and coopers; and finally there is Malt Master David Stewart who makes the decisions as to which casks will be bottled after 12 years and those that will be held back to mature for their 21, 30 Years Old or even older.

The tour is one of the best offered in Scotland and because everything is done on site the visitor is able to gain a full understanding of how whisky is made. By offering only three tours a day and

"ONE NOTED CRITIC HAS DESCRIBED ITS 15 YEARS OLD EXPRESSION AS THE BEST WHISKY IN SCOTLAND"

restricting each to eight people, the tour guide is able to go into much more detail, answer questions in depth and give the visitor the opportunity to see real craftsmen at work. At the end of the tour you can bottle your very own Balvenie in warehouse 24.

The Balvenie has built its reputation on doublewood maturation, using ex-Bourbon as well as ex-sherry casks to create a very distinctive flavour profile. In addition it has introduced a 14 Years Old Caribbean cask (ex-rum) and a 21 Years

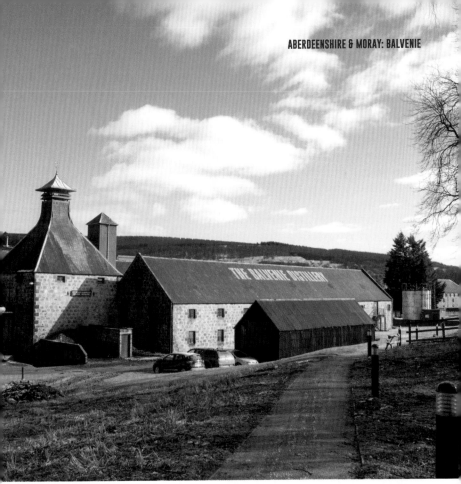

▲ *The pagoda roofs are a sign of traditional floor maltings*

Old Port Wood as part of the core range. The site is also home to another stillhouse, built in 1990 and christened Kininvie, whose washbacks are housed in an extension to the Balvenie building. Kininvie produces whisky for blending and only recently started to release single malts under its own name.

THE WHISKY The Classic Doublewood 12 Years Old 40% ABV, honeyed sultanas and grapes with Bourbon notes. Caribbean Cask 14 Years Old 43% ABV, Portwood 21 Years Old 40% ABV, and for something really special, try the 30 Years Old 47% ABV.

17 BENRIACH

⌂ Longmorn, Elgin IV36 3EB ✆ 01343 862888 ⟐ benriachdistillery.com ☺ Apr–Sep 10.00 & 16.00 Tue & Thu only; booking essential. Taken over by US company Brown-Forman in 2016, BenRiach soon appointed Rachel Barrie as master blender, who had been working with famous brands such as Glenmorangie (page 328), Ardbeg (page 304), Bowmore (page 302) and Laphroaig (page 311). At present there is not an established visitor centre but you can buy some whiskies in the small shop, after your tour.

18 BENROMACH

⌂ Invererne Rd, Forres IV30 8SJ ✆ 01309 675968 ⟐ benromach.com ☺ see website for details. A distillery with a distinctly chequered history, Benromach is one of an increasing number that have found their niche under independent and enthusiastic ownership. Acquired by the revered Elgin bottler Gordon & MacPhail, it has now been completely re-equipped. The new plant makes Benromach Speyside's smallest distillery

and one of its most visitable, too, with its award-winning Malt Whisky Centre complete with shop and a small museum. There are four tours to chose from and, if gin is your passion, then you can do a gin tour as they also produce Red Door gin on the premises.

19 CARDHU

⌂ Aberlour, Speyside AB38 7RY ✆ 01479 874635 ⟐ malts.com ☺ year-round – see website for details. They were good neighbours, John and Helen Cummings. Leasing Cardhu Farm in 1811, they promptly started making whisky illegally – Helen, according to legend, being the actual distiller – and when the gauger came they would sit him down to lunch while Helen went out with a big red flag to warn all the other moonshiners in the surrounding hills. Diageo, the present owner, has announced a huge investment in whisky tourism and Cardhu (previously called Cardow) will be among the beneficiaries. Despite the many new buildings, Cardhu's setting on rising ground overlooking the village of Knockando just off the B9102, its long views towards the hills and the retention of many charming stone warehouses and maltings, makes it a beautiful place to visit.

20 CRAGGANMORE

⌂ Cragganmore, Ballindalloch AB37 9AB ✆ 01479 874700 ⟐ malts.com ☺ Apr–Oct 10.00–17.00 daily. A smallish distillery whose product was always rated A1 by blenders, its

◀ *Benromach Distillery*
▶ *Bridge over the River Spey, Speyside*

single bottlings were never widely available, and Diageo surprised everyone except a handful of more knowledgeable aficionados by selecting it as Speyside's representative in its Classic Malt range in 1998. The quality of its output, combined with its tranquil location in a secluded glen overlooking the Spey near Bridge of Avon, make for a peaceful and informative visit, especially as it's not so well known and heavily frequented as some other Speyside distilleries. An upgrade to the Expressions tour earns you a tasting in the sumptuous Cragganmore Clubroom.

21 GLENALLACHIE

Aberlour AB38 9LR 01340 872547
theglenallachie.com Apr–Sep 10.00–16.00 Mon–Sat, Oct–Mar 10.00–16.00 Mon–Fri. Only

recently opened to the public, the distillery sits at the foot of Ben Rinnes and has taken on a completely new direction since being bought recently from the Chivas Brothers by master distiller Billy Walker and other investors. As part of the deal they also took on two blended Scotch brands, MacNair's and White Heather, which they intend to expand, including releasing a 21 Years Old blend. The fact that the distillery is small allows visitors to talk directly to production staff – with a choice of two tours, 'The Wee' and 'The Connoisseurs'.

22 GLENFARCLAS

Ballindalloch AB37 9BD 01807 500345
glenfarclas.com for tour details, see the website. Scotland only has two or three whisky companies that could be called 'family firms' in the

sense that the direct descendants of the founders still own or at least control them. One is William Grant of Glenfiddich; John Grant – no relation – is another. The Glenfarclas Distillery in Ballindalloch on the A95 five miles south of Aberlour was already 30 years old when John Grant bought it in 1865. But being family doesn't mean the Grants are stuffy: they opened a visitor centre way back in 1973, decorating it with panelling taken from an ocean liner, RMS *Empress of Australia*; they were also pioneers in developing a huge range of 'expressions' – bottling of various ages, strengths and finishes – which has been copied by many distilleries today. They are also well known for their 'sherry bomb' finishes – you should try the 10 Years Old which has a full and rich sherry finish, with a hint of fruit cake and citrus.

23 GLENFIDDICH

✉ Dufftown AB55 4DH ✏ 01340 820373 ✒ glenfiddich.com ◷ 10.00–16.00; for tours call ahead. Here at the home of the world's best-known malt whisky they will regale you with the biography of its founder, the truly remarkable William Grant. Born in 1839, the son of an ex-soldier, he worked his way up from farm boy to apprentice cobbler to distillery book-keeper, learning and saving as he went, until at the age of nearly 50 he seized the chance to buy a couple of clapped-out old pot stills at a bargain price, lease a bit of land and build a distillery of his own (and pretty much on his own, too, although all his seven sons were dragooned into labouring for him). William Grant died aged 89 in 1923, but the company is still owned and run by his direct descendants, and they have never

stopped innovating. In 1969 the distillery became the first to open its doors to the world when it created a visitor centre – recently refurbished at a cost of nearly £2 million.

24 GLENLIVET

See page 284.

25 GLEN GRANT

✉ Rothes, Aberlour AB38 7BS ✏ 01340 832118 ✒ glengrant.com ◷ see website for details. Meet the oldest of three dynasties of Grants. The brothers James and John founded Glen Grant in 1840 having previously leased the original Aberlour and (reputedly) distilled illegally on the family farm. The brothers were very forward-looking: they were influential in the building of the local railway line in 1851, and Glen Grant had the first electric lighting in the Highlands when a generator was installed in 1861. As one of the most handsome and elegant of Scottish distilleries, with its baronial-style pepperpot turrets and crowstep gables, Glen Grant was crying out to be opened to the public long before 2008, when a brand-new visitor centre was finally built in the old coach house and the fabulous 22-acre gardens were opened to the public. Glen Grant is also very much about Dennis Malcolm, who started working at the distillery when he was just 15 and is still there 50 years later making sure, as master distiller, that the whisky produced is of the highest quality. So why not try the core 10 Years Old 40% ABV, with hints of vanilla and toffee apple.

▶ *The gardens at Glen Grant Distillery*

24 GLENLIVET

HEY GEORGE, WHERE YOU GOING WITH THAT GUN IN YOUR HAND?

✉ Ballindalloch AB37 9DB ✆ 01340 821720 ✎ maltwhiskydistilleries.com ✆ Feb–Nov 09.30–18.00 daily.

One of Scotch whisky's biggest names, The Glenlivet was founded in 1823 by one of Scotch whisky's biggest characters, George Smith. The valley of the Livet, 14 miles long and six wide, was home to a reputed 200 illegal distillers before the Excise Act, and its whiskies were traded far and wide almost openly. The Smith family of Upper Drumin Farm, high on the barley-growing plateau, was no better than its neighbours and seems to have been moonshining since the 1770s; but sensing the opportunity presented by the 1823 Excise Act, George became the first distiller in Scotland to take out a licence.

This did not endear him to his neighbours, who saw that their business was being taken away; but permanently armed with a pair of pistols presented to him by the Laird of Aberlour (he only ever fired them in anger once, and that was to scare a braggart), George prospered. In the 1840s he leased a second distillery to cope with demand; but even two were not enough, and a new, much bigger plant was planned on a new site near the farm. Then in 1858 Upper Drumin was burnt down, so the new distillery on today's site at Minmore was completed in a rush.

Glenlivet remained family-owned until 1953, when it merged with J&J Grant of Glen Grant

(page 282) fame; 20 years later it merged again, this time with Longmorn. Then in 1977 at a time of depression in the world market, it was sold to Seagram and thus found its way into the hands of its current owner, Pernod-Ricard subsidiary Chivas Brothers. Today it is the number-one distillery in Scotland, with the capacity to make up to 21 million litres of new make a year; and it rides at number two for the most Scotch malt sold annually.

> **"THE VALLEY OF THE LIVET, 14 MILES LONG AND SIX WIDE, WAS HOME TO A REPUTED 200 ILLEGAL DISTILLERS"**

In 2015, many Glenlivet fans were appalled when the distillery announced that it would no longer make their bestselling 12 Years Old and that it would be replaced with a no-age statement whisky called Founder's Reserve. The problem was that like many other distilleries there was not enough aged stock. However, it still went on to become a very popular brand and some years later the 12 Years Old was reintroduced.

The distillery has doubled in size recently, and despite its dramatic setting on its windswept plateau, it isn't what you'd call picturesque.

▲ *A sculpture made from whisky bottles in the visitor centre*

Something very different from other distilleries is their Whisky Food Safari where award-winning writer and broadcaster Ghillie Basan gives a unique introduction to food pairings with Glenlivet whiskies, which she demonstrates in her own home.

THE WHISKY The classic Founder's Reserve, 12 Years Old 40% ABV, sharp plum with apricot and wine notes. If you want something different try The Nàdurra Oloroso NAS, cask strength at 59.1% ABV.

MALT 3

THRIFT IS ANY GREAT WHISKY'S SECRET INGREDIENT. WELL, THEY ARE BOTH SCOTTISH.

Barley's ability to flourish in poor soils and rotten weather is responsible for one of the greatest treats the human palate can ever hope to relish: single malt Scotch whisky. And those of you who believe that the monarch of the glen with his spreading antlers or the gleaming silvery salmon of loch and burn are the source of Scotland's finest contribution to world gastronomy need only gaze on a field of barley ready for the scythe to know that here is the country's real gold.

"SURELY IT CAN ONLY BE A MATTER OF TIME BEFORE WE ARE OFFERED A WHISKY MASHED WITH AMBER MALT, OR MILD ALE MALT OR VIENNA MALT"

The rolling hills of eastern Scotland, sheltered by mountains from the worst Atlantic weather, can sometimes seem like a great ocean swell of barley, and it's easy to imagine such bounty going to fill the huge industrial grain stills and lager breweries of the Central Belt. On the other hand, western Scotland is a different matter. The broken terrain and thin, often stony soil seem an unlikely starting point for a delicacy based on cereals of any kind. But the 'townships' or semi-cooperative villages that characterised the Highlands before the Clearances operated a system of transhumance – that is, driving their sheep and cattle to upland pastures over the summer, but bringing them down again after the harvest to overwinter on the township's patch of arable pasture. The arable land was therefore both well-trodden and well-manured, making for fertile soil that could produce surprisingly good yields of high-nitrogen barley; and the higher the nitrogen content, the more briskly and reliably the mash would ferment.

In many areas – and this is something that surprises many people – access to fuel was a real problem before coalmining was in full swing in the late 18th century. True, there were trees everywhere. However, demand for timber was so great – not just for housebuilding and fuel – but for shipbuilding, carts and wagons. Wood was also in demand for furniture, tools and implements of all shapes and sizes – from the handle of a hammer to the frame of a plough – as well as for all sorts of packaging, from jewellery boxes to beer barrels. There simply wasn't enough for malting. Many Scottish maltsters – and Irish, too – would therefore use peat to dry their grain. Depending on its make-up, peat contains phenolic compounds that smell and taste 'smoky' – ie: like Dettol – and many malt distillers, most famously those on Islay but also Talisker on Skye, Highland Park on Orkney and also Ardmore from Huntly on the far eastern side of the country, still make strongly phenolic whiskies from peat-dried malt.

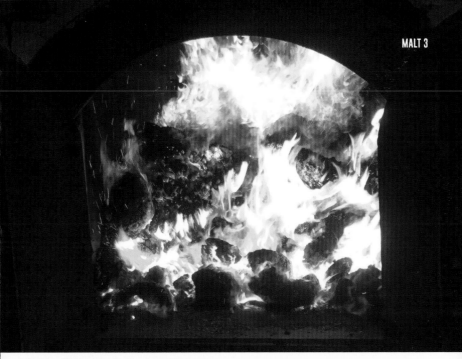

▲ *The kiln at Highland Park Distillery (page 340), burning peat*

One modern characteristic of distillers' malt that comes to us from those days is that it's as light as possible – as light as pale ale and lager malts, in fact. That's for a number of historic reasons: to keep the cost down, especially where a lot of charcoal was used; to rein in the peatiness; and also to charge the still with a (relatively) neutral wash that would bring its own character to the spirit but would also allow the oak room to express itself. In the brewing industry, malt is processed and kilned in all manner of ways to brew a gamut from lagers that are virtually colourless and flavourless to great big reddish-black barley wines. In the world of whisky, that's the function of oak; only recently have small artisan distillers started experimenting with ale and lager malts, but surely it can only be a matter of time before we are offered a whisky mashed with amber malt, or mild ale malt or Vienna malt.

Talking of artisan distillers, a last word on whisky malt. In history it was usual for whisky distillers to make their mash by maceration – that is, they didn't strain the wash off the grains before fermenting it. Maceration makes for a much more efficient extraction and a faster ferment. It's still part of the standard process in American rye distilleries but is long obsolete in Scotland. It was revived briefly by the Loch Ewe microdistillery, now closed and awaiting a buyer; again, it can only be a matter of time…

26 GLEN MORAY

Bruceland Rd, Elgin IV30 1YE
01343 550900 glenmoray.com see website for details. As Speyside's principal town, Elgin might almost be called the Capital of Whisky, but it only has one distillery actually within its bounds – Glen Moray. And not unnaturally, with Elgin full of tourists, Glen Moray is very welcoming to visitors. The last ten years have seen a transformation at the distillery with their core range gaining market share so make sure you try the 12 Years Old, giving you vanilla, pear drops and summer fruits. The positioning of the distillery in the Laich O'Moray gives it a good protection and allows even maturation in the warehouses.

27 KNOCKDHU

Knock, Huntly AB54 7LJ 01466 771223 ancnoc.com tours 10.00 & 14.00 Mon–Fri, call ahead. Standing over 305m (1,000ft) up on the slopes of the picturesque Knock Hills from which the distillery draws its water, Knockdhu's grey stone warehouse has something of the look of a hillfort on the Northwest frontier and indeed (purely coincidentally) it did actually serve as a barracks for Indian troops during World War II. It was bought and reopened by Inver House Distillers in 1989 and is now once again working hard for its living. Very hard, in fact, since in its new incarnation it produces not only fillings but also a very distinguished bottled range under the AnCnoc umbrella; An Cnoc being Gaelic for 'Knock Hills'. The AnCnoc family embraces possibly a wider selection of ages, finishes, expressions, vintages, special bottling and limited editions than any

other across the entire spectrum of characters – from menacingly dark and peaty to light-bodied, summery and lemony – making Knockdhu's tasting room the end point of every discerning whisky-lover's tour of choice.

28 STRATHISLA

Seafield Av, Keith, AB55 5BS
01542 783044 maltwhiskydistilleries. com Easter–Oct 10.00–18.00, Nov–Easter 10.00–16.30. Scotland's oldest operating distillery (and one of its prettiest) was founded by two local businessmen in a former mill on the banks of the River Isla in 1786 in an attempt to exploit the 1784 Wash Act that reduced the duty levied on small-scale Highland distillers. The visitor centre with its luxurious Dram Room was opened in 1995 as a showcase for the Chivas Regal blend and its family of expressions, but Strathisla as a single malt is also available at 12 Years Old in the brown bottle in which it has been sold since the 1920s. It is hugely prized by connoisseurs and is often described as Scotland's best-kept secret.

29 THE MACALLAN

See page 290.

30 THE SPEYSIDE COOPERAGE

Dufftown Rd, Craigellachie AB38 9RS
01340 871108 speysidecooperage.co.uk
09.00–15.30 Mon–Fri. The cooperage doesn't actually make any whisky, but if it wasn't here nobody else would either, because it takes three

▶ *A cooper at work in the Speyside Cooperage*

years in oak to make whisky into a single malt. Founded in 1947, it now has operations in Alloa, Scotland, as well as Kentucky and Ohio. Situated in the village of Craigellachie at the confluence of the two rivers most closely connected to the Scotch whisky industry, the Spey and the Fiddich, it repairs and refurbishes but also makes more than 100,000 hogsheads, butts, casks and puncheons a year. The coopers here still use traditional instruments, and judge their work entirely by eye. You can enjoy a dram of its very own 10 Years Old single malt in the coffee shop.

29 THE MACALLAN

FIVE HILLS TAKE SHAPE FOR THE NEW DISTILLERY.

✉ Easter Elchies, Craigellachie AB38 9RX ✆ 01340 318000 🌐 themacallan.com ⏱ 09.30–18.00 daily; book tours online.

The Macallan is whisky aristocracy. But although it was one of the first distilleries in the region established after the 1823 Excise Act, what you actually see when you arrive… well, it's more a hi-tech hobbit hole than a stately home.

Now one of Scotland's most highly regarded single malts, The Macallan was actually a bit ho-hum for its first 140 or so years. It changed hands a few times in its early history, then achieved a respectable stability in the early 20th century as a family trust that just plodded along. In the 1960s, though, a new management set about galvanising the old place, doubling its size and taking two pioneering decisions: first, to revive the extinct practice of finishing the whisky in old sherry casks; and second, promoting it as a single malt rather than just a blender's favourite.

> **"THE ROOFS ARE CLAD WITH TURF TO CREATE THE ILLUSION OF A RANGE OF GRASSY HILLS"**

The new, richer flavour, although deplored by some, was an instant hit. Equally quickly, The Macallan's world-beating potential attracted investors including Japanese distiller Suntory, which bought a 25% stake in 1986. Some ten years later it was bought by Highland Distillers and is today a stablemate of Highland Park in the Edrington Group. Despite all the adulation,

though, and despite its picture-postcard setting in the Elchies Forest just west of Craigellachie with views over the Spey to Ben Rinnes, the distillery was slow to throw its doors open to the public. To be honest, it wasn't actually all that attractive and a visitor centre didn't come until 2001. When it did, it was a huge success.

If you visited then, though, what you see now will totally blow your mind. Work started in 2014 on a totally new £140 million-plus plant as revolutionary in design and construction as the Adnams (page 156) distribution centre – and just as respectful to poor old Mother Earth. The successive phases of production are laid out in a series of cells, each with its own conical roof. The roofs are clad with turf to create the illusion

of a range of grassy hills. It's not just pretty, it's also a near-perfect insulator and, to cap it all, the heating and electricity are supplied by a £74 million biomass generator that also supplies low-carbon electricity to 20,000 homes.

The new plant produces 15 million litres a year, compared with the 9.5 million litres that the old (mothballed) plant could turn out. And the development also includes a completely new immersive visitor exhibition, a gallery and a café.

THE WHISKY Sherry Oak 12 Years Old 40% ABV, buttery with hints of Christmas cake and oranges. Double Cask 12 Years Old 40% ABV, where European and American sherry oak casks have been used for the maturation. Triple Cask 12 Years Old 40% ABV, allows gingerbread and vanilla to come through.

▲ *The Macallan collection*
◄ *The visitor centre and the five hills shape visible*

STILLS

FOR CENTURIES, DISTILLING HAS LED THE WAY IN SCIENCE AND TECHNOLOGY. IF THAT'S NOT WORTH A DRAM, WHAT IS?

It could be argued that distillation is the foundation of all practical science because the first humans to melt, by some now unimaginable accident, pure copper from its ore and then repeat the process deliberately were also the first humans to control the shape and nature of their world by brain rather than brawn. The manipulation of temperature was the key, for the discovery that all substances had their own melting, evaporation and condensation points made it possible to separate the desirable fraction from the dross. Metallurgy was just one form of distillation routinely practised in the ancient world; salt evaporation was another since it allowed the preservation of meat. The extraction of essential oils and volatiles from all sorts of plant matter was a third.

"COPPER BECAME THE USUAL MATERIAL AFTER DISTILLATION WENT SECULAR IN THE 16TH CENTURY"

The evaporation of ethanol from wine, however, was not a discovery of the ancient world but of the 8th-century Arab Enlightenment when the Persian chemist Abū Mūsā Jābir ibn Hayyān (721–815), known as the Father of Chemistry, first identified the flammable vapours given off by a boiling flask of wine and salt. His successor Al Razi (854–925), known to Christendom as Rhazes, appears to have been the first to condense these vapours into liquid ethanol. The name given to the apparatus capable of both evaporation and condensation – alembic – was derived from the Greek *ambix* or cup, suggesting that the Arab and Persian chemists were working with the same equipment that the Byzantines had used to make cosmetics and perfumes.

It is probable that these early alchemists used earthenware vessels since heat-resistant glassware only became widespread in the 14th and 15th centuries: fragments of glass alembics are routinely found in the ruins of abbeys and monasteries where infirmarers used them to make medicines. Copper became the usual material after distillation went secular in the 16th century, at which time distillers were making large volumes of beverage for sale rather than small quantities of physic for prescription-adapted brewing and household coppers for use as stills. But, although the materials and scale changed, the kit remained essentially unaltered: the still itself in which the alcoholic wash was boiled; the neck that collected the vapour; the worm or coiled copper tube that passed through a tub of cold water to recondense the alcoholic fraction of the vapour; and the receiver into which the spirit eventually dripped. The spirit had to be passed through the pot-still two or three times to get up to full strength, the

▲ *The pot stills at Highland Park (page 340) – on the left the pair of spirit stills and on the right the wash stills*

first pass producing 'low wines' of 25–30% ABV; and on each pass the stillman had to collect the first and last runnings separately because they were full of poisons such as methanol, which can make you blind. Furthermore, batch distilling leaves in the finished spirit a lot of aromatics from the original wash – most famously the peaty smokiness in malt whiskies like Laphroaig (page 311) – so that only the best and most expensive ingredients can be used (and which is why the pot-still is even now preferred by makers of single malt Scotch whisky, Cognac and most other prestige spirits).

The column, continuous or Coffey still, patented in 1830 by Aeneas Coffey, overcame these drawbacks to produce spirits of near-total purity from wash fermented from any old thing. It's a heat-exchanging loop into which the wash is continually pumped, vaporised by high-pressure steam, and then recondensed in a rectifying column. Each fraction of the wash has its own condensing temperature, so all the fractions – good and bad – can be liquefied and collected separately. The advantages are obvious; the disadvantage is the product has little if any character of its own and has to be processed or blended. To make vodka the pure spirit has to be filtered through charcoal; to make gin it has to be redistilled with botanicals; to make Scotch it has to be aged in oak for at least three years and then blended with single malts. And if you happen to visit a distillery where these huge and ingenious heat-exchangers are at work, then reflect on this: if they hadn't been invented, scarcely one of us would ever be able to afford spirits at all.

CHAPTER FIFTEEN
ARGYLL & THE ISLES

ISLE OF MULL

ARGYLL & BUTE

COLONSAY

JURA

ISLAY

CAMPBELTOWN

ARGYLL & BUTE

BREWERY

1 FYNE ALES

✉ Achadunan, Cairndow PA26 8BJ ✆ 01499 600120 🖰 fyneales.com 🕒 year-round 11.30, 12.30, 13.30, 14.30 & 15.30 daily. Situated on the Achadunan Estate, the brewery is part of a farm and the intention has always been to provide jobs but also to attract tourism. In a classic example of how to use your spent grain in the brewing process the owners invested in 27 Highland cattle that are now fed this very high-protein feed. The stunning 4,500-acre site is also home to sheep and a herd of red deer. A large range of beers are produced every year; some are small batch or one-offs but they also produce all year-round ones such as Jarl 3.8% ABV – a citra session blonde, Avalanche 4.5% ABV – a traditional pale ale, and Highlander 4.8% ABV – an amber ale.

▼ *The skyline of Oban*

WHISKY DISTILLERY

2 OBAN

⌂ Stafford St, Oban PA34 5NH ✎ 01631 572004 ✐ malts.com ☺ see website for details. Known as the 'gateway to the isles', Oban is the ferry port for both the Inner and Outer Hebrides and is also the point of departure for much closer islands such as Kerrera and Lismore. Although one of Diageo's smallest distilleries, Oban's whisky always features in their annual Special Releases and has a very light flavour as a result of long contact with the copper stills. Once it opened its doors to the public, the Sensory and Flavour Finding tour was soon attracting 35,000 visitors a year. There's also a more luxurious Exclusive Distillery Tour offering comparative tastings of different bottlings, or you can go for the top tour which is led by the distillery manager. If you are a fan of *Game of Thrones* then make sure you try one of the licensed bottlings such as the Night's Watch Oban Bay Reserve 43% ABV, giving you toffee, cereal and a hint of peat.

CAMPBELTOWN

GIN DISTILLERY

3 BEINN AN TUIRC

⌂ Lephincorrach Farm, Torrisdale, Carradale PA28 6QT ☏ 01583 431528 ✆ Kintyregin.com ⊙ shop 11.00–16.00 Mon–Sat, 12.00–15.00 Sun; check their website for tour availability. Beinn an Tuirc, or Wild Boar's Hill distillery, was installed in the old piggery buildings on the 1,200-acre Torrisdale Castle Estate in 2016. As well as ten commonly used botanicals its Kintyre Gin adds two that are grown on the estate: Icelandic moss and sheep sorrel, which give a spicy nose with floral notes in the finish. The estate enjoys stunning views over Kilbrannan Sound and out towards the Isle of Arran, and it has three self-catering cottages and a flat in the castle itself, all powered by sustainable electricity.

WHISKY DISTILLERIES

4 GLENGYLE

⌂ 9 Bolgam St, PA28 6HZ ☏ 01586 551710 ✆ kilkerran.scot/tours ⊙ year-round 11.30 & 13.30 Mon–Sat. Glengyle has a somewhat complicated history of ownership in that William Mitchell founded the distillery in 1872 and by 1919 had sold it, but 75 years later a descendant of his – the owner of the neighbouring Springbank – bought it back again out of mothballs, but didn't buy back the name with it. Glengyle is therefore now the home of Kilkerran single malt. A limited

range at the moment but try the 12 Years Old with peaty fruit notes; a heavily peated expression has also been released. All the malting of the barley for both distilleries is done at Springbank to create another of the barley-to-bottle enterprises that are becoming so popular in the independent sector.

5 GLEN SCOTIA

⌂ 12 High St, PA28 6DS ☏ 01586 552288 ✆ glenscotia.com ⊙ tours 11.30, 13.30 & 15.00 Mon–Fri, 11.30 & 15.00 Sat; shop 10.00–17.00 Mon–Sat. Prohibition in the US from January 1920 cut off a key whisky market, while Britain's return to the gold standard in 1925 made exports more expensive in general. In 1928 Glen Scotia became one of the 20 Campbeltown distilleries that closed between the wars and is supposedly haunted by the ghost of its then owner, the 81-year-old Duncan MacCallum, who was found

▲ *Casks awaiting filling at Glen Scotia Distillery*
▶ *View of Campbeltown*

298

drowned two years later having been tricked out of £40,000 by a gang of fraudsters. Unlike other Campbeltown distilleries, Glen Scotia reopened in 1933, the year Prohibition was repealed, supplying the very heavy, oily, peaty malt so prized by American blenders because it only needed to be used sparingly.

....

6 SPRINGBANK

✉ 9 Bolgam St, PA28 6HZ ✆ 01586 552009 ⬙ springbank.scot ⊙ tours Apr–Oct 10.00, 11.30, 13.30 & 15.00 Mon–Sat. For many whisky-lovers, Springbank would be the last dram before dying. Of all Campbeltown's malt distilleries it has suffered the fewest periods of being shutdown – it was silent during the latter years of Prohibition and again, briefly, in the 1980s – but the reputation of today's whiskies is towering. The distillery was founded by the Mitchell family in the 1820s and is still owned by a direct descendant. But Springbank doesn't only produce Springbank. Occasionally it peats its malt to make Longrow and by way of contrast it has also revived the name of another long-gone Campbeltown distillery, Hazelburn, for an unpeated, triple-distilled malt of contrasting delicacy. If you are looking for a really intensive in-depth introduction to whisky making, Springbank, every year, runs a Whisky School. Taking place over five days you will experience every stage of whisky production from helping to turn the malt right through to filling bottles.

COLONSAY

GIN DISTILLERY

7 WILD THYME SPIRITS
See page 300.

7 WILD THYME SPIRITS

COLONSAY – WHERE EVERY HOME HAS ITS OWN FRIENDLY SPIRIT.

⌂ Tigh na Uruisg PA61 7YR ✐ 01951 200082 ✐ wildthymespirits.com ⏱ 12.00–16.00 Tue–Thu & Sat; tours must be booked in advance.

Colonsay is only eight miles long and three wide with a population of just 135. Its unspoilt natural beauty and sandy beaches are among the reasons why so many tourists make the arduous journey. The wildlife is tremendously varied, making it a firm favourite with naturalists and birders too. You can either catch a ferry from Oban every day in summer and Monday, Wednesday and Saturday in winter or you can fly from Oban with Hebridean Air Services (✐ hebrideanair.co.uk). If you arrive without transport there's a limited bus around the island.

Finlay and Eileen Geekie – he an architect, she an HR professional – from Oxfordshire had owned a cottage here since 2007 before moving in permanently in 2016. Some work needed to be done to the place: the original building was demolished and rebuilt from scratch to create

Tigh na Uruisg, or 'Home of the Brownie'. Every house on Colonsay has its own friendly spirit, or in Gaelic 'Uruisg', to help with the household chores, although you won't see them because they only work at night. They tend to become attached to particular families or houses, and the two here, Doughal and Ferghus, are very helpful. And, of course, Tigh na Uruisg has a very different kind of spirit as well...

"THE WILDLIFE IS TREMENDOUSLY VARIED, MAKING IT A FIRM FAVOURITE WITH NATURALISTS AND BIRDERS TOO"

Along with the distillery tours Finlay and Eileen offer a long weekend with a difference. They aim to increase production at the distillery to provide work not only for islanders, but for incomers from the mainland as well, and perhaps persuade some of them to stay. So they have set up a Gin Lover's Retreat that provides full board for four people over a long weekend and includes sampling some of the 200 gins they keep in stock in addition to their own.

Their gin is based on the traditional juniper berry but many other botanicals are added including angelica root, calamus root and coriander. The others remain a trade secret.

THE GIN At 48% ABV the gin gives you strong juniper notes before the flavour develops into a delicate balance of spice, pepper and lemon sherbet.

ISLAY

BREWERY

8 ISLAY ALES

✉ Islay House Sq, Bridgend PA44 7NZ
✆ 01496 810014 🖫 islayales.com 🕒 tours
by arrangement. Founded in 2004, Islay Ales
is the only brewery on the island and is easily
outnumbered by its nine distilleries. (Although
you could argue that each of them is a brewery in
its own right.) A tiny four-barrel plant produces a
regular range of ten cask and bottle-conditioned
ales, some of them peated (well, this is Islay!), as
well as specials for the annual Feis Ile Festival to
celebrate Gaelic song and language that is held
every year towards the end of May.

WHISKY DISTILLERIES

9 ARDBEG
See page 304.

10 ARDNAHOE
✉ Port Askaig, Islay PA46 7RN ✆ 01496
840777 🖫 ardnahoedistillery.com 🕒 Mar–Oct
09.30–17.30 Mon–Sat, 10.00–17.30 Sun; food
served 09.30–11.00 Mon–Sat & 10.00–11.00 Sun.
A strikingly modern and indeed brand-new star
joined the constellation of Islay distilleries when
Ardnahoe was opened in 2018. Behind the venture
is Glasgow-based independent blender and bottler
Hunter Laing, founded five years earlier by whisky
veteran Stuart Laing, Bruichladdich-trained, and

his sons Andrew and Scott. The company had built
up a formidable stock of malts of all styles and
ages but still required a reliable source of whisky
stocks, so they decided to create their own. But
this is no perfunctory factory. It's designed, and
when you sit in the Illicit Still restaurant – or, even
better, on its balcony – and gaze across the Sound
towards the Paps of Jura and the Isles of Mull and
Jura, you'll know what designed means. Why, the
place even has its own tartan.

11 BOWMORE
✉ School St, Bowmore PA43 7JS ✆ 01496
810441 🖫 bowmore.com 🕒 Mar–Oct
09.30–18.00 Mon–Sat, 12.00–16.00 Sun, Oct–
Dec 10.00–17.00 Mon–Sat. Situated in the centre
of Islay's largest town, Bowmore was founded in
1799 by a farmer and 'merchant' (ie: legal dealer)
called Simson and is therefore Islay's oldest
distillery. The original building was later torn
down and enlarged, and what you see today was
built in about 1840 mostly of concrete – the first
such construction in local history. In the 1950s a
flooded warehouse became the town's swimming
pool using waste heat from the still.
As with so many other distilleries, housing was
once provided for the workers and five of these
cottages have been converted into holiday lets.
This is also one of the few distilleries left in
Scotland – or anywhere else for that matter –
where you can see a traditional floor maltings in
operation.

12 BRUICHLADDICH
See page 308.

▲ *Bunnahabhain Distillery is well situated for stunning views over the Sound of Islay*

13 BUNNAHABHAIN

✉ Port Askaig PA46 7RP ✆ 01496 840557
🖥 bunnahabhain.com ⊙ Apr–Oct 09.00–17.00
Mon–Sat, 11.00–16.00 Sun. One of Scotland's
harder-to-spell distilleries, Bunnahabhain has
the most beautiful setting on the Sound of Islay
overlooking the island of Jura, and sits a few miles
up a single-track lane from Port Askaig amid a tiny
hamlet of former workers' cottages. The place is
so remote – and Port Askaig, the nearest source

of diversion, is certainly no metropolis – that
a holiday spent there would be a meditative
experience indeed. Like all Islay's distilleries,
Bunnahabhain sits right on the seafront and still
has its pier, built in 1887, where steamers known
as 'puffers' unloaded the necessary malt and
loaded up the finished whisky. Although famous
for its unpeated malt, Bunnahabhain has recently
introduced a much more peaty bottling – Toiteach
– which is Gaelic for 'smoky'.

9 ARDBEG

ARDBEGGIANS – THOSE WHO ENJOY THE TASTE OF ARDBEG.

✉ Port Ellen PA42 7EA ✆ 01496 302244 🖊 ardbeg.com 🕐 check website for café opening hours & tour details; tours must be booked in advance.

▲ *The distillery situated on the south side of Islay – on a clear day you can see Northern Ireland*

The last three miles of the A846 might well be called Whisky Boulevard, since this short stretch of road passes three of Islay's best-known distilleries: first Laphroaig; then Lagavulin; and finally, just where the route turns into the narrow lane to Kindalton – Ardbeg.

Like many distilleries, Ardbeg was licensed in the early 19th century when legislative reform was driving the small semi-legal or plain illegal distiller out of business and favouring the formation of larger commercial concerns. The farmer here, John MacDougall, may have been a moonshiner himself – certainly the cove on which Ardbeg stands had previously been used by smugglers.

By 1981 it was mothballed and in a very sorry state after several changes of ownership, but fortunately in 1997 it was bought by the Highland distiller Glenmorangie (page 328). It is now back in full production, turning out some of Islay's most gloriously and unapologetically peaty malt whiskies from a site in a rugged cove that seems to epitomise all the island's distilleries. The long, low warehouse fronting the sea – almost in the sea at high tide – is kept painted a gleaming white, as much to protect the old stone from the constant salt spray as for any aesthetic reason. At the end of its track and with scarcely a human habitation in sight, the distillery seems far remoter and more

▲ *The distillery with casks waiting to be filled*

self-contained than it really is — it could be a Newfoundland or South Georgia whaling station just as easily as a Scottish distillery. Back in the 19th century all the barley was delivered by ship, which is why all the coastal distilleries on Islay have their names clearly marked in huge black letters on the white walls of their warehouses.

"TURNING OUT SOME OF ISLAY'S MOST GLORIOUSLY AND UNAPOLOGETICALLY PEATY MALT WHISKIES"

As well as guided tours, Ardbeg has the Old Kiln Café serving snacks and light meals. And if you really want to immerse yourself then you can stay at Seaview Cottage, the former home of the distillery manager, which sleeps up to six with

dramatic views from the balcony over towards Campbeltown and the Mull of Kintyre. Can't make it in person? Ardbeg Day forms part of Feis Ile, the annual Islay Festival held in the last week of May, and you don't have to be on Islay to celebrate as The Ardbeg Committee, or Ardbeggians, with more than 120,000 members, organises events throughout the world.

THE WHISKY The 10 Years Old 46% ABV, packs an enormous punch with powerful peat followed by vanilla, citrus and sea spray notes. Corryvreckan, named after the nearby whirlpool, moves away from the conventional Ardbeg and more towards a medicinal flavour to give you spicy, fresh fruit and some smoke.

NICHE SPIRITS

ARTISAN DISTILLING DIDN'T START WITH GIN. IT STARTED WITH FRUIT.

Dreadful expressions and rickety portmanteaus such as 'ginaissance' and 'gincredible', plus the mad proliferation of gin rectifiers, gin brands and gin variants, might mislead the casual observer into thinking that gin is the bedrock of the craft distilling revolution. Perhaps surprisingly, that wasn't the case on either side of the Atlantic. In both England and America the initial excitement was all about unusual speciality spirits, often with a pleasing element of eccentricity.

"THE LICENSING OF SOMERSET ROYAL IN 1989 WAS THE STARTING GUN FOR THE CRAFT DISTILLING REVOLUTION IN BRITAIN"

In the United States the pioneer was a German lawyer by the name of Jörg Rupf whose family had distilled their own Obstbrands for generations and who, inspired by the food and drink culture of San Francisco, bought a small still and in 1982 founded St George's Spirits. He quickly proved himself to be a master of both tradition and innovation, and his small-batch eau de vie of raspberries, pears, cherries and other locally grown fruits won him headlines, awards and a big following.

It was a different story in Britain, where the King Offa Distillery was founded at the Hereford Cider Museum (page 116) in 1984 to revive a different kind of fruit eau de vie: apple brandy. The museum

had been co-founded by Bertram Bulmer, retired but restless chairman of the eponymous cider giant, who installed an antique alembic ambulant or travelling still from Normandy as a working exhibit to recall the years from the 1660s to the 1820s, when cider was distilled both for the private enjoyment of the landed gentry and to be shipped in quantity to the taverns of the capital; it would also raise funds for the museum.

King Offa attracted media attention not only as a novelty but also because of the struggle Bulmer had to wage against the inertia and obfuscation of Customs & Excise to get the distillery licensed. One of the people he inspired was Julian Temperley of Burrow Hill Cider (page 44) in Somerset, who faced similar bureaucratic hurdles including the rediscovery of an ancient regulation dictating that the cidermaking and distilling must be carried out at different premises. The first still – French, like King Offa's – was therefore installed at a stately home called Brympton D'Evercy not far from Yeovil. Next the European Commission weighed in: cider brandy, it said, was not a legal definition. It must be apple brandy. It took perseverance and a certain amount of bloody-mindedness to overcome these obstacles, character traits that Temperley, like Bulmer, possessed in abundance.

The licensing of Somerset Royal in 1989 was the real starting gun for the craft distilling revolution in Britain, with HM Customs & Excise (now HM

▲ *Penderyn Distillery still house (page 208)*

Revenue & Customs) realising that craft distillers were not lunatics but potentially valuable sources of revenue, and 'reinterpreting' obstructive regulations would speed up its procedures. It helped that most of the new distillers were in Scotland – Speyside (1990), Isle of Arran (1995) and Kilchoman and Loch Ewe (both 2004) – where local customs were used to overseeing distillery licences. Many of these first-generation craft distillers showed a suitable wackiness. Loch Ewe was a reproduction of an 18th-century bothy distillery with a still less than a tenth of the legal minimum capacity. Penderyn (page 208) in Brecon, opened in 2000, and was Wales's first operational distillery for more than a century, while St George's in Norfolk (2006) was the first whisky distillery in England for 103 years.

England's first new gin distillery, Chase of Herefordshire (2008) (page 115), was also agreeably eccentric: potato grower William Chase had already built a successful brand of crisps by the name of Tyrrells and sold it for a fortune. He decided that mashing and distilling his potatoes to produce vodka and gin would be more entertaining and more rewarding than frying them, so soon afterwards he made headlines by turning his farm's cider into gin too.

A fresh outbreak of mild weirdness came in 2012 when dairy farmer and cheesemaker Jason Barber of Beaminster, Dorset, stopped throwing his whey away and instead started to ferment it with *Kluyveromyces fragilis* rather than yeast to which lactose is impervious, before distilling the wash to make Black Cow vodka. Meanwhile over in Devon, Cosmo Caddy started producing Italian-style grappa (or Dappa!) from pressed grape pulp collected from the region's wineries at the Devon Distillery (page 22).

12 BRUICHLADDICH

BEWARE OF THE PEAT MONSTER.

⌂ Bruichladdich PA42 7EA ✆ 01496 850221 ⊘ bruichladdich.com ☉ year-round; shop/visitor centre 09.00–17.00 Mon–Fri, 09.00–16.00 Sat.

If you're looking for innovation and experimentation in an industry that prides itself on tradition, look no further. Converted from a farm in 1881, Bruichladdich had not been operational for some time when in 2000 daring entrepreneurs Mark Reynier and Simon Coughlin stepped in to revive it... and started having fun. Avoiding the mass market, they went boutique to produce individual, experimental and short-run bottlings with three radically different whiskies – Bruichladdich, Port Charlotte and Octomore – at the forefront. One of them, Octomore, is the world's peatiest malt.

> **"ONE BOAST IS THAT THE ONLY COMPUTER IN THE PLACE IS IN THE ACCOUNTS DEPARTMENT"**

Producing whiskies that could frighten the horses wasn't the limit of their pranking, though.

In 2004 they started to grow their own barley, much of it organic; in the same year they also reopened the long-closed cooperage.

During its century of operational life Bruichladdich had changed hands quite often. A happy side effect has been a lack of inward investment, so much of the equipment and vattage the visitor will see, such as the Lomond still, is pretty much antique, extremely rare and utterly fascinating. It was all taken out and restored, piece by piece, after the distillery changed hands in 2000, and it's still operated by hand and eye. One boast is that the only computer in the place is in the accounts department. But while all this was going on the partners needed cash flow, so they did what is becoming common practice among start-ups: they distilled their own gin. The beauty of gin is that once you've determined your botanicals you can have a product on the shelves within three weeks rather than the three years it takes to bring whisky to market. Bruichladdich's Botanist Gin has become hugely popular: to its nine classic berry, bark, seed and peel botanicals are added a further 22 locally foraged herbs, that make it a very special gin indeed.

THE WHISKY For those who don't want the peat smoke then The Classic Laddie 50% ABV, with barley sugar and freshly cut flowers on the nose, and on the palate brown sugar and ripe green fruit. For the smoke then Octomore 10 Years Old third edition 56.8% ABV will give you malted barley at 167ppm and on the nose vanilla and caramel, while on the palate quite peppery with some pineapple notes.

◀ *Inside the visitor centre*
▲ *The spectacular views from the distillery*

14 CAOL ILA

✉ Port Askaig PA46 7RL ✆ 01496 302769
🖥 malts.com ◔ see website for details. Like
its neighbour Bunnahabhain (page 303), Caol Ila
enjoys a spectacular if somewhat hard-of-access
setting at the end of a steep and winding track on
the seashore facing Jura. It is somewhat older than
Bunnahabhain, having been founded in 1846, 23
years after the legislation that all but hounded
the illicit moonshiners out of existence while
making large-scale distilling a commercial
possibility. Today much of its production goes into
the Johnnie Walker blended label and, because
of this, Diageo (the owners) are going to spend
a considerable amount of money improving the
visitor experience over the next few years.

15 KILCHOMAN

✉ Rockside Farm PA49 7UT ✆ 01496 850011
🖥 kilchomandistillery.com ◔ Mar–Oct
09.45–17.00 daily, Nov–Feb 09.45–17.00 Mon–
Fri. When everyone else thought that Islay had
enough distilleries, along came Anthony
Wills to prove them all wrong. Kilchoman is
extremely proud to be one of the very few 'barley-
to-bottle' distilleries in Scotland – the whole
process from growing the barley right through to
bottling is all done on Islay. The first Three Years
Old spirit was released in late 2009. Try their grain-
to-glass tasting where you join one of the team
inside the warehouse to taste their new make
spirit followed by some of their currrent releases
such as Kilchoman Machir Bay.

◀ *Kilchoman and Laphroaig distilleries*

16 LAGAVULIN

See page 312.

17 LAPHROAIG

✉ Port Ellen PA42 7DU ✆ 01496 302418
🖥 laphroaig.com ◔ Apr–Oct 09.45–17.00
daily. Laphroaig was founded at the same time
as Lagavulin (page 312) just up the coast, and
also by a family named Johnston. By World War
II Ian Hunter was in charge and he appointed
Bessie Williamson who went on to become one of
Scotland's first female distillery managers. Bessie
became the major shareholder on the death of Ian
and anticipated the trend for single malt whiskies,
especially in the United States where Laphroaig
was to have a huge following. In the early
1960s she was appointed by the Scotch Whisky
Association to represent them in the United States
where she represented Islay whiskies to buyers
and distributors. Of all the widely available Islay
malts, Laphroaig has long been regarded as one of
the peatiest. For many it's an acquired taste that
marks out the true connoisseur; for just as many
others, its near-medicinal tang has been too high
a hurdle (although as a plus, its iodine flavour
persuaded the US authorities during Prohibition
that it was a medicine and could therefore be
prescribed as such). But love it or hate it, this
Marmite of a malt has long been a world-class
performer. The distillery has one of the best
visitor centres in Scotland, a very large shop and
a tasting bar where you can enjoy a dram looking
out over the bay. If you've made it this far make
sure you take in Lagavulin and Ardbeg (page 304)
distilleries close by.

16 LAGAVULIN

THE 16 YEARS OLD IS A CLASSIC FOR THE WHISKY CONNOISSEUR, AND YOU CAN HAVE SOME TOO!

⌂ Port Ellen PA42 7DZ ✆ 01496 302749 ⊘ malts.com ⊙ see website for details.

Ask anyone in the whisky world to name their top ten favourite whiskies and a pound to a penny the 16 Years Old Lagavulin will be among them, an absolute stalwart equally loved by Islay and non-Islay malt maniacs including the author. For Lagavulin is the perfect expression of Islay malt – as peaty as Laphroaig but fuller in body – and it is the heart of the world-famous White Horse blend.

Lagavulin lies on the south side of the island and the best way to visit is on foot. Start at Port Ellen and make your way up the Three Distilleries pathway, especially built to take pedestrians off the main A846. The first distillery you will come across is Laphroaig (page 311) then Lagavulin and finally Ardbeg (page 304). A walk of only four miles, but it takes in three of the very finest

distilleries on Islay if not the whole of Scotland. Lagavulin in Gaelic means 'the hollow on the mill' and in the late 1700s there were a large number of illicit stills operating in the bay. Alfred Barnard in his book *Whisky Distilleries of the United Kingdom* (published in 1887) applauded Lagavulin by describing it as one of the most prominent whiskies ever made.

On a peninsula close to the distillery lie the ruins of Dunyvaig Castle where in 2018 a team of archaeologists began an excavation funded by the Islay Heritage charity thanks to a donation from the Lagavulin 200th Legacy fund. This in turn raised funds by selling a special bottling of Lagavulin Islay single malt Scotch whisky single cask. Just 522 bottles were released with a selling price of £1,494 and bottle No.1 was held back

and auctioned, which raised a further £8,395. The Lagavulin Legacy Project raised a total of just over £500,000 for local community causes on Islay including the dig and the RSPB, as well as other organisations. By sheer chance, not long after excavations had started, a seal of Sir John Campbell of Cawdor (c1576–1642) was found. Sir John once owned the island back in 1615 and there was a continuing war between the Campbells and the MacDonalds for control of the castle, which was the main naval fortress of the Lordship of the Isles.

"AN ABSOLUTE STALWART EQUALLY LOVED BY ISLAY AND NON-ISLAY MALT MANIACS"

Lagavulin, now part of Diageo, is one of their flagship distilleries and indeed one of their most important and best-selling single malts. It's not all about the 16 Years Old – there is also the highly regarded Distillers Edition bottling where secondary maturation has been undertaken using ex-Pedro Ximénez sherry casks. This gives you a candied sticky sweetness, a touch of marmalade and finally some spicy peat.

▲ *The distillery and the ruins of Dunyvaig Castle*
▲ *On your tour watch out for the classic Porteus milling machine*

THE WHISKY The truly classic 16 Years Old 43% ABV gives a typical Islay amount of smoke but at the same time the smoke dissipates once on the palate and you get a gentle sweetness with a touch of sea and salt.

JURA

GIN DISTILLERY

18 LUSSA GIN

✉ The Stables, Ardlussa PA60 7XW
✆ 01496 82019 ✎ lussagin.com ⏲ tours 11.30
& 14.30 Mon–Fri, must be booked. Just to the
north of Islay lies the remote and mountainous Isle
of Jura, where George Orwell retreated to write
his dystopian masterpiece *1984*. Friends Alicia
McInnes, Claire Fletcher and Georgina Kitching
have all been drawn here for different reasons, and
it was a chance conversation in 2015 that inspired
them to epitomise the spirit of the island in gin.
Today they grow most of their own botanicals in
polytunnels, and what they don't propagate they
forage. Expect a gin redolent of wild flowers such
as honeysuckle and elderflower gathered from the
hedgerows and also bog myrtle from the island's
many peat bogs – incidentally, a superb deterrent
to the midges. The gin is fresh, zesty and smooth
with an aromatic finish.

▼ *The beach at Ardlussa, Jura*

WHISKY DISTILLERY

19 JURA

✉ Craighouse PA60 7XT ✆ 01496 820385
✎ jurawhisky.com ⏲ Apr–Oct 10.00–16.30
Mon–Sat; Nov–Mar 10.00–16.00 Mon–Fri. There's
much debate among whisky fanciers as to whether
Isle of Jura should be classified with the peaty
malts of its nearest neighbour, Islay, or with the
gentler liquors of the Highlands. Certainly Jura has
peat, but in ancient times the island was covered
with birchwood, unlike Islay, so the composition of
the peat is different and the flavours it confers are
less pungent. Thus it remained until 1960, when to
boost the island's faltering economy, landowners
Tony Riley-Smith of Ardfin and Robin Fletcher
of Ardlussa enlisted the help of MacKinlay's and
its renowned designer, William Delmé-Evans
(a Welshman!), to install a new distillery in
the shell of the old one. Since then it has gone
from strength to strength, supplying the malt
component for blends including Whyte & Mackay
(whose parent company now owns it), and is now
one of the best-selling single malts in the UK.

▶ *The Paps of Jura*

MULL

WHISKY DISTILLERY

20 TOBERMORY

✉ Ledaig, Tobermory PA75 6NR ✆ 01688
302647 🖊 tobermorydistillery.com. At the time
of writing the distillery was temporarily closed
for a thorough upgrade and refurbishment, so call
ahead or visit their website. The town was founded
in 1788 by the British Fisheries Society as one of 50
projected villages intended to improve the herring
fisheries in the west of Scotland. In the event only
three were built, as they failed to attract crofters
into the industry. Tobermory's distillery, founded
ten years later, provided employment for the failed
fishermen and was a respectable, tax-paying
alternative to moonshining. Since coming under
the ownership of Burn Stewart (who also own
Deanston, page 239, and Bunnahabhain, page
303) it has thrived, the distinctive squat green
Tobermory bottle becoming a familiar sight on
supermarket shelves. Burn Stewart has also gone
back to the Ledaig name for a heavily peated malt
in keeping with local tradition, and Tobermory has
also started to produce its own gin.

▶ *Tobermory waterfront*

CHAPTER SIXTEEN
HIGHLANDS
& ISLANDS

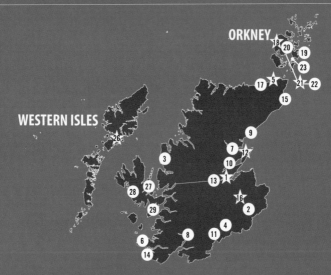

SHETLAND

25

24

ORKNEY

18
20
19
23
17 5
21 22
15

WESTERN ISLES

26

9
7 12
10
3
13
28 27
16
29 2
8 11 4
6
14

HIGHLANDS

1 BLACK ISLE BREWERY

SAVE THE PLANET – DRINK ORGANIC.

⌂ Black Isle IV8 8NZ ✐ 01463 811871 ⊘ blackislebrewery.com ⊙ year-round 10.00–18.00 Mon–Sat, Apr–Sep 11.00–17.00 Sun; book in advance.

▲ On the farm they keep Hebridean sheep

Lying (as many southerners seem to think it does) almost completely within the Arctic Circle, Scotland's propensity for growing plump, juicy barley ideal for mashing and fermenting is somewhat counter-intuitive, but the truth is that even northeast Scotland is actually at the northern extremity of that long eastern belt of soft, rolling and sheltered soil that stretches from Hertfordshire to Helmsdale and is perfect for ripening an even moderately hardy cereal. Of course the season this far north is not long, but then the growing day is so the hours of sunshine allotted to each little grain even out.

Black Isle Brewery's home, the 120-acre Allangrange Farm, has been growing barley since at least 1790 and its current proprietors have

▲ *The brewery shop*

wilfully burdened themselves with the sort of agricultural regime that prevailed back then – ie: they're completely organic. David Gladwin, who started the brewery in 1998, grows 40% of the barley he uses himself and has to pay dearly for the organic supplies he buys in: twice the usual price for malt and three times as much for organic hops that come all the way from New Zealand and the west coast of the United States. He also has to pay for his organic certification,

"ALLANGRANGE FARM HAS BEEN GROWING BARLEY SINCE AT LEAST 1790"

but fans evidently think the higher prices for beers such as Yellowhammer IPA, Red Kite Ale and the strong pale Goldeneye are well worth paying, as attested by a metaphorical trophy cupboard full of award certificates and the four brand-new 10,000l fermenters David has recently installed in the brewhouse.

Tours of the brewhouse start every half-hour, but there's a lot more to see at Allangrange than just a load of great big buckets. Marvel at the mural in the brewery shop painted by Loch Fyne-based artist Fin Barge using eco-friendly paints. Wander the farm, making the acquaintance of the 200 black Hebridean sheep and other livestock. And have a good old nose round the gardens, picking up a few tips about biodiversity, digging and dividing, propagation, composting, pruning and tying in climbing plants, collecting seeds and all aspects of green gardening. The farmhouse now offers bed and breakfast accommodation too, with four letting bedrooms. And, if you want something a bit different, then stay in the shepherd's hut, ideal for two.

THE BEER Altstadt 4.8% ABV lager, Yellow-hammer 4% ABV, straw-coloured beer with a grapefruit aroma, or try Hibernator 7% ABV, an oatmeal stout.

BREWERY

2 CAIRNGORM BREWERY

⌂ Dalfaber Industrial Estate, Aviemore PH22 1ST ✆ 01479 813303 ⌨ cairngormbrewery. com ◷ 10.00–17.30 Mon–Sat. Situated on an industrial estate in Aviemore, the heart of Scottish skiing and inside the Cairngorms National Park, the brewery was founded in 2001 after Aviemore took over Tomintoul and merged their operations on a single site. Thanks to highly regarded brands such as Trade Winds, Stag and Wild Cat, Cairngorm has grown into an operation that can produce up to 40 barrels a day on its 20-barrel plant. In 2016 Cairngorm and regional hotel chain Cobbs jointly took over Loch Ness Brewery. Cairngorm donates part of the proceeds of all beer sales to the Highland Tiger Project, a conservation charity aimed at preserving the Scottish wildcat. To add to a long string of awards, Cairngorm Black Gold was Champion Beer of Scotland in 2016 and 2017. The brewery shop is the start and finish for tours, which should be booked in advance.

GIN DISTILLERIES

3 BADACHRO

⌂ Aird Hill, Badachro IV21 2AB ✆ 01445 741282 ⌨ badachrodistillery.com ◷ 11.00–14.00 Mon–Fri, tours May–Sep 14.00 Mon–Thu; book online. Badachro Distillery only opened in 2017, but for globetrotting business couple Gordon and Vanessa Quinn it was the culmination of many years' dreaming and planning. A local couple, they met in the Badachro Inn. He achieved success as an advertising agent, she in the hotel trade, and their career took them round the world – only to come home after 20 years, build their own house and open their own small-batch distillery in partnership with Delilah, their veteran Portuguese copper pot-still. Badachro is a must-visit even if you don't care much for gin: the countryside and sea views are breathtaking and the locally caught seafood is among the best in the world. The three gins with their locally picked botanicals, including wild myrtle, rosehip and gorse blossom, are pretty special too.

4 DAFFY'S GIN SCHOOL

⌂ Strathmashie Distillery, Strathmashie PH20 1BU ✆ 01528 544755 ⌨ daffysgin. com ◷ sessions 10.00–13.00 & 15.00–18.00 daily; book online. At its home in a range of distinguished-looking stone barns in the grounds of Strathmashie House on the southwestern edge of the Cairngorms National Park, Daffy's was founded in 2018 by Chris Molyneaux and his wife Mignonne (who is the face that features on the label). It produces a wide range of sophisticated and beautifully packaged gins and liqueurs distinguished by a base spirit of French wheat and with Lebanese mint as a signature botanical. The gin school, however, has rather less of the cosmopolitan and urbane about it, and you will have to scramble about the surrounding hills and fields foraging your own botanicals before they allow you back indoors and take you step by step through the arcane rituals and lore of creating your very own gin. The distillery incorporates two holiday lets.

5 DUNNET BAY DISTILLERS

See page 324.

WHISKY DISTILLERIES

6 ARDNAMURCHAN

✉ Glenbeg, Ardnamurchan PH4 36JG ✆ 01972
500285 🖉 adelphidistillery.com ⏰ Apr–Oct
18.00–10.00 Mon–Sat, 17.00–10.00 Sun; tours
at 15.30 & 14.00 ,10.00. If you want to attract the
whisky-loving tourist, let Ardnamurchan show you
how to do it. For a start it's remote, which is always
a plus point among visitors to western Scotland.
It's also one of the many attractions on the
Ardnamurchan Estate on the shore of Loch Sunart,
along with the outdoor sports and activities,
nature trails and the delightful Glenborrodale
Castle. The estate and surrounding holiday
parks also offer a range of accommodation from
campsites to holiday cottages. The distillery itself
is entirely newly built but to a traditional design
and it prides itself on its environmentally friendly
energy, hydro-electric power and woodchip
boilers. They expect to launch their first single
malt in 2021.

7 BALBLAIR

✉ Edderton, Tain IV19 1LB ✆ 01862 821273
🖉 balblair.com ⏰ Apr–Sep 10.00–17.00
Mon–Fri, 10.00–16.00 Sat; Oct–Mar 10.00–16.00
Mon–Fri. Ken Loach fans will recognise Balblair
from the film *The Angels' Share*, in which the
distillery is featured towards the end when a cask
of Malt Mill single malt is put up for auction. But
Balblair is more than just a movie set: it's also
one of the oldest, best-documented and most
scenic distilleries in Tain. One John Ross started
distilling here in 1790 but struggled against the
moonshiners who continually undercut him until
1823, when tax reform came to the rescue of legal
distillers. Balblair flourished from then until 1911,
when it failed and was closed. It was bought and
reopened in 1948 but continued to struggle and
was once more threatened with closure until 1996
when it was bought and cherished by its current
owner, Inver House Distillers. The whole story is
told in the Time Capsule room, where visitors can
also experience the sights and sounds of the past
years when Balblair Vintages were created.

▼ *Loch Insh, Cairngorms National Park*

5 DUNNET BAY DISTILLERS

THE VIKINGS BELIEVED ROCK ROSE GAVE THEM STRENGTH. THE MURRAYS BELIEVE IT GIVES THEIR GIN FLAVOUR.

✉ Dunnet, Thurso KW14 8XD ✏ 01847 851287 ✇ dunnetbaydistillers.co.uk ☉ 16 Mar–30 Nov 11.00–14.00 Mon–Sat; book online.

Dunnet Bay was started up in 2014 almost as a lifestyle business by oil engineer Martin Murray and his wife Claire. They were living in France and wanting to return to Dunnet (her hometown) in the Highlands, when Martin's employer offered him a posting to Nigeria. It was no contest. But what to do for a living? Well, he had had to make a choice between petrochemicals and distilling while a student at Heriot-Watt and had jumped the wrong way: here was a chance to put it right.

Dunnet Bay's first product, Rock Rose dry gin, attracted a lot of attention owing to the choice of botanicals. Some were locally foraged, including *Rhodiola rosea* (rose in the rocks), also known as rose root, which gives a superb aroma and floral notes; Vikings were believed to have eaten it to give them strength. Sea buckthorn is a silver-leafed shrub that grows along the coastline and produces oil-rich berries. Few trees can withstand the battering winds up on the Caithness coast but the rowan is one of them, and with it come sharp, bright-red berries. From further afield Dunnet Bay also uses juniper from Bulgaria, which carries sherbert lemon notes, as well as juniper from Italy that gives a real warmth and depth to the gin. The character of the botanicals was enhanced by the Murrays' decision to opt for vapour infusion (hanging the botanicals up in the neck of the still to allow the alcohol vapour to extract their volatiles) rather than straightforward steeping.

The first batch sold out in 48 hours, but there was still no question of giving up the day job. Then, dear reader, you – or an awful lot of people very like you – came to the rescue. The distillery has the huge advantage of being listed on the North Coast 500 official website (✎ northcoast500. com). The route, starting and finishing at Inverness Castle and hugging the north coast, was created in the very year of Dunnet Bay's nativity by the North Highland Initiative to foster economic growth in the North Highlands. It worked very well. Visitor numbers rocketed as more and more people discovered the sheer beauty of a scenic route through some of the most spectacular and stunning parts of Scotland.

"THE FIRST BATCH SOLD OUT IN 48 HOURS, BUT THERE WAS STILL NO QUESTION OF GIVING UP THE DAY JOB"

By 2017 it was obvious that the distillery had to expand, and the Murrays approached Highlands and Islands Enterprise for funding. They secured a £64,000 grant towards a £248,000 development that has allowed them to install another still, build a new warehouse and, most importantly, create a visitor centre with shop and tasting room. They've also added a vodka to their range, Holy Grass, which is flavoured with the eponymous Scandinavian aromatic first reported growing in Scotland by local baker and amateur botanist Robert Dick in 1854.

▶ *The tasting room and the still house*
◀ *The shop*

THE GIN Rock Rose with Scottish botanicals 41.5% ABV, bright berries, followed by waves of soft florals (heather and rose), savoury maritime hints and lively juniper. Rock Rose Navy Strength 57% ABV, or Rock Rose Pink Grapefruit 41.5% ABV.

▲ *Clynelish Distillery*

8 BEN NEVIS

✉ Lochy Bridge, Fort William PH33 6TJ
✆ 01397 702476 ⊗ bennevisdistillery.com
⊙ Easter–Oct 09.00–17.00 Mon–Fri, 10.00–16.00
Sat, Jun–Aug 09.00–18.00 Mon–Fri, 10.00–16.00
Sat, 12.00–16.00 Sun. If you're unfamiliar with Ben
Nevis as a single malt, that's because the distillery
is owned by Asahi Breweries and up to 75% of
the new make is shipped to Japan to go into Black
Nikka blend. But with a foundation date of 1825 –
just after the Excise Act that made legal distilling
commercially worthwhile – it's one of the country's
older-attested whisky distilleries. It was started by
Long John McDonald, a man of legendary height
(well, 6' 4" which was perhaps more impressive then
than it is now), which makes it all the stranger that
the fictional character who promotes the whisky in
the visitor centre is a cartoon giant named Hector
McDram. Surely one genuine giant is more than
enough? The current distillery incorporates a sister-
plant, Glen Nevis, built right next door in 1878
when Scotch was overtaking gin as the drinker's

favourite in England; the signature blend, Long
John, was one of Britain's top sellers for decades.
After the usual bout of corporate pass-the-parcel,
Asahi bought it in 1989 and the current visitor
centre, Hector McDram and all, was created from a
warehouse and bottling hall in 1991.

9 CLYNELISH

✉ Brora KW9 6LR ✆ 01408 623000 ⊗ malts.
com ⊙ Mar–Oct 10.00–17.00 Mon–Sat, Nov–
Feb 10.00–15.00 Mon–Sat. Despite its generally
agreed excellence, the heavily peated Clynelish
malt has rarely been seen in bottle. Founded
in 1819 by the Dukes of Sutherland, it was at
first sold only to private customers and later to
blenders. Disappointed by its performance, in
1896 the Duke sold it to a commercial blender
who saw its potential and built an entirely new
distillery to make more of it. That was superseded
in turn in 1968 when the state-of-the art Clynelish
you see before you was built, while the original
distillery soldiered on under the name Brora until

1983 when it closed and was converted for use as warehousing. The new Clynelish became a star performer as one of Diageo's Classic Malts range and distillery tours, with the visitor centre and shop, quickly became extremely popular year-round attractions. The big news is that the old distillery is to be brought into use again and that the visitor centre will be appropriately extended, enhanced and improved.

10 DALMORE

⌂ Alness IV17 0UT ✆ 01349 882362 ✆ thedalmore.com ⏱ Nov–Mar 10.00–17.00 Mon–Fri; Apr–Oct 10.00–17.00 Mon–Sat; all visits & tours must be booked in advance. A cluster of dignified grey stone buildings on the northern shore of the Firth of Cromarty, Dalmore would look good on the lid of any shortbread tin. Built in 1839 by the local landowner on the site of an old mill, the distillery was rented out to a succession of lessees, the last of them being an enterprising family called Mackenzie who in 1870 exported the first boatload of malt whisky to Australia, doubled the capacity of the distillery and eventually in 1891 bought the freehold. In World War I it was used as a munitions factory until someone was careless with a match and blew the whole place up. It was repaired in 1922 and in 1960 merged with Whyte & Mackay, which was already one of its biggest customers. For a while there was a lot of speculation that The Dalmore would be used only for blending. However, it is now recognised as a very superior single malt, so prized that a collection of 12 rare examples fetched £987,500 in 2017.

11 DALWHINNIE

⌂ General Wade's Military Rd, Dalwhinnie PH19 1AA ✆ 01540 672219 ✆ malts.com ⏱ see website for details. One of Scotland's highest distilleries at 355m (1,164ft) above sea level, Dalwhinnie can be a difficult place to reach in winter even though it's right on the A9 and still has an operating railway station. It is also officially Scotland's coldest place – hence, perhaps, Dalwhinnie's continuing dependence on outdoor worm tubs, making it one of only 16 distilleries that still uses them. Perhaps its remoteness has contributed to its chequered past: the consortium that started it in 1897 went bust before the building was even finished; in 1905 it was auctioned for just £1,250 to an American firm, just in time for Prohibition; and the Scottish firm on which the Americans quickly unloaded their unwanted purchase was forced to sell up to The Distillers Company. Then it was burnt to the ground in 1934 (the rebuilding took until 1938) and in 1940 it went silent for the duration of World War II. One of the main reasons why Dalwhinnie keeps getting another chance is that the whisky is so good. Another is its magnificent setting, with astonishing views of the Cairngorms to the east and the Monadhliath range to the north. Its visitor centre, shop and four levels of tours and tastings (must be booked) are among the industry's most popular, attracting some 50,000 visitors a year.

12 GLENMORANGIE

See page 328.

12 GLENMORANGIE

ORANGE, IN THIS CASE, IS THE ONLY FRUIT.

✉ Tain IV19 1PZ ✆ 01862 892477 ✎ glenmorangie.com ⏰ year-round 09.45–17.00 daily; tours should be booked in advance.

The first thing people ask about Glenmorangie is how to pronounce it: the correct answer is to scan with the fruit, but actually people in the know just call it Glenmo.

Glenmo has always stood out from the crowd, not just for its unforgettable and (to some) unpronounceable name but also because of the height of its 12 stills, which at 4.8m (16ft 10in) are the tallest in Scotland and flank an aisle to give the stillhouse the appearance of a cathedral: the cathedral of whisky. And there's a reason for that. The distillery was installed in a former brewery on Dornoch Firth in 1843, using secondhand pot stills bought from a gin distiller who was going over to the newfangled patent column stills. Tall stills and long necks increase the amount of contact the spirit and its vapour have with copper. Contact with copper turns sulphites into sulphates, which precipitate more efficiently to leave a purer, lighter-bodied spirit – exactly what you want with gin. When they want to replace a still or add a new one, whisky distillers generally install an exact replica of the original in order to safeguard their product's distinctive character, and that's what happened here. What you see is therefore the nearest thing on earth to an 18th- or early 19th-century English gin distillery.

Don't let that fool you, though: Glenmorangie has never been any kind of a fossil. For example, it was the first to switch from direct firing its stills

▲ *The tallest stills in Scotland*

"IT IS ALSO AT THE FOREFRONT OF THE GREEN REVOLUTION THAT IS SWEEPING THE SCOTTISH DISTILLING INDUSTRY"

to using much more controllable steam coils: the steam engine in question is the star exhibit in the museum. It is also at the forefront of the green revolution that is sweeping the Scottish distilling industry: here, the focus is on renewable energy. All distilleries create waste: draff from the mash house, lees from the spirit still, pot ale from the wash stills: at Glenmo, a 12,000l charge yields 4,000l of low wines and 8,000l of pot ale. All these waste products are now converted into methane-rich biogas that accounts for 20% of the distillery's energy needs. Meanwhile anaerobic digestion now purifies up to 95% of its wastewater before it is discharged into the Firth, and Glenmorangie is financing a project to recreate the Firth's once renowned oyster reefs.

Another area where Glenmo has long been a pioneer is the use of different casks in which to mature and finish its whiskies. Perhaps because its whisky in its purest form is so light, Glenmorangie has long finished it in ex-port, sherry and Madeira barrels. Each year since 2009 a new expression has been produced using a different kind of cask or to experiment with a different ingredient. In 2015, for instance, an expression was produced using Maris Otter barley, more commonly used for brewing. In 2018, an expression was finished in American rye casks. Most of these bottlings are now only available at whisky auctions.

THE WHISKY The Original 10 Years Old, The Lasanta finished in Oloroso and Pedro Ximénez sherry casks, or The Quinta Ruban 14 Years Old, finished in ruby port casks.

13 GLEN ORD

✉ Muir of Ord IV6 7UJ ✆ 01463 872004
🔗 malts.com 🕑 09.15–18.00 Mon–Fri,
10.00–17.00 Sat–Sun; for tour times check
their website. One of Diageo's less well-known
distilleries in its home territory, Glen Ord's malt,
bottled as Singleton of Glen Ord, is one of its best
sellers in the Far East. The distillery, like so many
others, was opened in the 1830s as part of the
local laird's campaign to drive illegal distillers off
his estate so that he could profit from doing it
legally. The pleasant-enough stone buildings you
see today date from later than that, though: the
original was burnt down in 1878 and rebuilt pretty
much from scratch. The huge 1990s complex next
door is not so pleasant, but it is important: it's a
huge maltings that produces 36,000 tonnes of
malt a year to supply Glen Ord itself and a number
of its sister Diageo distilleries. A visitor centre with
a rather splendid exhibition was opened in
the 1990s.

14 NCN'EAN

✉ Drimnin, By Lochaline PA80 5XZ
✆ 01967 421698 🔗 ncnean.com 🕑 book
tours online. This is not the easiest distillery to
reach – situated on the Morvern peninsula, it's a
45-minute drive from Lochaline. This all-organic,
all-sustainable distillery was founded in 2016 as
part of the restoration of the 7,000-acre Drimnin
Estate on the Morvern peninsula. It occupies
outbuildings at the old Home Farm and while
waiting for its new make whisky to mature it has
been producing a hybrid that is neither gin nor
whisky. Botanical Spirit is essentially new make

sent to Beinn an Tuirc (page 298) to be rectified
with local botanicals. The first whisky will be ready
for release in 2020.

15 OLD PULTENEY

✉ Huddart St, Pulteneytown, Wick KW1 5BA
✆ 01955 602371 🔗 oldpulteney.com 🕑 Oct–
Apr 10.00–16.00 Mon–Fri; May–Sep 10.00–
17.00 Mon–Fri, 10.00–1600 Sat. Pulteneytown
was laid out in the early 1800s and named
after Sir William Pulteney, once the wealthiest
man in the country as well as the governor of
the British Fisheries Society that provided the
finance. In those days Wick, on the other side of
the river, was one of the biggest fishing ports in
Scotland and very much dependent on herring,
with at times over 1,000 boats moored up in
the harbour. The distillery was founded in 1826
and went along happily enough until 1930,
outlasting neighbours such as Brabster, Murkle,
Greenland and Gurston who all perished as a
result of the 1900 collapse of the fraudulent
Paterson Brothers blending and bottling empire.
In 1925 it was bought by the Distillers Company,
but in 1930 the Depression caught up with it,
compounding the disappearance of the herring
fishery thanks to overfishing and the loss of US
sales during Prohibition, and it was mothballed.
It was reopened in 1951 by an independent
entrepreneur called Bertie Cumming, and after
several changes of ownership was bought by Inver
House Distillers to become the stablemate of such
distinguished names as Speyburn, Balmenach,
Knockdhu and Balblair. The core expression is the
12 Years Old, known as The Maritime Malt, and

2018 also saw the release of a 15 and an 18 Years Old. There's also an *hors d'age* called Huddart after Captain Joseph Huddart, a hydrographer who worked for the British Fisheries Society. Huddart has been finished in ex-Bourbon casks that had previously held heavily peated whisky, which gives it a distinctly smoky nose unlike any other Old Pulteney expressions.

---

16 TOMATIN

See page 332.

---

17 WOLFBURN

Henderson Park, Thurso, KW14 7XW 01847 891051 wolfburn.com Nov–Mar 10.00– 15.00 Mon–Fri, Apr–Oct 10.00–16.30 Mon–Fri; 14.00 tours daily, book online. Mainland Scotland's most northerly distillery is a reincarnation, at least in name, of Thurso's previous distillery that flourished from its foundation in 1821 until its unexplained closure in the 1850s. Excise records from its early years show it to have been the biggest producer in Caithness; the 1872 Ordnance Survey map marks it as a ruin. Then in 2012 a consortium of South African investors found an ideal location on an industrial estate only 350yds away and revived the name when their brand-new distillery opened in 2013. Their first new make was bottled as a Three Years Old in 2016 and distillery manager Shane Fraser – ex-Oban and Glenfarclas – pronounced it to be as good as many much older malts. Wolfburn was never intended to be an open distillery and has no visitor centre, but its proximity to the North Coast 500 route drew many tourists, and tours are now held at 14.00 every weekday with an opportunity to buy whiskies at distillery prices – it must be booked, though. Private group tours can also be arranged at weekends.

▲ *Casks being filled at Wolfburn Distillery*

16 TOMATIN

HOW THE MIGHTY HAVE FALLEN... AND HOW THEY GOT UP AGAIN.

⌂ Tomatin IV13 7YT ✆ 01463 248144 ⌕ tomatin.com ◷ Jan–Mar 10.30–16.30 daily, Apr–Sep 09.30–17.30 daily, Oct–Dec 10.30–16.30 daily.

▲ *The distillery is just 16 miles south of Inverness and only 5 minutes off the A9*

High in the hills and miles from anywhere you'll find what used to be Scotland's biggest malt distillery. To us the choice of such a remote location for a factory seems crazy. To the founders back in pre-internal combustion engine 1897, ease of access to raw materials – especially water – trumped ease of distribution of the finished product, which could always come down the mountain by train. Hence the existence of Tomatin,

1,000-odd feet up what is now the A9 halfway between Inverness and Aviemore – so remote that the workforce still lives in the tied cottages built to house their predecessors.

Tomatin's gradual expansion started in the 1950s as post-war austerity began to relax. Its reputation for providing the blenders with sound, high-quality fillings saw capacity added in successive bursts over the next 30 years until

at its height Tomatin was operating 23 stills with an annual output of 12 million litres. Then in the late 1970s three disasters struck all at once: many of the stills were beginning to wear out; there was a huge downturn in international demand for Scotch; and as it had always rubbed along just supplying fillings, Tomatin had never developed a brand of its own. As a result it went bust in 1984.

"AT ITS HEIGHT TOMATIN WAS OPERATING 23 STILLS WITH AN ANNUAL OUTPUT OF 12 MILLION LITRES"

Only two years later, this great distillery was bought and reopened by the distiller and blender to which it had supplied vast quantities of fillings. The development, although welcome, was also met with some scepticism because the rescuers –

Takara Shuzo – were Japanese: how serious could they be? Very serious, as things turned out. They cut production to less than two million litres and reduced the number of stills to ten; they marketed high-quality blends including Legacy, The Antiquary range, The Talisman and Big T around the world; they released single malts at various ages and finished in different oaks. A limited-edition peated malt, Cù Bòcan, is released annually. So Tomatin has been drastically slimmed down, but thanks to its trim new figure and its development of an identity of its own – it has been saved.

THE WHISKY Tomatin Legacy 43% ABV NAS, lemon, panatella and pine forest with some vanilla and then cracked pepper and sweet barley with pineapple. Cù Bòcan Signature 46% ABV, light smoke and citrus notes.

▲ Bottle your very own single malt

333

WATER

BEER IS MOSTLY WATER, AND THAT MAKES WATER PRETTY IMPORTANT STUFF.

It's often said that ale and beer were so popular and so ubiquitous in days of yore because you couldn't drink the water. That may have been true of certain places at certain times – downstream of a pool or ford used by livestock, for instance, or the River Fleet between Smithfield and the Thames or pretty much anywhere in London during the cholera outbreaks of the mid-19th century – but for most Britons throughout most of our history the water was safe enough. But why put up with water when you could have good, healthy ale to regulate your digestion and give you energy, strength and stamina?

"MOST OF THAT WATER THEY USE COMES FROM BOREHOLES TAPPING INTO ARTESIAN WELLS, EACH WITH ITS OWN MINERAL PROFILE"

Containing no hops, medieval ale wasn't boiled. But the combination of alcohol and carbon dioxide generated by fermentation was lethal enough to kill any bugs and bacteria that might be lurking, so ale was pretty sterile even if it was mashed with river water (as often happened, although Guinness was never brewed with water from the Liffey and Bass was never brewed with water from the Trent). Beer was even more sterile, of course, thanks to the 90-minute boil required to extract all the good stuff from the hops. More important to the brewer than the water's microbial content, therefore, is its mineral content.

Everyone knows that the water in different regions carries different minerals: that's why kettles fur up in hard water areas and why you can't rinse the shampoo out of your hair in soft water areas. What many people perhaps don't realise is how important these differences are to brewers – although it's a given that nearly all beer is more than 90% water, so it should come as no surprise. Most of that water they use (which brewers always call 'liquor' – water is for washing out the buckets) comes from boreholes tapping into artesian wells, each with its own mineral profile. If the rock through which the rain that fills the wells has percolated is impervious, the water takes up almost no minerals and is soft. If the rock is sedimentary, the water dissolves and collects the various minerals and is hard.

The minerals of interest to the brewer are chalk (calcium bicarbonate) and gypsum (calcium sulphate). They have no flavour of their own but they affect the behaviour of the liquor and contribute to the final character of the beer, either helping or hindering the various enzymes at every stage from mash to fermentation and affecting the liquor's pH value. Gypsum reduces mash acidity, enhancing extraction. It mellows the astringency

▲ *A borehole draws gypsum-rich brewing liquor from deep below the ground*

of the hops somewhat, allowing you to make the most of their aromatic properties, and will also smooth and round out the hop bitterness. Its ions also aid clarity, flocculating and precipitating many of the particles that can make a beer hazy. The artesian well water of Burton upon Trent is rich in gypsum, which is one of the reasons why Burton was the birthplace of pale ales and why water treatment is known throughout the brewing industry as Burtonisation. Chalk, though, breaks down during the boil and deposits limescale on the brewer's boiler exactly as it does in your kettle. It also raises the acidity of the mash, reducing its extraction efficiency, enhancing the crude bittering characteristics of the hops and reducing the amount you can use; and its ions even interfere with fermentation. In short, brewers don't really want a lot of it! (Brewers often claim that they can't exactly replicate the water from a brewery's own well when, for instance, production of a brand is transferred from one plant to another. But they can. They do it all the time.)

Of course most of the water that flows through a brewery never goes anywhere near the beer. A fair bit of it is used to cool down liquid that's just been heated up for one reason or another, but most of it goes for washing and rinsing – and if you want water that's really not safe to drink, that'll be it!

ORKNEY

18 THE ORKNEY BREWERY

LEARN A FEW THINGS ABOUT BEER... AND VIKINGS.

✉ Quoyloo, Stromness KW16 3LT ✆ 01856 841777 🖱 orkneybrewery.co.uk 🕐 Apr–Oct 10.30–17.00
Tue–Sat, 12.00–17.00 Sun; for details of daily tours & tastings see the website.

There can't be many breweries whose visitor centres are as evocative of the schoolhouse as they are of the brewhouse. Well, there's only one, actually. This one. When Roger and Irene White washed up on Orkney's shore in the late 1980s they were determined to revive a tradition of brewing that had died out nearly half a century earlier. Orkney is, after all, at the extreme northern tip of the barley belt and has made some pretty choice whiskies for generations. So they bought the former North Sandwick School at Quoyloo and, with the help and guidance of the Godfather of Microbrewing himself, Peter Austin, cobbled up a ten-barrel plant and got brewing.

"THE BREWERY HAS SKARA BRAE AND THE RING OF BRODGAR ON ITS DOORSTEP"

The quality and distinctive character of the beers made Orkney a success from the start. Coming from a brewery that has the North Atlantic pretty much lapping at its back garden they tend to be full-bodied and warming: Raven, the 3.8% ABV session ale, includes crystal malt for those

▲ The visitor centre, shop, bar and restaurant

comforting toffee notes; Dark Island at 4.6% ABV is vinous and chocolatey. Note the nod to Orkney's Norse heritage; in fact, the brewery attracted more than a little criticism for naming its 8.5% ABV barley wine Skullsplitter. Supposedly such an aggressive name attached to such a strong beer was an incitement to violence; actually Skullsplitter was the mob name of Thorfinn Torf-Einarsson, a Norse Jarl of Orkney; and far from being a Special Brew wannabe, Skullsplitter is as perfect an expression of the style as you will find.

In the 1990s the brewery had to be extended to house a brand-new brewplant, complete with

▲ *The converted schoolhouse with the distinctive pagoda roof*

the decorative lantern-style pagoda that normally ventilates a distillery maltings. But it has never forgotten its origin as a school. At the same time, a visitor centre with shop, bar and restaurant was opened. With two of Orkney's – and indeed the world's – great archaeological sites, Skara Brae and the Ring of Brodgar, on its doorstep the brewery is beautifully located to cater to the interest and thirst of tourists, as well as to educate them in the ways of beer. It is also mindful of the needs of tourists' children: the restaurant is laid out in rows like the old-fashioned schoolroom it is, and you eat at desks (try the kids on dragon sausages and Viking burgers: of course there are no dragons in the sausages because dragons don't exist, but are there Vikings in the burgers?); there are special (alcohol-free) tours for children and they can even dress up as Victorian school pupils.

There's something else the brewery hasn't forgotten, either: the Atlantic. Next time you have friends over from Brittany or the South of France, challenge them to *fruits de mer* Atlantic-style in the form of a seafood platter here: Dark Island smoked salmon; hot-smoked honey-roast salmon; smoked mackerel pate; marinated herring. And you can keep your Muscadet!

THE BEER Cliff Edge IPA 4.7% ABV. Dark Island (4.6% ABV) is their flagship beer, or try Northern Light 4% ABV, with citrus and apricot notes.

GIN DISTILLERIES

19 DEERNESS DISTILLERY

⌂ Newhall, Deerness KW17 2QJ
✆ 01856 74164 ⌖ deernessdistillery.com
🕐 Apr–Sep 11.00–17.00, tours 11.00 &
13.00 daily, phone ahead for availability. As an
international project manager and a pharmacist
respectively, Australian-born Stuart Brown and his
wife Adelle were well qualified to turn their hobby
into a business by designing and commissioning
their own distillery – and to formulate their own
botanicals! Set in the rugged and mysterious
extreme east of Mainland and yet only 12 miles
from downtown Kirkwall, the distillery produced
its first gin and vodka (Sea Glass and Into the Wild)
in 2017. Since then it has also produced Scuttled
to commemorate the centenary of the scuttling of
the German High Seas Fleet in Scapa Flow, and is
working on a rum and a range of liqueurs. There's
a shop (with 30 tonics!) and also a tasting room.
No café at the time of writing, only snacks, hot
drinks and ice cream to take away, but things are
happening fast so check their website for updates.

20 ORKNEY DISTILLING COMPANY

⌂ Ayre Rd, Kirkwall KW15 1QX ✆ 01856 875338
⌖ orkneydistilling.com 🕐 10.00–17.00 Mon–
Thu, 10.00–13.00 Fri–Sat; tours 11.00 & 14.00
Mon–Sat; book online. Opened in a strikingly
modern new build on Kirkwall's harbourfront in
2018, Orkney Distilling has its feet firmly rooted
in the past and its eyes just as firmly fixed on
the future. Stephen and Alyson Kemp have gone
back to Orkney's Norse heritage to name their

gins Kirkjuvagr (church bay, the origin of today's
Kirkwall), Harpa and Ark-Angell and to select
botanicals including Norwegian angelica, found
growing wild nearby, wild rose and borage,
which are grown for them by the University of
the Highlands and Islands Agronomy Institute
overlooking the bay. For the future, the Kemps are
working with Edinburgh Napier University and the
Scottish government to perfect the world's first
zero-carbon hydrogen-powered still. The distillery
building includes a harbourside shop and licensed
café and a function suite.

WHISKY DISTILLERIES

21 HIGHLAND PARK
See page 340.

22 SCAPA

⌂ St Ola, Kirkwall KW15 1SE ✆ 01856 873269
⌖ scapawhisky.com 🕐 shop opening hours &
start times of tours/tastings vary with the season
– always check website or ring ahead. Built in
1885, Highland Park's lesser-known neighbour has
always been something of a workhorse, quietly
producing fillings for the blenders almost without
interruption. In 1959 it was almost completely
rebuilt and was equipped with the newly designed
Lomond still, a hybrid between pot and continuous
still, rather like Penderyn's Faraday still (page 208),
that enables the stillman to make a range of styles
on the same plant. These were once widely used
but now only two are left: this and one recently
recommissioned at Bruichladdich (page 308).
Scapa was briefly mothballed during the recession

of the 1990s but soon came back to life, and in 2004 was treated to a £2 million restoration. This was the prelude to its sale to the French-owned Chivas Brothers, who started bottling Scapa for the first time as a 16 Years Old and in 2015 decided to challenge Highland Park for some of the tourist limelight by opening a shop and running guided tours. Scapa isn't the prettiest distillery in Scotland by a long chalk, but its functional hangar-like buildings enjoy such a spectacular view of Scapa Flow and the long and rugged coastlines that flank it that a walk along the seafront actually forms part of the tour.

WINERY

---

23 ORKNEY WINE COMPANY
⌂ Lambholm KW17 2SF ✆ 01856 781736/878700 ⏱ orkneywine.co.uk ⏲ Apr–Sep 10.00–16.00 daily. Let's face it, Orkney is not exactly known for its endless rows of vines. However, eastern Scotland as a whole is prime territory for soft fruit that in the right hands

makes very good wine. And Emile van Schayk's are indubitably very capable ones. Emile took up winemaking as a hobby in 1995 and eventually found himself compelled to equip his garage with industrial flooring, drainage and extraction, install 14,300l of stainless tankage and start selling what he produced. After seven years the enterprise outgrew the garage and moved to a factory on the tiny island of Lambholm, at precisely 58.8° North, where flora including strawberry, bilberry, gooseberry, elderberry (and flower), rhubarb, cranberry, gorse and Viking berry (regarded, not unnaturally, as a superfood) go crushed (but not pressed) into the vat for a full maceration ferment. In 2016 the van Schayks branched out and started a small distillery next door to make rum. J Gow Fading Light is named after the twice-hanged pirate John Gow who was captured in Orkney, first hanged at Execution Dock in London in June 1725 and then hanged a second time shortly afterwards because the first noose broke. The rum is aged in chestnut casks rather than oak, which is the coming thing. All products are vegan.

21 HIGHLAND PARK

THINGS ARE WHAT THEY USED TO BE.

⌂ Holm Rd, Kirkwall KW15 1SU ✐ 01856 874619 ⬙ highlandparkwhisky.com ☺ Apr–Oct 10.00–17.00 daily, Nov–Mar 10.00–17.00 Mon–Fri.

▲ *The sixth-oldest distillery in Scotland*

Scotland's most northerly distillery is also one of the oldest, having been founded in 1798 by Magnus Eunson, part-time clergyman, part-time smuggler and part-time illicit distiller. This is a nicely symbolic location, since the history of whisky in the late 18th and early 19th centuries concerns the struggle of legitimate commercial distillers and their allies in Customs to suppress illicit small-scale distilling and smuggling. Eunson is not your typical Scottish name such as The Macallan, Macduff or Macmillan, because between AD800 and AD1468 Orkney was ruled first by the

Norwegian and then by the Danish Crown. In 1468 the islands were reunited with mainland Scotland as part of a marriage settlement between the Danish and Scottish crowns, but even today most Orcadians would consider themselves to be more Scandinavian than Scottish.

Highland Park was a well-kept secret until 1979. In those days Orkney had fewer tourists than it does today, and very little of the mildly peated product was released to merchants for independent bottling. Connoisseurs (including Winston Churchill) praised it, but other than that

▲ One of the two kilns

▲ Traditional floor malting

its honeyed, heathery delights were known only to the blenders who prized it so highly. In 1979, after living for so many years in the shadow of its more illustrious stablemate The Macallan (page 290), it 'came out' as a widely available distillery bottling and soon became one of the most popular single malts in the world. A radical overhaul in 2017 saw Highland Park draw more deeply on its Viking heritage with the release of the 10 Years Old Viking Scars, Viking Honour 12 Years Old, and the 18 Years Old Viking Pride.

"MUCH OF HIGHLAND PARK'S CHARACTER COMES FROM A DETERMINED ADHERENCE TO TRADITION"

Much of Highland Park's character comes from a determined adherence to tradition. It has its own floor maltings and its own peat bog at Hobbister Moor some seven miles away; it can still therefore produce 20% of its own malt. The whisky is aged in sherry casks for a slight oloroso sweetness and the peat imparts a very faint smokiness. Cool maturation owing to the low temperature range and cask harmonisation further ensure a really smooth whisky.

Highland Park's on-site visitor centre was already well visited and highly regarded when the company decided that the huge number of cruise ships coming into Kirkwall (170 were due in 2020) justified the expansion of its visitor facilities. Highland Park has therefore tapped into the expanding tourist market by opening a shop in the town centre. The opening coincided with Viking Day and as well as selling a complete range of Highland Park whisky and merchandise it also hosts a gallery featuring work from local artists.

THE WHISKY The classic 12 Years Old 40% ABV, floral, smooth and honey with a gentle hint of smoke. The 18 Years Old 43% ABV is an absolute classic but if you want something really different then try Twisted Tattoo 16 Years Old 46.7% ABV, finished in ex-Bourbon casks and then in Rioja wine-seasoned casks.

SHETLAND

BREWERY

24 LERWICK BREWERY

🏠 Ladies Dr, Old North Rd, Lerwick ZE1 0NA
📞 01595 694552 🌐 lerwickbrewery.com
🕐 09.00–17.00 Mon–Fri; tours 10.00 & 14.00
daily; Brewery Experience 11.00 Mon–Fri. Started
in 2013 by brothers John, Jimmy and Graham
Mercer, Lerwick can claim to be the most northerly
brewery in the UK at 60° North (the name of its
lager). The Shetlands have a surprisingly mild
winter and an unsurprisingly mild summer,
which helps the brothers produce a consistent
product. The exceptionally pure water from the
brewery's own borehole is another advantage of
the location. The brewery now has a core range of
six ales, including an oatmeal stout called Tushkar,
which has become particularly popular. The tour
and subsequent tasting are also becoming very
popular among cruise passengers, although many
have found the stiffish uphill walk from town a
little challenging.

GIN DISTILLERY

25 SAXA VORD

🏠 Haroldswick, Unst ZE2 9EF 📞 01957 711217
🌐 shetlandreel.com 🕐 tours & tastings
Apr–Sep 12.00 Tue, Thu, Sat, must be booked
in advance. Saxa Vord was set up by whisky
industry veterans Stuart and Wilma Nickerson in
a resort carved out of what used to be Britain's

most northerly RAF base. It produces its own
Shetland Reel small-batch gin, whose botanicals
include local apple mint, and it also bottles
different expressions of Glenglassaugh (page
279) – which Stuart helped rescue from closure
– under the name Shetland Reel whisky. There's
no visitor centre as such, but the resort includes
a restaurant and bar as well as self-catering and
hostel accommodation, and the distillery has its
own tasting room. Getting there is quite a trek: fly
to Lerwick and take the A970 then the A968; take
a short ferry ride to Yell, then back on the A968
north, then another ferry to Unst, then the A968
again to Haroldswick, then an unclassified road
for the last couple of miles.

▲ *Tasting samples from Lerwick Brewery*
▶ *Looking northwest from Compass Head, Shetland*

WESTERN ISLES

26 ISLE OF HARRIS DISTILLERS

BORN OUT OF IDEALS, BUT HARD-HEADED WITH IT.

✉ Tarbert, Isle of Harris HS3 3DJ ✆ 01859 502212 ✆ harrisdistillery.com ⊙ tours Mar–Oct daily, times & frequency vary so ring ahead to check & book.

It took American-born musicologist and organic farmer Anderson Bakewell seven years to raise the £11 million he needed to finance his dream; but he reckoned it was worth the cost and stuck at it, and in September 2015 the Harris Distillery laid down its first new make and was officially open for business.

And it is a business, too, despite the tag Bakewell has attached to it: 'the social distillery'. It was conceived and built to create jobs – 20 so far – and to be a social hub for all sorts of cultural and leisure activities in a region that's been plagued by economic ill-health and its consequent depopulation. Bakewell had already restored and revitalised the deserted island of Scarp off the Harris coast and was determined to do the same again on an even bigger scale. But you can't do that without money, and while its whisky – laid down to mature in ex-sherry and bourbon casks – awaits its epiphany, the distillery pays its way with an eponymous gin specially formulated to accompany the seafood for which Harris is renowned: one of its nine botanicals is sugar kelp, which can almost be gathered from the distillery's harbourside front door.

To demonstrate further that he meant business, Bakewell developed and runs Harris Distillery in cahoots with a trio of big industry names: the legendary and alas late Dr Jim Swan was technical consultant, while former Glenmorangie (page 328) director Simon Erlanger and Whyte & Mackay CFO Ron MacEachran provided the business brains. Nor has he been afraid to invest in marketing: the bottle and label came from top London design agency Stranger & Stranger, whose creatives were invited to Harris to gain inspiration and who came up with the ripple effect to evoke the sea. The distillery has also been working with cult bartenders and foodie legends including Nigella herself to put the gin up on the very highest of top shelves.

So what will you find when you turn up for your tour? The distillery is equipped with two custom-made pot stills for the whisky along with a small gin still, all designed and built by the coppersmith Frilli, based near Siena, Italy. The technical team also opted for wooden washbacks made of Oregon pine. There is much discussion within the industry as to the relative advantages

▲ *The distillery which acts as a social hub*

of wood and stainless steel, and wood seems to be winning right now, with other distilleries including Highland Park (page 340) in support. But although you'll be made very welcome, you won't find an all-singing all-dancing visitor centre with interactive display consoles and Italian coffee and fine-dining restaurant serving locally caught

"IT WAS CONCEIVED AND BUILT TO CREATE JOBS – 20 SO FAR – AND TO BE A SOCIAL HUB"

seafood gussied up to within an inch of its life. It's all a bit cosier than that: there's a peat fire always burning in the grate in the still room; there's a shop that sells all manner of local produce including essential oils and cosmetics from Amanda Saurin, who also gathers the botanicals for the gin; and there's a staff canteen where the ten distillery workers take their lunch and where you, as their honoured guest, are welcome to take yours too.

Isle of Harris seeks to reach out, too: in order to promote distilling in the Hebrides, it was deeply involved in the Hebridean Whisky Festival, which was inaugurated in 2019. Working alongside Raasay and Skye the festival included free tours, tastings, music and other special events. For more information visit ⊘ hebrideanwhisky.com.

> **THE GIN** One style only, the original at 45% ABV. A well-defined juniper note with pine needles, immediately followed by the fresh citrus notes of bitter orange and grapefruit. Sugar Kelp adds to the complexity.

GIN DISTILLERY

27 ISLE OF RAASAY DISTILLERY

⌂ Borodale Hse, Raasay By Kyle IV40 8PB
✆ 01478 470178 ⬡ raasaydistillery.com
☉ tours year-round 10.00, 11.00, 13.45, 14.45, 15.45 & 17.00 daily; must be booked online. Another relative newcomer to the Scottish distilling scene, Raasay laid down its first new-make spirit in September 2017 and will be able to release its first true whisky in 2020; meanwhile, it has released a gin to generate revenue with the juniper being foraged wild from the island slopes. Borodale House, its HQ, is an 1870s villa that was for a long time a hotel, then an outdoor pursuits centre and is now a hotel once again – a bang-up-to-the-minute hotel with every mod con and possibly the most magnificent views of all the gin joints on all of the tiny Hebridean islands in the world, looking as it does over the sea to Skye and the peaks of the Cuillins.

WHISKY DISTILLERIES

28 TALISKER

⌂ Carbost IV47 8SR ✆ 01478 614308 ⬡ malts.

com ☉ tours daily but times vary with the season – check website for availability & booking information. For many years (until Torabhaig was opened) the island's only distillery, Talisker has benefited greatly from the increase in tourism that followed the abolition of the Skye Bridge toll in 2004, and more than 60,000 visitors a year now make the 12-mile scenic pilgrimage along the B885 and A863 from Portree to Carbost (making sure they head southwest to the correct Carbost, not north on the A87 to the alternative, distillery-free Carbost). When people get there what they see leaves some a little underwhelmed. Talisker, like so many seafront distilleries, was not built to decorate the lid of a shortbread tin but to meet the challenges of manipulating temperatures in an uncertain environment, which is pretty much what distilling is hereabouts. In short, it's chunky. The setting, by contrast, is rather overwhelming, with the Cuillins in the background making their bold statement about the majesty of Creation and the fjord in the foreground sometimes lapping, sometimes crashing. The distillery was founded in 1830 by local landowners, who like so many others set about improving the value of their estate first by packing most of their tenants off

to Canada (and burning down their cottages so they couldn't come back) and replacing them and their cattle with sheep, then by building the distillery to add value to the barley they still grew on the more arable land. On behalf of those so harshly evicted you might feel inclined to cheer that in its early years the venture did not flourish. The local minister thundered against it as 'one of the greatest curses that could befall'; the laird wouldn't allow a pier to be built until 1900, so casks had to be floated out to waiting ships (some didn't make it); and several of the earliest owners went bust. Only when phylloxera destroyed grapevines and caused a worldwide shortage of Cognac in the 1860s and 70s was Talisker's quality given its due and its future secured. Not forever, though: a disastrous explosion in 1960, caused when spirit from an unsecured valve leaked into a coal-fired furnace, more or less destroyed the stillhouse. The building itself was rebuilt in the rather brutal form you see, but the obliterated stills were replicated in minute detail, including the distinctive kinks in their lyne arms that give the whisky its peppery finish; and it was perhaps this near-catastrophe that made people appreciate the malt they almost lost. Today Talisker has almost more ages and expressions than any other, and almost every year Diageo includes a variation among its special releases because it has become such a prominent and top-selling brand. Unlike many attractions on Skye, Talisker has plenty of parking although there are buses to and from Portree as well; the welcoming visitor centre has the Talisker Boat Bar and although there's no restaurant, there is a pub, the Old Inn, pretty much next door.

29 TORABHAIG

⌂ Teangue, Sleat IV44 8RE ✆ 01471 833447 ⌂ torabhaig.com ⊙ year-round 10.00–17.00 Mon–Fri, 10.00–16.00 Sat–Sun. A recent addition and only the second distillery to be built on Skye. Converted from a redundant farm building, they have only been making whisky since 2017 but, being owned by Mossburn Distillers, they have access to a range of blended whiskies created from other distilleries called Mossburn's Signature Casks, which are all blended malts. There is also a range of vintage casks; see ⌂ mossburn.com. Based in Teangue, a small fishing village, you can also enjoy a meal here and there is a small shop where you can buy some of their whiskies.

GLOSSARY

acqua vitae – literally translated as 'water of life', *acqua vitae* was used as a generic term for all types of distillates during the Middle Ages

barm – the froth created during fermentation

botanicals – the extracted parts of plants used in the making of gin

butt – a 105–110-gallon oak wine barrel

cask – a generic name for any size of oak barrel

condensing rectifying column – part of a patent or continuous still in which alcohol is separated into its constituent parts, ie: ethanol, methanol and other heavy alcohols

cooper – a maker and repairer of wooden casks

coppersmith – a maker and repairer of copper vessels

degorgement – the process of removing the lees from Champagne: the bottles are turned upside-down, the necks are frozen, and once the solidified lees are removed the bottle is refilled with fresh wine and a little sugar and sealed with a mushroom or pressure cork

dunnage warehouse – a traditional warehouse with casks stacked in three tiers without racks

eau de vie – clear fruit-based spirit, a speciality of Alsace and many parts of central Europe

expression – a particular or distinctive method of maturing a whisky, eg: ageing in sherry barrels

fillings – malt whiskies used for blending

finings – a collagen preparation used to clear beer of protein haze and yeast particles by electrolysis

floor malting – traditional method of converting barley to malt by spreading the grain over a gently heated floor and turning it repeatedly

gyle – a batch of beer

hogshead – a 108-gallon traditional wooden barrel

hopnik – a vessel in which hops are steeped in beer; an alternative to boiling

hops – bines related to nettles and cannabis whose flowers or cones contain preservative and aromatic biochemicals

lees – or spent lees as it should be referred to. Spent lees are a waste product at the end of the distillation process where the ABV is approximately 1%.

lyne arm – the spout of a pot still

marc – the grapes contained in the wine press and the residue, as skins and pips, remaining after the juice is expressed

mash tun – the vessel in which ground malt is steeped in hot water to produce the sugary syrup from which beer will be brewed

méthode champenoise – the process of finishing the wine's fermentation in a strong bottle, removing the lees and adding enough yeast and sugar to produce a persistent CO_2 sparkle

NAS No Age Statement. Scotch Whisky Association rules state that if the whisky is an aged statement whisky it must state the youngest whisky in the bottle, so a 12 Years Old could have different aged whiskies within the bottle, but the youngest is 12. With No Age Statement whiskies the distiller does not have to state how old the youngest whisky is.

new make – unaged spirit too young and immature to be described as whisky

perry – cider made from varieties of pear

pomace – the pulp left after grapes, apples or other fruits have been crushed for their juice

pot stills – the basic and traditional form of still: at its simplest a copper vessel with a heat source underneath and a condenser on top

ppm – parts per million

puncheons – traditional barrels of 110 gallons; informal alternative to 'butt'

pupîtres – racks in which Champagne bottles are placed upside-down to allow the lees to clump in the neck, prior to freezing and removal

real ale – ale which has been filled into casks unfiltered and unpasteurised to continue its secondary fermentation

rectifying column *see* condensing rectifying column

Saison – a sour, summer beer from Belgium and northern France

spirit still – the second still in a whisky distillery in which the coarsely processed wash is refined, ready to be racked into cask and matured

Union set – an arrangement of troughs and barrels unique to Burton upon Trent, in which beer is purged of surplus yeast while undergoing primary fermentation

vineyard vs winery – a vineyard is where the grapes are grown; a winery is where the wine is made. Fewer than half of UK vineyards have their own winery, and there are some contract wineries which grow no grapes of their own.

viticulture – the cultivation and harvesting of grapes

wash still – the first still in a whisky distillery, where the fermented malt liquor or wash is distilled to a strength of 23–30% alcohol

washback – the vessel where the wash is fermented ready for the still

worm tub – a primitive form of condenser: a vessel full of circulating cold water through which the spirit vapour from the still is passed in a coiled pipe or worm. The condensate is collected in a receiver and the first and last fractions, which contain methanol and other undesirable compounds, are collected separately and discarded.

LOCATION INDEX

CATEGORY INDEX

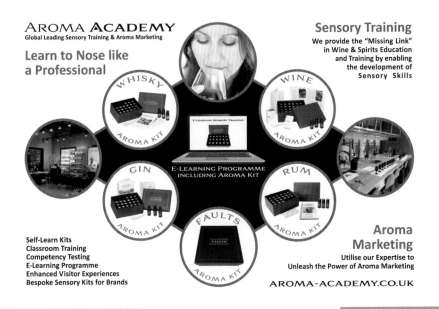

gin
MAGAZINE

Each issue has extensive and informative articles, regular features include tastings, bars to visit, cocktails to try, ask the expert, plus all the very latest consumer news and product launches!

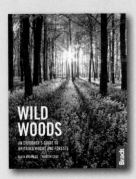
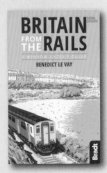

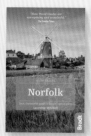

Posthouse Publishing

The Craft Distillers' Handbook

- Get inside information on developing the necessary skills, calculating the finances, and finding the right premises.
- Find out what equipment you'll need.
- Learn all about satisfying the requirements of Her Majesty's Revenue & Customs.
- Formulate and market your own brand of top-quality spirits and liqueurs.

Size: 218 x 145mm
Pages: 256
Binding: Paperback
RRP: £12.95

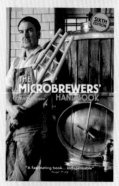

The Microbrewers' Handbook

Instead of distilling why not try brewing? This guide takes you through all the stages of starting a microbrewery.

Size: 210 x 135mm
Pages: 256
Binding: Paperback
RRP: £12.95

The Wine Producers' Handbook

The complete guide to starting your own vineyard which comes with a **free** map detailing all the vineyards in the UK.

Size: 218 x 145mm
Pages: 256
Binding: Paperback
RRP: £12.95

The Sustainable Smallholders' Handbook'

Author Lorraine Turnbull guides you on how to set up your own smallholding and how to make a profit.

Size: 210 x 135mm
Pages: 223
Binding: Paperback
RRP: £12.95

www.posthousepublishing.com